A Congregation of Learners

Transforming the Synagogue into a Learning Community

Edited by
Isa Aron, Sara Lee, and Seymour Rossel

Introduction by
Seymour Rossel and Sara Lee

UAHC Press
New York, New York

ACKNOWLEDGMENTS

Productive educational change, like productive life itself, is a journey that doesn't end until we do.

Michael Fullan, *Change Forces*

We are grateful to the Mandel Associated Foundations and the Nathan Cummings Foundation for providing the generous support that makes the journey of the Experiment in Congregational Education possible.

We are grateful, as well, for the courage and commitment of the following congregations who are our companions on the journey of exploration that the Experiment in Congregational Education has undertaken:

Congregation Beth Am, *Los Altos Hills, CA*
Congregation Emanu-El, *San Diego, CA*
Congregation Shaare Emeth, *St. Louis, MO*
Leo Baeck Temple, *Los Angeles, CA*
The Temple, *Atlanta, GA*
Westchester Reform Temple, *Scarsdale, NY*

Library of Congress Cataloging-in-Publication Data

A congregation of learners: transforming the synagogue into a
   learning community/edited by Isa Aron, Sara Lee, and Seymour
   Rossel; introduction by Seymour Rossel and Sara Lee.
     p.   cm.
   Includes biographical references.
   ISBN 0-8074-0538-8 (alk. paper)
   1. Jewish religious education—United States.   2. Jews—United
States—Identity.   3. Reform Judaism—United States.   I. Aron, Isa.
II. Lee, Sara.   III. Rossel, Seymour.
BM75.C665   1995
296.6'8—dc20

95-23259
CIP

Designed by Helayne Friedland

10 9 8 7 6 5 4 3 2 1

CONTENTS

Acknowledgments   2

Introduction   5
Seymour Rossel and Sara Lee

SECTION 1: The Argument for Transformation

Toward a "Unified Field Theory" of Jewish Continuity   14
Jonathan Woocher

From the Congregational School to the Learning Congregation   56
Are We Ready for a Paradigm Shift?
Isa Aron

Vignette #1   78
Congregational Education at Temple Lomdei Torah
Isa Aron

Vignette #2   82
The Chavurah School
Jonathan E. Kraus

Vignette #3   87
Higher and Higher: Reflections on the Sefirot Program
Richard Abrams, Kenneth Carr, and Susan Cosden

SECTION 2: The Context for Transformation

When School and Synagogue Are Joined   93
Joseph Reimer

Changing Public Schools and   119
Changing Congregational Schools
Larry Cuban

Reflections on the Social Science of American Jews   139
and Its Implications for Jewish Education
Riv-Ellen Prell

SECTION 3: The Process of Transformation

An Organizational Perspective on Changing   155
Congregational Education: What the Literature Reveals
Susan Shevitz

Reimagining Congregational Education   185
A Case Study of a Work-in-Process
Linda Rabinowitch Thal

A Pilgrim's Progress: Educational Reform and Institutional   228
Transformation at Congregation Beth Am
Richard A. Block

Process of the Beth Am Education Task Force   242
Eddie Reynolds

Contributors' Biographies   254

INTRODUCTION

Seymour Rossel and Sara Lee

or American Jews the findings of the 1990 National Jewish Population Study, which indicated that we are an ever-shrinking population, constituted a call to arms. It was evident that something had to be done immediately to stem or reverse the trend. And it was equally apparent that our arsenal of tools was limited. In earlier generations Jewish identity had been held fast on the positive side by traditions inherited from our European roots; by the solidity of the Jewish family; by identification with the State of Israel; and on the negative side by overt anti-Semitism in America and by the after-effects of the Holocaust. Time and distance have combined to lessen the traditional values of our European roots. Intermarriage and social integration have rendered the Jewish family more susceptible to the vicissitudes of the American family in general. Although Israel continues to exercise a positive influence on American Jews, ironically Israel's growing strength and success have diminished the need for concern and made Israel less of a factor in the shaping of Jewish identity in America.

At the same time the steady passing of both time and the actual survivors of the Holocaust have, for the most part, relegated the Holocaust to museum status. While it continues to exercise an influence on the moral thinking of both Jews and non-Jews, the Holocaust does not seem to convey (at least, as it is presently conceived and taught) the essential lesson that the Jewish philosophers had hoped to impart, namely, that the disappearance of the Jewish people would grant a posthumous victory to those who had sought to destroy us. Indeed, little of the meaning of Jewish history has managed to convey this lesson to a Jewish people that has found itself more and more comfortable identifying as Americans first, rather than as American Jews. This lessening of the impact of Jewish history upon the Jewish psyche has come at a time when the problem of anti-Semitism rarely raises even so much as a single eyebrow and social barriers that prohibit Jewish success in the general society have all but disappeared.

More and more of our hopes to create continuity and insure the continuing importance of Jewish identity have come to rest upon

Jewish education. Imparting the meaning of the Holocaust has been a part of this education. Although Zionism was once an activity of American Jews, it has increasingly become an educational issue for American Jews who now identify with the State of Israel through the use of modern Hebrew and educational pilgrimages to the Holy Land. Anti-Semitism has itself become a subject of Jewish study. And even the Jewish family structure has become as much a subject of historical and sociological interest as it is a living entity.

It is no wonder that we have begun to look seriously at the state of Jewish education in America. The 1990 National Jewish Population Study reported that 40% of the core Jewish population is affiliated with a synagogue. At the same time, the number of Jews who will receive a Jewish education at some point in their life has been estimated at 80%. This means that, despite all other demographic changes, a great majority of Jews still see fit to continue the tradition of Jewish schooling for their children. Thus, changes in the way in which we educate children may have far-reaching implications for the continuity of the Jewish community in the United States and Canada.

In 1987 the number of school-aged Jewish children in North America between the ages of three and seventeen was estimated to be between 937,000 and 1,107,000. In that year approximately 120,000 Jewish young people were enrolled in Jewish day schools, while 280,000 were enrolled in supplementary schools. Just under 100,000 young people participated in some form of Jewish camping in that year. About the same number were members of youth groups, although this figure included 25,000 who were only occasional participants. Approximately 100,000 Jewish students were at least occasional attendees at functions of Jewish college programs, and about 600 colleges and universities offered courses and academic programs in Judaica.[1]

Little was known about the state of Jewish education for adults beyond the college years. Most adult education consisted of programs offered by synagogues and Jewish community centers. Although there were fourteen training institutions for Jewish teachers and educators in 1987, only 358 students were enrolled in B.A. and M.A. degree programs, and only 100 were expected to graduate annually. A few programs for senior educators existed in Israel, but the number of graduates of these programs who returned to North America each year was estimated to be less than twenty.

Of course, figures such as these cloud the issue of Jewish education. Statistics concentrate on what is calculable. They, therefore, confuse Jewish education with "schooling" or "camping." They tend to portray the Jewish learner as one who is enrolled in a formal or informal program. It is important to make a distinction here. The number of Jews who are candidates for Jewish education is, in truth, identical with the total number of Jews. Jewish literacy—knowledge of the tenets, life-style, history, customs, and ceremonies of the Jewish people—is the stuff of lifelong Jewish learning. If Jewish education is to be successful, it must not be confused with Jewish "schooling." If Jewish education is to be the cornerstone of Jewish continuity in America, it must shake off the impression that schooling or camping or even educational trips to Israel are the only or even the proper means of Jewish education. That is one of the main purposes of this volume.

In fact, if we must confuse Jewish education with any other aspect of Jewish existence, the only one we should endeavor to confuse it with is Jewish living. It is through the activities of Jewish living that we truly inculcate the values, feelings, and understandings that are Jewish learning. It is when what we know translates into how we act that Jewish learning becomes a reality. It may seem that youth groups, community center programs, retreats, trips to Israel—in short, informal Jewish programming— combined with day school education are the obvious answer. They are, after all, ways of translating learning into living. And assuredly they are important steps in the right direction. Yet each and every one of these is a small measure of Jewish living within the context of the far longer life span of a Jew. To the extent that we assume that education is only for young people, we continue to ignore the vast majority of potential Jewish learners.

If we are serious about bringing Jewish learning to the Jews of North America, we must look to the one institution in which the vast majority of Jews take part, which is the congregation. It is estimated that at one time or another in their lives fully 75% or 80% of Jews are affiliated with a congregation. To transform Jewish education we must transform the congregation. As the title of this volume indicates, we must create a congregation of learners. By doing so, we will by definition create a congregation of Jews who live their lives Jewishly.

The papers in this volume, with the exception of the opening essay, were commissioned on behalf of the Experiment in Congregational Education (ECE), undertaken by the Hebrew

Union College-Jewish Institute of Religion Rhea Hirsch School of Education and the Commission on Jewish Education of the Union of American Hebrew Congregations, the Central Conference of American Rabbis, and the National Association of Temple Educators. The ECE has been funded by generous grants from the Mandel Associated Foundations and the Nathan Cummings Foundation. The essays were commissioned as background papers for a consultation of scholars, educators, and congregational leaders held in Malibu, California, in May 1993, at which the foundations for the ECE were laid. To date, seven congregations have joined the project, whose purpose is to reconceptualize and reconfigure education in the congregational setting and to study the process of this transformation, so that other congregations will benefit from this knowledge in the future.

This volume, therefore, proposes to begin the discussion of how Jewish education could be changed, rather than answer the question of what Jewish education should be like in the future. It is meant to be exploratory—to begin and not to end the process. Although the editors have carefully arranged these essays in a sequence that we believe will elicit deeper and deeper reflection, we could have chosen to arrange the articles differently within the context of the discussion. Indeed, each essay stands virtually on its own. For this reason it may be wise to indicate the logic that we used in our arrangement of the various papers.

In the opening essay Dr. Jonathan Woocher, Executive Vice President of the Jewish Education Service of North America, provides us with an overall context. He argues that "the historical dynamic governing North American Jewish life has been one of a gradual dissipation of Jewish identity, culture, and community together." Despite this bleak assessment, he finds ways in which Jewish learning can be made to serve Jewish living. Each of these ways constitutes a possible overall theory by which Jewish education can be transformed. As he understands this transformation, "[F]or education to be maximally effective, there must be a living Jewish community in which what is being taught and learned is already visible and valued." Yet, he continues, "[t]his is not an argument for a purely 'experiential' Jewish education....A holistic Jewish education, anchored in the life of real Jewish communities and capable of interpreting and communicating the depth and complexity of that life is the only kind of Jewish education likely to have a decisive impact on Jewish identity development." Our Jewish institutions must seek to provide their members with a deep understanding of the sacred nature of our task, not only the forms of Jewish living but the substance of Jewish knowledge to inform it. We must build Jewishly religious communities. Although Woocher's focus then turns to the issues of how this can be accomplished through Federations and Jewish community centers, the implications for the renewal of congregational life are equally clear. This, then, is the context within which the remaining papers can be understood.

In her essay on the possibility of creating a paradigm shift in the way we understand and enact Jewish education in our congregations, Dr. Isa Aron of the Rhea Hirsch School of Education of Hebrew Union College-Jewish Institute of Religion opens by recounting the main elements of the history of Jewish education in America. She argues that there are conflicts in the patterns established for Jewish supplementary schooling that grow out of its roots in the earlier Talmud Torah model and that were never resolved. She then proceeds to call for a radically different change in Jewish education—a paradigm shift—to an education that encompasses not only programs for young people but programs that seek to transform the lives of all members of our congregations.

Immediately following the Aron paper are three vignettes, fictitious futuristic models of what congregational education might become: one by Aron herself; one by Rabbi Jonathan Kraus of Beth El Temple Center in Belmont, Massachusetts; and one that was written jointly by Richard Abrams of the Brandeis-Bardin Institute, Kenneth Carr, currently a rabbinical student at HUC-JIR, Cincinnati, and Susan Cosden, Educator at Congregation B'nai Israel in Sacramento, California. If we contrast and compare these three models, the interplay of common elements and the differences among them provide us with an excellent starting point for discussing the ways in which our congregations might seek to reinvent their educational structures. All three models seek to build community even as they provide the ways and means of effectuating educational change within the community.

Dr. Joseph Reimer of Brandeis University's Hornstein Program in Jewish Communal Service reports on his study of two Reform synagogues in his article "Where School and Synagogue Are Joined." He explores the need for change evinced by both synagogues and the diverging answers that each eventually adopted. This article helps us to understand the kind of ferment that the attempt to change emphasis and direction in education causes. How should policies be rethought? Who are the real players? How did various synagogue members respond to the changes? And, finally, can educational change in a congregation be legislated by the leadership of the congregation? This paper introduces the second major theme of *A Congregation of Learners*, namely, the effects of change on the congregation and the prospects for successfully changing our present model of Jewish learning within the congregation.

It is the question of change in education generally—and the prospects for change in congregational education specifically—that Dr. Larry Cuban of Stanford University explores in his paper. He notes that both the public school system and the congregational school had endured nearly five decades of criticism and reform. He begins by addressing the question of what is meant by the term "change" and then turns to an examination of the many similarities between secular and congregational schooling, the crucial differences that make the reform of Jewish education the more challenging of the two reforms, and what congregations can learn from the process of change undertaken in the public sector. In the end he considers Jewish education and especially the Jewish supplementary school to be "a unique invention." Here, too, Dr. Cuban also explores the difference between "schooling" and "learning," suggesting that a fundamental rather than an incremental change might be in order for the supplementary school. He speaks of creating "mini-communities" that are more than schools for the young, in which individuals, families, and children are constantly mixing, performing, and serving. The goal is to create small Jewish communities of adults and children in which living Judaism, as defined and continually revised by each congregation, is meaningful enough to create a far stronger attachment than currently exists. He concludes by adducing several specific suggestions for those who are seeking to create change in the educational models of their congregations.

In an essay titled "Reflections on the Social Science of American Jews and Its Implications for Jewish Education," Dr. Riv-Ellen Prell of the University of Minnesota explores the social dynamic of Jewish education within the structure of the larger American Jewish society. She examines the peculiar contradiction that portrays Jewish education at one and the same time as "a disaster" and the primary means for the building of "a sense of identity." Through a brief review of recent social scientific studies of American Jewish life, she attempts to show what each approach can provide in terms of direction for the reform of Jewish education. She concentrates on four elements: (1) How do Jews create meaning? (2) What contributes to Jewish social cohesion? (3) What promotes Jewish behavior? and (4) What do Jews believe? She concludes with the proposition that recent sociological research on American Jews "has provided Jewish educators with a powerful picture of the ideologies, behaviors, and sources of cohesiveness that characterize Jewish life." For Prell, the future depends on how Jewish institutions will create for their members "a meaningful religious experience that will not disrupt their secular lives, but will not abandon them to that world either."

The next paper, by Dr. Susan Shevitz of Brandeis University's Hornstein Program in Jewish Communal Service, explores the literature of change. What seems at first to be a theoretical exercise soon reveals itself to be a very practical enterprise. There are essential stages in which fundamental change takes place. Errors in judgment and perception can all too easily cause change to go awry. One must view the congregation and its school from the outset as an "organizational system" in order to understand the impact that any change may have. Although the subject of this paper is educational change, the understandings and assessments that it presents, along with the many examples that Dr. Shevitz includes, become a guide to the initiation of any change within the context of a congregation. Because of this paper's larger scope, we have chosen to close the academic portion of the present volume with this essay.

At the end we turn to actual practice—two congregations that have not only committed themselves to change their model of Jewish education but have documented the process so that others may understand its implications. The changes undertaken by Leo Baeck Temple in Los Angeles are discussed by Linda Thal, its Education Director; the process of restructuring at Congregation Beth Am in Los Altos Hills, California, is described from two different perspectives, that of Rabbi Richard Block and that of Eddie Reynolds, currently the congregation's President. Some may read these as "thick descriptions" of the theoretical principles outlined in the earlier papers. Others will no doubt be fascinated by the flexibility that is possible within what we consider normative congregational models. Still others will respond to these instances as a challenge. What may be said of these two instances may also apply to the entire body of the Jewish community.

There is no question that education has moved to the forefront of the discussion about Jewish continuity in America. There are many questions about how the future of Jewish education should differ from its past. Thanks to the ongoing Experiment in

Congregational Education, this volume marks just the beginning of that discussion. As new congregations respond to the challenges presented in these papers, the ECE's researchers will continue to document and analyze their responses. The researchers' analyses and suggestions for choices to be made in continuing the process will form the basis for future volumes.

Whether we consider these papers as cautionary, as indications that change may be possible, or as active calls for changing our congregations, on one thing all readers will no doubt agree: To attempt to change Jewish education without rethinking the form and structure of the synagogue as a whole is to overlook the vast majority of Jewish learners. It is within the synagogue that Jewish ritual and Jewish action are informed by Jewish texts and Jewish values. It is the synagogue that holds the greatest potential for transforming Jewish learning into Jewish identity.

The Bible records that just after the Second Temple was built, the Israelites assembled as one in the square before the gate and asked Ezra the scribe to bring the Torah to them.

> Ezra the priest brought the teaching before the congregation, men and women and all who could listen with understanding. He read from it, facing the square before the water gate, from the first light until midday, to the men and the women and those who could understand; the ears of all the people were given to the scroll of the Teachings. ... Nehemiah the Tirshatha, Ezra the priest and scribe, and the Levites who were explaining to the people said to all the people, "This day is holy to the Eternal your God...."

One might ask, as the commentators did, "What does 'and the Levites who were explaining...' mean? Was Ezra's reading not sufficient? Was he unable to explain the text?" To us the inclusion of the Levites means that reading and explanation were not sufficient, that discussion and dialogue were integral to the process. We hope that this volume engenders the discussion and dialogue that will be needed to transform our synagogues into congregations of learners.

Notes

[1] These figures are taken from *A Time to Act,* The Report of the Commission on Jewish Education in North America, published in 1990.

THE ARGUMENT
FOR TRANSFORMATION

TOWARD A "UNIFIED FIELD THEORY" OF JEWISH CONTINUITY [1]

Jonathan Woocher

Physics and the Jewish Condition

t may be wise to begin with a word about the title of this paper. The term "unified field theory" is borrowed from physics, where it designates the long-sought, but not as yet found, megatheory that will relate all of nature's primary forces (gravity, electromagnetism, and the strong and weak nuclear forces) to one another. A unified field theory will thereby enable us to tie what occurs at the subatomic level to what happens at the cosmic level. All of nature will be comprehensible as a seamless, integrated whole.

I borrow this term with tongue in cheek but also with a serious intent. The Jewish continuity agenda is the most complex and far-reaching that the North American Jewish community has ever taken on. By its very nature, the effort to promote Jewish continuity touches the innermost recesses of the individual psyche—where that mysterious phenomenon we call "Jewish identity" ostensibly resides—and, at the same time, the collective historical, social, and political passage of the Jewish people in the modern world. Success in this effort will almost certainly require that, on the one hand, we find and employ powerful new techniques for changing individuals and, on the other hand, we transform and reconfigure our communal institutional system to an extent and with a rapidity unprecedented in our modern organizational experience.

The endeavor that we are now beginning—attempting in a systematic way to mitigate or even reverse historical trends that are deeply rooted and largely welcomed by the very population (including ourselves) upon which we are seeking to impact—is, at the very least, audacious. To launch such an endeavor without a guiding theory of what we are doing—without a conceptual road map that alerts us to the difficulty of the journey, highlights the critical junctures along the way, and suggests the directions along which we must move—is foolhardy and perhaps even irresponsible.

To label such a theory "unified field theory" is apt in another sense. The contemporary Jewish condition cannot be described, much less transformed, within the framework of a single discipline. We must call upon psychology, sociology, history, anthropology, religious studies, and political science to begin to make sense of who we are and where we are as Jews today. In fact, each of these disciplines has made contributions to the efforts that have been mounted thus far to promote Jewish continuity. But we have not yet drawn our partial insights together and conceptualized the connections between the microscopic—the lived experience of individual Jews—and the macroscopic—communal policy-making—in ways that promote confidence that our endeavors in the latter arena will make a difference in the former. For this we need a holistic understanding of the dynamics of contemporary Jewish life at the individual and collective levels that goes beyond demography or survey research (illuminating as these may be). To be sure, historians and analysts of contemporary society and culture do not fully agree about these dynamics and their implications. But we need to work from some conceptual base or we run the danger of simply skimming the surface of the challenges we face and finding, two or ten or twenty years down the road, that our responses were hopelessly inadequate.

This paper most assuredly is *not* a "unified field theory" of Jewish continuity. Rather, it should be read as an attempt to articulate the challenge and initiate the discussions that will be required if such a theory is to emerge. Almost nothing in this paper is new. What I have tried to do is to weave together a large number of ideas and initiatives that are already in circulation and to set them in an overarching context. As with the search for a unified field theory in physics, this effort focuses not so much on rewriting the individual theories but on finding the connections among them in the hope that our drive for Jewish continuity will not founder on our inability to appreciate the complexity and singularity of what must be done.

Modernity and Postmodernity: the Impact on Identity and Community

The conventional starting point for understanding the American Jewish condition today is the two-century process of "modernization," of which we are perhaps the quintessential exemplars and beneficiaries. Modernization, as it has impacted Jewish life, includes at least three key elements:

(1) The breakdown of traditional (organic) communities and the belief systems and cultures that characterized these communities.

(2) The rise of individualism (free choice) and rationality as the bases for action and knowledge.

(3) The ascendance of the nation-state as the dominant form of political organization, which demands primary behavioral loyalty.

For Jews, modernization has had profound specific effects on what we call Jewish identity. These effects are the result of the complex processes – social, behavioral, and intellectual – by which Jews negotiated and continue to negotiate their entrance into and participation in the societies, states, and cultures of the modern world. Only at times were the changes in Jewish thinking and behavior the products of well-formulated and formally articulated programs (although it is these programs that we tend to know best). Often the changes that were made were simply the accumulated result of numerous ad hoc adjustments made in the course of responding to new environments, opportunities, and challenges. Nevertheless, and especially over time, modernity put a distinctive stamp on Jewish identity that forms the backdrop for nearly every discussion of Jewish continuity today (understanding always that generalizations are just that, and not necessarily descriptive of any particular individual's situation).

Typically, Jewish identity in the modern world has become:

- Hyphenated, i.e., existing alongside other group identities as part of an individual's self-definition.

- Fragmented, i.e., broken up into components affecting specific areas of an individual's cognitive, affective, and behavioral life-space, without integrating these as a whole.

- Truncated, i.e., *not* impacting certain areas of the life-space, which are, therefore, devoid of Jewish influence.

- Episodic, i.e., salient only intermittently in the course of one's daily life or life cycle.

- Pluralized, i.e., found in many variations that may or may not be or regard themselves as compatible with other variations.

- Marginalized, i.e., operative primarily in areas distant from the core of self-definition.

• Homogenized, i.e., blended with elements of other identities so as to reduce the Jewish identity's distinctiveness.

Empirically, it seems that for most Jews in contemporary America, being Jewish, while neither shameful nor distasteful, is simply not a prime feature or determinant of selfhood. Jewishness no longer provides the meaning for significant segments of the individual's life; it no longer integrates other roles and identities; nor does it induce the individual to commit to sets of norms that guide behavior (whether ritual or general) on a daily basis. For many Jews, Jewish identity is residual – a self-attribution with minimal practical consequences whose expression is confined at best to clearly demarcated times and places – and is not being operative throughout their life-space.[2]

What is more, the *content* of Jewish identity is frequently meager compared with the fullness of the Jewish cultural system to which it is linked.[3] The typical Jew chooses only selected elements of the Jewish cultural system (itself often only vaguely and amorphously understood by the individual) to adopt as the substance of his/her Jewish identity. Some choose more, but many choose very little to fill whatever Jewish "space" they carve out in their lives. Furthermore, what they choose as being Jewish may represent secondary associations rather than primary cultural contents. In its most vulgar form, the process whereby primary content is replaced by secondary associations is epitomized in the gastronomic Jew whose Jewish identity revolves around certain foods and involves little more. But this process operates more subtly as well. The oft-made observation that political liberalism has become the content of Jewishness for many American Jews is an historically significant manifestation of the same dynamic.

The displacement of some Jewish cultural contents and the addition of new ones is not in itself a negative process. Indeed, Judaism could not evolve without it. In assessing the state of Jewish identity we may, as Steven M. Cohen has pointed out, unduly neglect or dismiss new manifestations of Jewish behavior – e.g., political action for Jewish causes – and focus only on more traditional ritual indicators of Jewishness. Still, in the contemporary environment, the combination of widespread Jewish cultural illiteracy and essentially unlimited choice leads many Jews to construct versions of Jewishness that lack substantial traditional content. The Jewish identity that results, is therefore, often not only intermittently relevant but also shallow and idiosyncratic.

From the standpoint of a concern for Jewish continuity, the

voluntarization of Jewish identity—the fact that the meaning and expression of one's Jewishness has in fact taken on the character of a choice, not a fate or destiny—is perhaps the most critical element in its overall attenuation. The unwillingness or incapacity of many Jews to accept norms of communally sanctioned behavior as necessary correlates of the fact of their Jewishness not only takes them outside the realm of *halachah*, it also renders all forms of Jewish collective action, social structures, and shared culture—without which it is hard to envision continuity—problematic. Obviously it is not the case that these have disappeared from North American Jewish life, any more than that halachic living has disappeared. However, the maintenance of reasonably stable Jewish social and behavioral structures certainly is more difficult when Jews must be repeatedly persuaded to give these structures their loyalty and commitment than when that commitment is seen as the inevitable and appropriate consequence of one's Jewishness. The voluntaristic and highly selective model of Jewish identity that is dominant in American Jewish life, especially the extreme psychologization of identity that is often heard ("I feel Jewish. Isn't that enough?"), is problematic as a basis for continuity because it places the locus of Jewish meaning in the individual rather than in the collective enterprise of the Jewish community, where it must reside if continuity is to be a persuasive value.

It may seem that in making this argument we are placing the blame for the changes that have rendered continuity problematic on individual Jews who have valued their freedom more than their Jewishness. In fact, locating the problem of continuity solely in the choices that individuals have made and continue to make is itself problematic, both as analysis and as strategy. From an historical and sociological perspective, this does not do justice to the social and political dimensions of modernization that have strongly influenced the responses that Jews have manifested. When the Jewish community lost both its organic and its authoritative character, most Jews, willingly or not, were thrust into a vastly different social environment, which made the individualizing of Jewish identity almost inevitable.[4]

If we accept the insights of social psychology and the sociology of knowledge – both of which argue that beliefs and behavior are powerfully shaped by the character of the social realities and relationships in which individuals live – then we must regard the attenuation of Jewishness as a life-shaping force for most Jews as a *social* phenomenon as much as an *individual* one. We need not deny the reality of free will in order to acknowledge at the same time that the social and cultural settings in which individuals live and work strongly influence how they think, feel, and act. Much of life is lived in a realm of unconscious choices, in which taken-for-granted patterns of action and meaning hold sway. These patterns acquire their power not primarily because they are rationally persuasive but because they are omnipresent and continually reinforced by social structures and environments, what Peter Berger calls "plausibility structures."[5] For individual actors these social forces and the behavioral patterns they sustain become almost literally natural, i.e., part of nature itself.

In fact, they are not natural, as we discover when social realities change, communities break down, and ideologies and behavioral norms once thought unassailable lose their potency. Even in times of social stability, individuals retain the ability to transcend their social environments and to choose values and patterns of behavior that lie outside the socially sanctioned norm. But such choices require both an awareness of attractive alternatives and the motivation to act on this awareness, which in turn are rendered more likely when alternative "plausibility structures" are available as well.

Thus, from a strategic as well as an historical perspective, we would do well to focus not just on individual choices and actions but also on the existence or absence of Jewish social realities that are likely to affect the cognitive, affective, and behavioral systems of Jewish individuals. Most Jews live, work, spend their time in and derive their knowledge and values from settings that are not Jewish—certainly in their cultural content. To expect these Jews to muster the psychic energy to make their Jewishness a determinative force that guides their life decisions (i.e., a source of norms and not merely intermittent goods) is to ask more than is reasonable. Today being actively Jewish is no longer natural and we cannot make it natural through intellectual or even emotional appeals alone.

According to this analysis what would be needed in order to counter the attenuation of Jewish identity are more powerful Jewish plausibility structures in the contemporary world—effective surrogates for the organic, encompassing, authoritative Jewish community that exists no more. What we call the Jewish community today is really a set of institutions designed to meet specific individual needs, in which Jews are not likely to spend a substantial amount of time. On the continuum of engagement ranging from participant to member to consumer, Jews increasingly find themselves relating to these institutions and hence to the community as a whole in the latter role. Because the Jewish community is highly pluralized and delimited, it lacks sufficient weight and coherence to function in its totality as a powerful plausibility structure in supporting Jewish identity. As a set of voluntary institutions, each making partial and sometimes competing claims for attention, the contemporary community may in fact actually reinforce the individualizing and marginalizing of Jewish identity.

Serendipity or a special act of will is required to make most Jews today a part of a Jewish social reality that is sufficiently encompassing and engaging to shape their life-space in a significant and substantial way. Except for a minority, the natural collective settings and processes (family, neighborhood) in and through which Jews were enculturated into a semiorganic community no longer function effectively, and the institutional substitutes that we have devised have proven inadequate in performing this role except for a small minority of Jews.[6]

In sum, the historical dynamic governing North American Jewish life has been one of a gradual dissipation of Jewish identity, culture, and community together. Almost as if entropy were at work, Jewishness in all of its key aspects has moved from being well structured to being diffuse. As a result, the gap between the social, cognitive, and experiential bases for serious, committed Jewish living and what most contemporary Jews have access to is enormous. This gap, not the presumed indifference of individual Jews, should be the starting point for our strategizing about Jewish continuity. Indeed, given the weaknesses of the Jewish plausibility structure, the miracle is that as many retain some sense of attachment to Jewish life as they do!

This is, perhaps, a rather bleak picture (which some might view as an appropriate gloss on the rather bleak statistics that emerge from the 1990 National Jewish Population Survey that stimulated the recent wave of concern for Jewish continuity).[7] However, in the last few years, commentators have drawn attention to the possibility that the dynamic of modernization described above in its particular Jewish version may no longer be the guiding force of contemporary history. Some are claiming that we now live in a postmodern world that has a different dynamic. To be sure, postmodernity has simply accentuated many of the trends that have already been noted as characteristic of modernity (in this sense, we might better speak of a "hypermodern" world). Talk about the saturated self that is overwhelmed with choice, with no fixed identity anchor, and about a relativistic world that has no fixed truths hardly sounds conducive to supporting the reemergence of strong Jewish communities and individuals prepared to commit to stable, collectively defined life patterns.

But recent years have also seen the emergence of sociocultural, or at least intellectual, directions that do provide the basis for a critique of modernity and perhaps even a countermovement. The evident dysfunctions of hyperindividualism expose a need for community that has already found expression at various places within the Jewish world. The postmodern critique of rationalism and universalism as unassailable master values allows room for the reemergence of spirituality and particularity (cf. the rapid spread of multiculturalism). Systems approaches that are beginning to dominate thinking in areas ranging from the natural sciences to business management emphasize linkages and relationships as the keys both to understanding and changing the world. Communications technology is perhaps the most powerful symbol (both literally and figuratively) of postmodernity's accentuation and counterbalancing of the dynamics of modernity. The promise of contemporary technology embraces both vastly expanded individual choice and control over the information flow we receive and the possibility of immediate access to virtual time, space, and communities that will permit connections far beyond those allowed by physical reality alone.

There is no question that postmodern trends and values carry their own dangers: fundamentalism, tribalism, and authoritarianism in the guise of community; moral and intellectual relativism in the guise of challenging a homogenizing universalism. But these trends also point to openings for a reconstruction of Jewish life that allow us to hope that at least some of the impacts of modernization can be mitigated if not altogether reversed.

Toward a Strategic Vision for Jewish Continuity

With the above analysis as our starting point, the question is how to frame the basic strategy for promoting the continuity of Jewish life. Where shall we begin? What shall we emphasize?

One possibility is to tackle the problem head-on, to try to convince Jews that there are good reasons for them to be more Jewish. It is not difficult to find such reasons, ranging from the benefits that Jewish practice can bring to lives often lacking in intimacy, structure, and dignity to the moral values that a Jewish community embodies in a world that appears desperately in need of an ethical compass. However, for the reasons cited above, it is not clear that such a strategy can work on a large scale. The process of the dissipation of Jewish identity that has brought us to our current situation was and is largely an unconscious one and a concomitant of other processes that are generally valued by Jews (i.e., modernization and social integration). In this context, direct efforts to convince people to be more Jewish are likely to appeal only to those few who are actively seeking to change their lives, unless these efforts involve drawing Jews into new social settings and relationships at the same time. "Why be Jewish?" is an important question but not necessarily one that is being asked by many of those whose Jewish identity is already attenuated.

We should also recognize at the outset that for many of these individuals, no strategy will produce radical change. For many Jews, we can hope at best to reposition Jewish identity to give it a bit more life-space in which to operate and to move it somewhat closer to the center of self-definition. Seeking to accentuate the value-added dimension of Jewishness for these Jews, without fundamentally disturbing their other identities, is a worthwhile goal in its own right. However, from the standpoint of a concern for Jewish continuity, even success in this effort will probably not be decisive. Out of the ranks of these "consumer" Jews will come some of the members and participants needed to sustain a collective Jewish social and cultural enterprise, but it is the strength and quality of this enterprise itself that will ultimately determine our continuity. This means that at least equal attention from a policy and programmatic view should be given to the question of how we increase to a critical mass the number of Jews for whom Jewishness will serve as a primary identity integrating other identities and expressing itself across large segments of the individuals' life-space.

The burden of my argument thus far is that this can be done only by reconstructing social/experiential/cognitive realities—communities and cultures—that can nurture and sustain strong Jewish identities. If *Jewish identity* is the cart we wish to move along the path of growth, *Jewish community* is the horse that will pull that cart. Focusing on individual identity solely at the programmatic level, in isolation from the larger task of community- and culture-building, is likely to prove frustrating. Community provides the context and culture the content for Jewish identity.

Ideally the Jewish family should be the cornerstone of this effort to reconstruct Jewish community and culture. It is in the family that the initial experiences and attachments of Jewishness take root. When the family does provide a positive Jewish environment, when it is the microcosm of a Jewish community, it can have a major impact on shaping Jewish identity.

In the modern/postmodern world, however, many Jewish families are ineffective in this role. They do not provide strong Jewish environments. They are themselves weak in experiential, social, and cognitive resources to transmit. The response in recent years to this reality has been an explosion of interest in Jewish family education. From a strategic point of view, this is an entirely reasonable response, and the continued growth and qualitative improvement of family education must be encouraged.

However, merely trying to reinforce and reempower the Jewish family as a Jewish social-cultural system is not a sufficient response. Even under the best of present circumstances, many other influences, especially mass culture, dilute the impact of the family on shaping identity. Furthermore, we are increasingly coming to recognize that identity development is a lifelong process, that early family influence is often neither sufficient nor decisive. Both for this reason and because, in practical terms, neither the individual nor the family is accessible to those seeking change without a mediating agent, the community must be regarded as the social reality and mediator of experiences, knowledge, values, and behaviors (i.e., the culture) that is most likely to serve as the engine of reconstruction in Jewish life.

Of course, a strategic focus on the community (rather than the individual or family) is not without its own difficulties. After all, the breakdown of community is no small piece of the problem we are trying to address. In fact, one could argue that it is far easier to change individual lives, using tools that we know are available and do work, than to imagine that we can transform a fragmented but highly institutionalized community, best known for its "culture of organizations," into an effective plausibility structure for dramatically enhanced Jewish identity and commitment.

Nevertheless, without such a transformation, I believe it is unlikely that our efforts to change individuals can produce more than marginal gains in the prospect for Jewish continuity. In order to retain and create the critical mass of committed Jews needed to sustain a significant collective enterprise over time, the community must, in effect, become a self-reproducing system. The demographic studies indicate that this is not happening today. Successes in helping even a fairly substantial number of Jews become a little more Jewish—a result by no means currently within our grasp—will not be enough. What is required is the creation of many more intensely Jewish Jews, and this, in turn, will require the development of significantly stronger plausibility structures suited to nurturing and sustaining this level of commitment.[8]

This means that for a substantial segment of the Jewish populace, the Jewish community will begin to function as the "home" community from which individuals go out to participate in other social/cultural contexts and to which they return for their primary connections.[9] In light of the diversity of the Jewish population in life circumstance, background, temperament, and interests, we will need multiple realities (multiple communities) that will engage different individuals and even the same individual at different times. But, in order to form an overarching plausibility structure for Jewish life, these subcommunities will also need to recognize and seek to realize a substantial measure of commonality and connectedness to one another.[10]

In practical terms, the shift in emphasis from the individual to the community means focusing less on the ideological bases for Jewish identity and more on the social and behavioral bases for Jewish involvement and commitment. We must try to create sites and settings in the collective life-space we call the Jewish community that invite attachment and can subsequently provide ideological legitimation for that attachment. The strategic paradigm is to engage the individual in a community that has identifiable Jewish characteristics (in material culture and behavioral patterns) and, using the social influence of such communities, to build a sense of commitment to the community and its culture.

Of course, this will not be a unidirectional process. The relationship of the individual and the community is always dialectical: Once the individual becomes a participant in a community's social and cultural reality, he/she also helps to shape that reality. But, as proponents of "in-reach" to marginally involved Jews have reminded us, it is primarily the intensity, character, and quality of the community they encounter that determine whether individual Jews who do enter Jewish institutions become strongly attached to them (and hence are likely to give something back) or remain "consumers" who eventually turn elsewhere to buy a different product.

How, then, do we make our Jewish community more "community-like," more effective in providing a social /experiential/cognitive reality that will attract engagement and build commitment? We must begin by reconsidering the ways in which traditional communities effectively anchor and embrace individuals' lives so as to cement both the bonds between and among them and their bonds with the collective as a whole. There are several points where the community can try to give structure and content to individuals' lives that will reinforce attachment by responding to some of the problematics of postmodern life.

One is by providing the nurturance, warmth, and security that are often missing in a highly individualized and institutionalized society. The existence of so many cults should teach us how powerful these experiences can be in not only creating intense personal bonds but also in securing a commitment to what in the case of these cults are often highly unbelievable ideologies. We need more emphasis on the community's role in caring for its members before we can ask more of them.

In practical terms, this argues for the importance of organizing our institutions for the *mitzvot* of *gemilut chasadim* in ways that emphasize their personal, concrete, and participatory aspects. Again, making an ideological claim about the worthwhileness of Jewish values can certainly follow, but probably cannot precede, presenting these values at the level of lived experience. (This applies both to the performers and the beneficiaries of the *mitzvot*.) The objective of being a visibly and palpably warm and nurturing community should make us think about how we have organized our social services, one of the jewels in the crown of organized Jewish life. Is it possible that our social services have become too professionalized, too divorced from the larger matrix of collective Jewish living? Perhaps these services will have more impact if they are delivered in the context of multidimensional Jewish communities, synagogues, and centers, rather than in the offices or treatment rooms of agencies, no matter how Jewishly committed and sensitive the personnel are.

A second way in which our institutions can address the need for structure and content in individuals' lives, and thereby take on more of the aspects of the traditional community, is by guiding the use of time. This is more than a matter of filling leisure time with activities. Postmodern life is often perceived as an endless rush of events. People are looking for the proverbial quality time—time that is measured, purposeful, and shared. (Research on Jewish family education indicates that the promise of such time for both parents and their children is one of family education's strongest attractions.)

Of course, ritual life is in a large measure about just this: rendering the passage of time meaningful by giving it both structure and attention. For most Jews today, infusing time with Jewishness will not recreate the traditional Jewish experience of time, whereby the day, the calendar, and the life-cycle are tightly organized and experienced entirely in Jewish terms. But we can try to add Jewish markers to these domains. Making Shabbat a focal point for intensified familial and congregational Jewish activity, as is now almost universally urged, is a worthy centerpiece for such efforts. The development of new nontraditional life-cycle rituals, such as a trip to Israel as an adolescent rite of passage, makes eminent sense in this context as well.

The aim of these efforts should be to create Jewish regularities in the experience and use of time to counteract the regularities that are imposed by the dominant non-Jewish culture. There is a principle in education that also seems valid in this context: The more time on task, the more learning. Research on Jewish youth programs conducted by Hanan Alexander indicates that they are most effective when they engage young people over extended periods and in intensive, concentrated ways, i.e., when they occupy significant amounts of time and when they fill that time fully. (Partisans of Jewish camping have long recognized this principle.) Quite simply, this would argue for whatever strategies we can devise that will capture more time for Jewish activities in any form and in any setting. Not only quality but sheer quantity matters.

Efforts to "re-ritualize" the calendar and the life-cycle of Jews will be more effective if at the same time Jewish institutions can help individuals cope with the issues posed by the pressured rhythms of daily life and life's critical passages. I suggest that there is a connection between the credibility of a call for Shabbat observance and the ability of those making that call to help families deal with the perceived difficulties of managing multiple careers, providing quality education and childcare, and having time for self-enrichment and fellowship. Similarly, providing individuals with emotional, financial, and social assistance in facing difficult times and major life transitions (e.g., divorce), as well as meaningful contexts in which to connect these experiences to Jewish symbols and values, is likely to establish in them a more powerful sense of being part of a community than either response alone.

A third way in which Jewish communities can draw individuals into a Jewish social reality by addressing typical postmodern needs is by providing them with explicit opportunities for personal meaning-making in a Jewish key. Although the question What is my life about? is not always at the forefront of consciousness, it is for most people one that resurfaces repeatedly in the face of our mortality, begging for serious answers that contemporary culture is hard-pressed to provide. Judaism and Jewish life have traditionally excelled in answering this question, offering Jews an opportunity to link their personal histories to the destiny of a messianic people serving the one God of the universe. The life of Torah, around which the community organized its daily existence, assured its members that this answer would be felt and enacted, not merely believed in the abstract.[11]

Can contemporary Judaism and the Jewish community provide similarly effective answers today for a substantial number of Jews? If it can, it will likely do so through the same vehicle that traditional Judaism (and many other religious traditions) employs so well: the power of stories to confer and express meaning.[12] In a period when propositional theology holds little appeal, narrative as a way of making sense of the world and of one's life seems to be faring better. Our ability to understand the human experience as an unfolding story and to link this experience to other, more encompassing stories may represent our best hope for snatching meaning from a chaotic world. Certainly, the enduring power of myth in human experience is well attested, whether the narrative emanates from sacred texts or Hollywood studios.

The key question from the standpoint of Jewish continuity is whether nontraditional Jews can be brought to see that their personal stories are connected to traditional and historical Jewish narratives ("master stories") and to a living community that tells and enacts these stories and then made to view these narratives as norm-giving. For this to occur, three things must happen: First, Jews must be encouraged to become storytellers and to share the narratives of their lives with other Jews. Second, Jews must have the opportunity to hear and grapple with the master stories, not as dicta to which they must conform but as templates that they can use to give their personal stories increased scope and resonance. (These master stories include not only textual narratives but the stories emanating from Jewish history as well. Understanding the ways in which Jews have lived in the past provides us with additional templates for our own efforts to construct meaningful Jewish lives in vibrant Jewish communities.)

Third, the Jewish community must continue to struggle with how to *enact* its master stories — how to realize and call attention to the behavioral implications implicit in them. Just as ritual lends potency to myth, so, too, our Jewish master stories will be more persuasive if they are seen as being able to generate collective behavior. The American Jewish community has done this superbly with the story of Holocaust to Rebirth. Regardless of whether one feels that the Holocaust and the State of Israel (separately or together) have come to play too prominent and too exclusive a role in the contemporary Jewish consciousness, one must acknowledge that few, if any, other Jewish stories have had a similar ability to inspire twentieth-century American Jews to individual and collective action. There are other Jewish stories, e.g., the call to be a "holy community," whose contemporary behavioral parameters have been far less fully explored, and the challenge for the community is to seek to translate these stories as well into programs of action.

The Jewish community must, in effect, become one in which large numbers of stories – traditional, historical, and personal – are exchanged. We hope that gradually the configurations of shared stories (and shared meanings) will emerge and out of these stories, which are likely to contain many traditional elements, mutual commitments to live in accordance with the stories will likely emerge as well.

These are but three ways in which the contemporary Jewish community might strengthen its capacity to serve as a plausibility structure for intensified Jewishness. In laying these out rather straightforwardly, as I have done, I do not wish to imply that implementing my suggestions will be easy. Designing attractive and Jewishly authentic communities is challenging enough. But we must also provide individuals with both the opportunities and incentives to utilize these contexts. Issues of visibility, cost, and accessibility are not irrelevant. Requiring Jews to be highly aware and committed *before* they are likely to enter or utilize our most potent contexts for Jewish experiences (e.g., day schools, Jewish summer camps, Israel trips, which are all comparatively expensive) immediately reduces our prospects for success. Nor is this only an issue of funding. Jewish settings that may function reasonably effectively as communities for their active members often find it difficult to genuinely welcome those who do not share the insiders' code.[13]

Thus, we dare not underestimate the extent of the effort that will be involved to make the Jewish community more "community-like." Even were we to make substantial progress, some might rightly question whether efforts along these lines could possibly have sufficient impact to outweigh the fact that, for most Jews, American society and culture are and will remain the primary context for and influence on the shaping of their beliefs, values, and behaviors. This recognition opens up an additional strategic direction for consideration: seeking to infuse public space and time with Jewish presences to the greatest extent possible.

Although North America represents the most benign and supportive diaspora environment in which Jews have ever lived, the public arena on this continent remains by and large neutral to negative in its impact on Jewishness because it provides relatively few positive cues or reinforcements for Jewish behavior. However, this arena is accessible to efforts that are designed to provide positive Jewish images and messages. Increasing attention has been given in the past few years to the possibilities for employing a variety of media—from television to computer networks—in ways that will foster Jewish pride, supply Jewish knowledge, or build Jewish connections, especially for many who are not drawn to Jewish institutions.[14] (In today's telecommunications world, people speak of "virtual communities" of individuals who interact, sometimes quite intimately and over long periods, only electronically. As anyone who has checked out the Internet lately can confirm, there are thriving Jewish "virtual communities" dealing with almost every imaginable concern and interest throughout today's cyberspace.) Some have urged that the tools of modern marketing and advertising be mobilized to foster Jewish consciousness. Even traditional American Jewish opposition to the placement of religious symbols in public spaces has been called into question as groups like the Lubavitcher Chasidim have erected large *chanukiot* in parks and in front of city halls.

In this context, we must address the question of the impact, both actual and potential, of what is unquestionably the most powerful Jewish plausibility structure of our era—the State of Israel. Israel has and continues to play many different roles with respect to North American Jewish identity.[15] For most American Jews it is a multivocal symbol—of Jewish tradition, post-Holocaust revival, continuing vulnerability, mutual responsibility, social justice, heroism, etc. Yet some of these symbolic resonances appear to be fading or becoming muddy, and as a result, Israel's position as the symbolic center of American Jewish life, what some have regarded as a pseudoreligion in its own right, appears to be weakening.

But Israel is not just a symbol. It is a real place and unquestionably a Jewish one, soon to be the largest Jewish community in the world. In Israel not only are Jews a majority, but public life and popular culture are thoroughly infused with Jewish referents and dimensions in a way that can never be in North America. At its best, Israel offers Jews the opportunity to connect their Jewishness to every aspect of their and society's life. Israel as Jewish plausibility structure may play a more powerful role in the future than Israel as symbol in shaping North American Jewish identity.

Inevitably, however, this will be a highly paradoxical role. Israel's power lies precisely in its being what the Jewish Diaspora is not. Like other experiences of intensive Jewish communality in which Jewish plausibility structures dominate—Jewish summer camps and retreats—Israel can inspire an intensification in Jewish consciousness and commitment, but unless one chooses to remain in that environment through *aliyah*, one faces the challenge of transferring and sustaining this level of identity in one's "normal" environment, where Jewish plausibility structures are weak.

Certainly those (and I am among them) who are urging today that as many Jewish young people as possible spend extended periods of time in Israel must be aware of this problem.[16] Israel can fulfill the vital role of exposing Diaspora Jews to the possibilities (and challenges) of creating and living in a Jewish society and can thereby expand the horizons of one's Jewish identity in manifold ways. Israel, as some educators have claimed, is a laboratory of Jewishness. But it cannot by itself solve the problems of Jewish identity and continuity for those who will live most of their lives in North America. The challenge of creating viable, attractive Jewish plausibility structures here persists.

It is not yet clear whether it is in fact possible to add to the plausibility structure for Jewish living in North America by using the public arena as a supplementary source of Jewish messages. Even if media and marketing can create a more hospitable climate for explicit community- and identity-building endeavors, it is doubtful that they can serve as substitutes for the latter. (We should recognize also that opening up public spaces carries the risk that Jewish messages may be overwhelmed by others that are inimical to our concerns.) The best rationale for marketing efforts and the use of media is, therefore, not that these are likely to transform behavior in their own right but that they may enhance the receptivity of Jews to intensive efforts to involve them in uniquely Jewish environments and settings.

The attempt to carve out Jewish space within the larger public space of American life leads to a broader question: How should we seek to position our community-building efforts in relationship to our surrounding society and its prevailing culture? If the plausibility structure that we are seeking to erect is to be both attractive and enduring, it seems that we must walk a thin line between linking these contexts/communities (and the Jewish cultures they embody) closely to the general society and culture and establishing areas of uniqueness and even dissent. If we do not present some familiar elements, if we are not conversant with the idioms of contemporary culture, and if we do not address issues that emanate from it, our Jewish settings will probably not be attractive or relevant to more than a handful of those whom we seek to engage. Indeed, one can take the argument a step further: Unless we work to insure that Jewish community and culture are in dialogue with the full range of contemporary art, literature, science, professions, and politics, we are impoverishing their ability to respond to ultimate questions by cutting them off from possible sources of insight and creative self-expression.[17]

But the Jewish partner must also have something to say in such a dialogue. If Jewish communities do not speak in a unique voice and do not offer additions or alternatives to some of the norms and meanings of the larger culture, there is little chance that they will be able to embody a worldview and ethos that is sufficiently distinctive and powerful to motivate any serious reconsideration by Jews of how they live their lives.[18] Without embodying a "no"—or at least a "yes and . . ."—and not simply a "yes" to contemporary society, Jewish identity is unlikely to be able to resist the pull toward homogenization and marginalization, the kind of purely symbolic ethnicity that Herbert Gans describes.

The arena of social and political action presents an excellent test case for the proposition that Jewish participation in the concerns of the larger American society can in fact be carried out in such a way as to enhance Jewish identity as well. There is no question that for a substantial number of Jews today, social issues and causes— equal rights regardless of gender or sexual preference, the environment, poverty and homelessness, international peace and justice—exercise a pull far stronger than any explicitly Jewish context or content. Some make no connection between their social commitments and their Jewishness. Yet for others these concerns are regarded as emanating from and expressing Jewish values and identification. The question is whether it is possible to capitalize on this sense of linkage and on the fact that Judaism certainly does have something to say about a wide range of social and political issues (even if what it has to say is often more complex than

ideologists of either the left or the right are prepared to acknowledge, abortion being a good example).

There have been both calls and initiatives in the last few years
to revive what some perceive as an ebbing tradition of Jewish
involvement in social causes as a way of drawing more Jews,
especially younger ones, into contexts where they can express some
of their deepest concerns with other Jews and perhaps even in a
Jewish idiom. If pursued with these goals in mind, these efforts
hold promise of providing a segment of the Jewish population with
gateways into both more extensive Jewish social relationships and
a fuller encounter with the cultural contents of Jewish tradition.
Although tapping political idealism is hardly a new strategy for
stimulating and activating Jewish consciousness, it may acquire a
new significance within the framework of the continuity agenda.
The key, however, may be whether those who follow this route are
serious about building the linkage to Jewish community
and culture. A "reductionist" approach that merely equates an
ostensibly Jewish political position with current thinking (whether
"correct" or otherwise) will not serve ultimately as the basis for a
genuine dialogue between a Jewish subculture and the larger
American society.

I have not yet spoken explicitly about what is probably the most
widely touted weapon in the arsenal of Jewish continuity—Jewish
education. My delay in doing so is in no way intended to cast doubt
on the critical importance of education, understood as a deliberately structured process of socialization and enculturation, in shaping
and strengthening Jewish identity. But all that I have said thus far
leads toward a particular view of how Jewish education's potential
impact can best be realized. *For education to be maximally effective,
there must be a living Jewish community in which what is being
taught and learned is already visible and valued.*

This principle explains why, on the one hand, the most effective
programs for Jewish identity development are those that create (or
expose participants to) functioning Jewish communities, and why,
on the other hand, temporally brief and isolated experiences (even
so-called transformational ones) are not in themselves sufficient to
guarantee success in changing identity. Day schools, summer
camps, youth group programs, trips to Israel, learning in *chavurot*
are all (or at least can all be) especially potent because they
typically place Jews in the company of other Jews for more than
just a formal learning experience and in environments in which
lived Jewish behavior is modeled and practiced over a period of

time. That the experience of community and the development of behavioral norms are important elements in the educational process apart from whatever content is transmitted is suggested by research that shows that the impact of such educational experiences often declines fairly rapidly once the individual is removed from the supportive social environment. The growing support for what Isa Aron has called an "enculturation" rather than an "instructional" model for elementary Jewish education in general also reflects acceptance of the proposition that it is difficult if not impossible to teach what hasn't been experienced.

This is not an argument for a purely experiential Jewish education. Communities and cultural systems are not built on shared experiences alone. Experiences without a language through which to interpret and connect them remain mute. Such a language involves highly sophisticated cognitive and symbolic components that must be encountered and mastered if the experiences are to yield their full of meaning. Performing Friday night rituals without knowing some measure of the historical, theological, literary, and halachic dimensions and resonances of Shabbat is rote behaviorism, not Jewish observance. The challenge for education is to curricularize the socialization/ enculturation process over time and for various target groups in all its dimensions: cognitive, affective, social, and behavioral. A holistic Jewish education, anchored in the life of real Jewish communities and capable of interpreting and communicating the depth and complexity of that life, is the only kind of Jewish education that is likely to have a decisive impact on the development of Jewish identity.

The Content of Community

There is, then, a consistent bottom line to my analysis of the potential strategies for promoting Jewish continuity: To be significantly more successful than we are today, we need to create many more and richer contexts in which Jewish culture is the prevailing socially operative framework within which activities are being undertaken and interpreted. That is, we need more Jewish *community*, not just more Jewish *programs*.[19]

To stop here, however, raises a critical question: What should the content and the culture of these Jewish communities be? Communities are defined by more than the relationships among their members. Martin Buber emphasized that a true community has a Center—a shared vision, purpose, and commitment—to which its members are linked like the spokes to the hub of a wheel.

It is this common relation to the Center that binds the members together. Any social reality communicates meaning implicitly through its structure, the norms of behavior it sanctions, and the codes of communication that govern day-to-day relationships within it. But communities also provide meaning explicitly by articulating ideologies and worldviews and by telling and interpreting the kinds of master stories referred to above that lend meaning to the individual lives of their members.

These explicit meanings are not the same from community to community. Not all societies and cultures share the same worldviews, the same values, the same moral or aesthetic sensibility. Earlier we suggested if Jewish communities are to constitute viable plausibility bases for a distinctive Jewish identity, they must embody distinctive cultural contents at some level. But what can these contents be in the contemporary, postmodern world, and what truth claims can be made on their behalf? What version (or versions) of Judaism will work today and be transmissible across generational boundaries so as to insure continuity?

Clearly the cultural contents of different Jewish communities will and must be diverse. If there ever was an era in which Jewish culture was unitary and monolithic, that time is long since past. Yet the pure existentialist position that claims that Jewish is as Jewish does (i.e., whatever Jews choose to do in the name of Jewishness has equal validity) also cannot be accepted as a framework for designing serious Jewish communities. The framing of the key questions, if not the answers themselves, must come out of a common storehouse of cultural categories that, for better or worse, we call Jewish tradition. What Shabbat means and how it will be celebrated in various Jewish communities may differ. But that there must be Shabbat (and that it must be on Saturday) seems inescapable if a community is to call itself Jewish.

This means that we will need major efforts to acquaint a largely unlearned Jewish population with the contents of classical Jewish culture. As was noted above, Jewish education, conceived as both socialization and enculturation, is rightly regarded as central to Jewish continuity. In fact education is itself in a profound sense the content of both Jewish community and culture. We are a Torah-centered people who ultimately refuse to separate study and action into means and end. In a more practical sense, all the characteristics that would enable a Jewish setting to take on the attributes of a Jewish community are tied into the traditional vocabulary of Jewish life. Without the ability to understand, use, and perhaps even add to this vocabulary, an individual cannot be expected to be an active and satisfied participant in the life of the community. And this facility cannot be achieved without textual, historical, and experiential learning.

By identifying Jewish tradition as the cultural storehouse for Jewish communities, we raise the question of whether contemporary Jewish communities and cultures must be religious in the ways in which we have conventionally understood this term. Today many are arguing that genuine and transmissible Jewish commitment can only be nurtured in explicitly religious contexts and via religious language. And indeed, attempts that have been made to construct alternative secular Jewish ideological and value systems in the modern period have largely failed.

The issue is a difficult one for several reasons: First, there is the empirical question of whether the religious ideologies operative among Jews today play any significant role in shaping behavior, at least outside Orthodox and elite circles. We have argued that the development and expression of Jewish identity probably owes more to the presence or absence of Jewish plausibility structures in which particular Jewish behaviors are manifest than to the communication of rationales for Jewish identification and commitment. (If this were not so, many of our current efforts to nurture Jewish identity should be more effective than they apparently are.) Community must have a content, but it may be that this content needs to be made explicit primarily at the behavioral level, not through religious or secular ideology.

Still, it is hard to dismiss the role of articulated ideologies and values altogether, given the fact that humans are rationalizing creatures who, at a minimum, seek to give their behavior legitimation in ideational and moral terms and who may well be motivated to act by these same considerations. It may be fairer to say that there *is* a connection between Jewish ideology and behavior in which each in some way reinforces the other, although the precise dynamics of the relationship may vary and are difficult to pin down. However, this does not resolve the question of whether Jewish ideologies must be religious in order to exert a significant impact.

Historically an important element in the power of religious ideologies has been their ability to invoke the experiences (individual or collective) of the sacred to legitimate their claims. When Jews are asked to accept behavioral norms (i.e., *mitzvot*) that are traditionally perceived and promulgated as reflecting the will of a Sacred Power, their ability to experience that Power in their lives

35

is surely one (although not the only) determinant of the persuasiveness of this call. (That is to say, Torah without Sinai, without the experience of its revelation, is not quite so authoritative.) The ability to invoke powerful spiritual experiences is one of the advantages that religion has over purely secular meaning systems in asserting its influence, one that secular authority frequently seeks to mimic through theatrics and other means.

Most surveys, however, show that American Jews are highly secularized, perhaps the most secularized segment of American society. Some would argue that this secularity is experiential even more than it is ideological. Many Jews simply don't experience the sacred in their lives, or if they do, they don't recognize and name it as such.

What is certainly true is that many American Jews don't experience the sacred in the ways and places they have been told to expect to find it—in explicitly religious institutions. If it is true that Jewish identity detached from a religious base is inherently tenuous (at least from the point of view of transmissibility, as seems to be the case) and that religious ideology has difficulty sustaining itself as impactful without religious experience to support it, and if the religious institutions that have serious ideologies often fail to be effective mediators of religious experience (on this score, statistics on synagogue attendance are chastening), then a major priority must be not the repeated reiteration of the ideological claims (which are likely to fall on deaf ears) but the reinvigoration of religious experience itself.

Religious institutions must look carefully at which elements of religious life and language resonate for Jews today as pathways to the experience of the sacred and the acceptance of behavioral commitments (*mitzvot*) and which do not. Theology and large group prayer (the typical worship experience in many synagogues) may be ineffectual, while Judaic text study, family ritual, personal participation in acts of *tzedakah* and *gemilut chasadim*, and more intimate *chavurah*-style worship may prove to be quite potent. Religious institutions must also acknowledge that religious experience, and hence even some measure of ideological validity, can be found in settings that are not conventionally religious. What I have called the "civil religious" settings and institutions of the contemporary Jewish community—among which I would preeminently list the Land and State of Israel—are also sources of sacred experience for many Jews, with or without religious ideological interpretation.

For most American Jews, Jewishness remains a complex, poorly conceptualized mixture of ethnic, cultural, and religious components. We must use all these elements in seeking to create social/cultural frameworks within which a sense of commitment can be nurtured. We will need systems of meaning to undergird Jewish behavior, but these may well be, as Riv-Ellen Prell has suggested, dialogic and partial rather than comprehensive and systematic and lead to Jewish practice without constituting full-fledged systems of obligation.[20] "Signals of transcendence" (in Berger's phrase) can be found for different individuals in different places. In fact, there is a serious theological current in modern Judaism, exemplified in such diverse figures as Kaplan, Buber, Borowitz, and Greenberg, that argues that this era is characterized by a blurring of the boundaries between the sacred and secular realms. Some people go even further and contend that the goal of instilling a sense of "holy secularity"—of effecting the interpenetration of these two ostensibly distinct sensibilities—may be read out of (or into) the texts and ideologies of classical Judaism that go as far back as the Bible itself.

Does this "opening up" of the sacred accentuate or diminish the importance and impact of explicit religious institutions and ideologies? The answer is not clear. It may be that we will have and need a variety of languages in which to express this sensibility, some traditional and some not. It is probable that as the purely ethnic components of Jewishness recede, and as Jewish popular culture grows less familiar (What does that Yiddish phrase mean?) and/or distinctive ("You don't have to be Jewish to . . ."), religious symbols and behaviors *will* grow more important as the elements of a shared Jewish culture. Religious language does represent our richest and most widely shared vocabulary for explicating Jewish life. Despite all of its problematics, other languages are even less potent. However, religious language itself is increasingly likely to appear as hybrid meaning-constructions with intertwined religious and secular elements. These "messy" constructs, and not movement ideologies per se, may well be the primary cognitive and value frameworks for most Jews, even those who affiliate with religious institutions.

It is thus even more essential that religious vocabulary and symbols do not become formulaic and objectified but remain actively in use for shared meaning-making. This then is the challenge that religious institutions face: Having won the ideological battle with secularism, can they prevent their victory from becoming pyrrhic? Religious institutions make a grave error if they believe that the decline of secularism is ipso facto a sign of their own strength. Nor do the indicators of a spiritual/ religious revival in Jewish life (whose dimensions are unclear) constitute an unreserved vote of confidence in the ideologies of our major religious movements. Only by insuring that religious ideology and values are tied—and exposed—to the life of real Jewish communities, where they will be measured against individual and collective experience and their power to help shape Jewish life-space will be tested, can these elements of Jewish culture achieve significant impact. Content as culture cannot precede community. It can only emerge along with it, even if its roots are in the most ancient texts and traditions.

I conclude once again, therefore, that the linchpin of our continuity efforts must be the construction of Jewish communities (social/cognitive/experiential realities), some of which will be explicitly and conventionally religious and some of which may experience and articulate their center – their unifying vision – in nontraditional ways.

From Strategy to Tactics: How Do We Build Communities?

We come now to the *tachlis*. It's fine to speak about the need for creating Jewish communities, but just how shall we do this, especially in light of the analysis suggesting that the loss of community is one of the characteristic features of modern Jewish life? It seems to me the only practical answer is to work with what community we do have, namely, the elaborate set of existing institutions that constitute the public domain of American Jewish life.

We may hope that new forms of community will emerge from time to time to challenge, catalyze, supplement, or fill the spaces between existing organizations. We need experiments in community building and new types of institutions. Indeed, there are many Jews for whom the current institutional infrastructure of American Jewry is at best irrelevant and at worst repelling. Some of these Jews have founded or formed their own Jewish communities, often nearly invisible to the dominant structures and their leadership. Others are still seeking (or may have despaired of finding) connections to Jews who share their particular interests or dispositions.

There is no loss and much potential gain for Jewish life in welcoming and even seeking to assist such nascent or countercultural communities. Helping them to grow and to establish linkages with other like-minded Jews adds to the sum total of community in Jewish life. Some may worry that such communities will foster highly idiosyncratic, marginal forms of Jewishness, not only further fragmenting the weak Jewish plausibility structure but also blurring the boundaries between Jewish and non-Jewish cultural contents. Still, in an already highly pluralistic, at times fractured, Jewish world, it is unlikely that these communities represent a real threat to communal and cultural integrity. It is far more likely that without such communities, a not insignificant portion of the Jewish populace will simply be lost to Jewish life.

Having said this, I still believe that the primary arena in which the efforts to strengthen community and to build a powerful Jewish plausibility structure must take hold is that of our current institutional infrastructure—especially the synagogues and their associated institutions, as well as the Federated system of agencies. (Most new institutions will probably be absorbed into this infrastructure in some fashion, either directly as organizations that work alongside those that exist today or by becoming attached to existing institutions, much as has happened with the *chavurah* movement. And, although one day perhaps "virtual communities" will diminish the role of institutions altogether and allow unmediated connections through electronic interfacing, this is neither an immediate nor, for many, an entirely encouraging prospect.)

Today's institutions, however, fall short, often far short, of what is needed for them to be effective identity-nurturing and identity-sustaining communities. Increasingly, the realization is spreading that the core of the continuity agenda is an agenda of profound institutional strengthening and transformation, both internally and in relation to one another. Institutions must be capable of offering a menu of high-quality programs to educate, socialize, and enculturate, but just as important, they must be capable of binding participants into groups in whose relationships, behavior, and conversations the educational content is anchored.

In recent years, many Jewish institutions have adopted a consumer orientation in their activities, emphasizing programs and services that they think will be attractive to prospective participants. To some extent, this approach is driven by economic necessity. However, it can also reflect a healthy openness to continual self-assessment and a desire to be responsive to genuine needs. In this sense, a marketing mentality can help create an engaged constituency and give an institution the opportunity to have an impact on life-choices. But customer service must ultimately be transcended as a definition of institutional *purpose* and as the content of an institution's culture because it too easily accepts an ethos that regards Jewishness as entirely voluntaristic and selective. Attracting consumers of Jewish programs and services is the beginning of community but not its full realization.

One can argue further that what is most likely to attract new participants to Jewish institutional life is the likelihood of their finding therein an attachment to a community that is active and authentic. This seems to be one of the lessons we can learn from those in the Jewish world who have enjoyed the greatest success in outreach. A delicate dialectic links the principle of "meeting people where they are" with the need to "be what you are." People must reach out from a place that is itself rich, vibrant, and contentful, as well as open, sensitive, and adaptive; otherwise when the invitation for others to join in has been accepted, there may be no "there" there to sustain the engagement.

In the effort to transform institutions into true communities, the synagogue is the institution that is the most directly on the firing line because more Jews look to it for primary Jewish community than to any other institution. The classical ideal of the synagogue, at once a *bet knesset* (house of assembly), *bet tefilah* (house of prayer), and *bet midrash* (house of study), is almost a paradigm for what a contemporary Jewish community should seek to be. Few synagogues today are this paradigm for more than a handful of their congregants. But the fact that a wide variety of Jewish activities of every type can take place under one roof and the fact that multiple subcommunities can pursue their own Jewish needs and interests and still come together and feel the power of being a single *kahal* (congregation) give the synagogue an enormous potential as the cornerstone of a revitalized Jewish plausibility structure.

This is the stake that every Jewish institution has in the success of synagogue renewal efforts. There are already a few model congregations worth emulating and a number of promising initiatives for promoting synagogue transformation.[21] What many of these efforts share is the belief that synagogues must move from being simply institutions that offer diverse programs to multiple constituencies (which is how many in fact operate) to being true communities in which a substantial number of the members are committed to and involved in realizing a shared vision of what their community is about.

This vision may be inward looking—for example, a congregation that is engaged in serious Jewish learning, spirituality, or *gemilut chasadim*—or outward looking—for example, a congregation that is devoted to social action, outreach, or service to specific populations, such as new Americans or singles. A congregation may embrace a complex defining vision or even a cluster of visions, for example, a commitment to promoting the Jewish growth of families and young people through excellence in Jewish education and active engagement with other institutions in the community. What seems critical, however, is that the synagogue define itself as a community that is striving to help its congregants become fellow participants in a shared endeavor that will enrich all concerned.

Organizing congregational life around a central vision is a challenging process, especially if that vision is to be relevant to the many different types of individuals who are "affiliated" with a particular congregation at a specific moment in time. Not all congregants may wish to be asked to become more involved in their affiliation, even if they are promised that they will get more out of it in return. The transformation process also offers challenges to the professional leadership to take on new and perhaps uncomfortable roles. Realistically, synagogues probably need to balance a desire to be vision driven and to have a core value or set of values inform the entirety of their programming and collective life with the need to maintain a diversity of foci in order to appeal to different age groups, interest, and life-cycle needs. But the process of bringing congregants into a new relationship with the synagogue and with one another seems vital if the institutional infrastructure of American Jewry is to succeed in rebuilding a substantive Jewish community for any significant number of Jews. The challenge to the synagogue is monumental, and the evident weaknesses of other institutions in Jewish communal life today should be cause not for complacency or triumphalism among synagogue leaders but for serious efforts to realize the synagogue's enormous potential.

Synagogue transformation is critical, but it is not sufficient as a recipe for strengthening Jewish community. I believe that no one would seriously disagree with the statement that we need a multiplicity of institutions of different types to meet effectively the needs of our tremendously diverse Jewish populace and to fulfill the multiple purposes of collective Jewish existence. (Whether we need quite as many as we have is another question.) But if these institutions are to add substantially to the sum total of Jewish community available to Jews, they must be sensitive to the same issues of how to forge genuine connections among Jews and how to develop norms of shared behavior, linked to Jewish experiences, language, and meanings, that synagogues should be preoccupied with.

All Jewish institutions can – and some are even beginning to – address this mandate. The Judaization of some Federations through the incorporation of study, ritual, and intensive experiences of fellowship established during retreats and on missions is one example of what can be done. The Hillel system has embarked on a major effort to reshape itself as a more open, encompassing structure capable of serving both as a visible, attractive, and relevant Jewish presence on campus and as a nurturer of Jewish growth along a wider spectrum of dimensions and for a broader array of students. But there is still a long way to go to engage the full ensemble of organizations that could transform themselves into more effective Jewish community-building instruments—membership organizations, social service agencies, community relations bodies—in this agenda.

Along with the synagogue, the institution that probably has the best chance to make a substantial contribution to the expansion of Jewish community is the Jewish Community Center (JCC). Historically the JCC has been a primary institution of Jewish acculturation to American life. However, for at least the past decade the dominant thrust among the leadership of the Center movement has been to refashion the JCC as a Jewish identity-building and educational instrument. Significant changes have already taken place: the hiring of Jewish educational specialists for JCCs; Judaic training of staff and lay leadership (especially in Israel); expanded Jewish content in Center programming in such areas as adult education, early childhood education, family education, and summer camping; the celebration of Jewish holidays and increased efforts to create a Jewish ambience in Center buildings.

The challenge that Centers now face is whether they can consolidate and extend these changes in order to transform the fundamental culture of the JCC. Certainly the Center has unique capabilities as a potential Jewish plausibility structure. It does reach and engage a broad spectrum of Jews across both age and ideological lines. There is evidence that JCCs are especially effective as gateways to Jewish experience, association, and even learning for populations that are reluctant or not ready to participate in synagogues. The large and diverse membership of Centers, the wide variety of activities they offer, and their often impressive physical plants constitute a Jewish plausibility structure in their own right. Center leaders speak today of aspiring to become a "new Jewish neighborhood," replete with the sights, smells, and sounds of Jews and Jewishness in action. Centers also have superior abilities to mobilize modes of expression, such as the arts, that are often neglected as vehicles for building engaging Jewish communities and culture.

However, JCCs do face significant challenges if they are to become powerful mediators of Jewish community for substantial numbers of Jews. Perhaps more than any other Jewish institution they are bound to a consumer ethos and a market-oriented strategy of engagement. This is both a strength and a potential weakness for the building of communities of commitment, as I have noted above. People come to Centers for many reasons and with many expectations. Often these reasons and expectations have nothing to do with a desire for Jewish experiences. For some JCCs this fact motivates efforts to become more creative in introducing Jewish elements into all aspects of their work and for larger numbers of their "customers." But this is rarely easy, and amidst the competition for attention and resources (and with staff often limited in their Judaic knowledge and skills), the Jewish component is frequently minimal.

Centers must also grapple with the question of the content of the Jewishness they sponsor. Some people still look to the JCC movement as the potential generator and transmitter of a nondenominational, secular Jewish ideology and culture.[22] Others doubt both that such a form of Judaism can today have an impact outside institutional settings and that it is transmissible. It may not in fact be necessary (or desirable) for JCCs to develop a unique, integral Jewish culture in their own right in order to make a contribution to the sum total of Jewish community, especially if their role is primarily that of gateway and adjunct to other Jewish settings. But, as Center leaders themselves are increasingly recognizing, neither can Centers be satisfied with being the sponsors of a minimalist, least common denominator version of Jewishness that is largely associational, expressed only within the walls of the institution (and then primarily in symbolic form), and inconsequential in terms of its impact on individual behavior and commitments.

A third major complicating factor faced by JCCs is that their very efforts to become more Jewishly substantive often cause tension between them and synagogues and other educational institutions. I know of no evidence that as Centers become more Jewishly vigorous and as they (presumably) thereby strengthen the Jewish plausibility structure for their members, synagogues are weakened. But turf and the perception of competition that is destructive are realities in Jewish organizational life, and Centers must develop strategies (hopefully with the cooperation of synagogues) that minimize the perception that their efforts at institutional transformation may negatively impact on others. The most desirable way to do this, on both practical and theoretical grounds, is to develop positive collaborations in which the community-building, culture-transmitting endeavors of multiple institutions are actually advanced. Happily, a growing number of examples of this type of collaboration can be found.[23]

This highlights the fact that transformation must take place not only *within* institutions but *between* them as well. Mordecai Kaplan imagined (and urged) that American Jewish life be organized as a "community of communities." New institutional relationships are an indispensable element of the community-building agenda. Pragmatically, we will need not just the involvement of multiple institutions but also their collaboration and mutual support if we are to have a sufficient number of high-quality contexts and programs for identity development and expression. In order to rebuild a powerful plausibility base for Jewishness, the face we present to Jews cannot be one with gaping fissures. Synergies and smooth transitions between institutions and programs are a requisite if Jews are to feel that they are part of an overarching community, one that places priority on their welfare and growth and not on preserving institutional interests. When multiple options and entry points become unconnected, not to say jealous, suitors for the allegiance of individual Jews, all of the claimants eventually suffer. This is why individual institutions that view Jewish affiliation as a zero sum game are not only wrong (the rule in Jewish identity is "the more, the more") but also self-defeating.

This does not mean that institutions should abandon their particularity or that one size can fit all. On the ideological level we face the challenge of developing a nonrelativistic pluralism of multiple but aligned Jewish cultures.[24] (We face a similar challenge vis-à-vis the outside world. Can we position ourselves in the emerging multicultural framework of American life as strong supporters of both pluralism and an overarching value framework and at the same time assert the truth claims of Jewish values and norms, at least for Jews?) On the practical level the challenge is to coordinate our respective institutional efforts to enculturate and socialize so that we take maximum advantage of the full (albeit limited) array of available resources, do together those things that can best be done in concert, and still give each institution the freedom to pursue its own vision of what Jewish community can and should be.[25]

This is a formidable challenge indeed, amounting to a cultural revolution in Jewish life. Change on this scale will require a combination of individual institutional initiatives and community-wide systems of support. We have learned from educational reform efforts in the general society in recent years (in some ways a less ambitious initiative than being urged here) that neither bottom-up nor top-down models of change work alone. Both thrusts are needed. We are seeking to affect the inner life and deepest structural regularities of institutions that developed with different self-understandings, populations, vocabularies, and survival strategies. If change at this level is to take place, institutions need to build up their capacities for envisioning, managing, implementing, and interpreting such change.

This capacity building must encompass:

- *Leadership education* Leaders must be willing to change and know how to overcome the inevitable roadblocks to doing so.

- *Personnel development* A sufficient number of professionals capable of guiding and facilitating community life must be trained.

- *Knowledge dissemination* Successes and failures must be understood and shared.

- *Matchmaking with external resources* Institutions must be guided and given access to sources of assistance for the complex process of change.

- *Incentivizing change* Rewards and recognition must be given to those willing to take the risks of seeking fundamental transformations and effecting new institutional relationships.

Each of these tools and supports for helping institutions transform themselves requires its own design and implementation system. This means that in addition to specific interventions at the institutional level, we need to create a supportive and to some extent demanding climate at the transinstitutional level that can alternately guide, assist, and drive the individual efforts. Communities will need agents of change at the institutional level, change facilitators at the transinstitutional level, and change coalitions to establish the environment in which self-improvement and cooperation become the accepted norm for institutional behavior. None of this can take place without major infusions of human and financial resources, directed not only at individual institutions but also at the development of high-quality support systems. (The need for the latter is still often overlooked or dismissed by some advocates of change today. I do not see, e.g., how it is possible to produce major improvements in the scope and quality of educational programming, sure to be one of the centerpieces of any continuity effort, without a strong and capable central educational body that serves as a change facilitator and resource.)

This is the primary arena of challenge and opportunity for Federations with respect to the agenda of Jewish continuity. The concept of community has been central to the Federation movement's self-understanding as it has evolved from a league of local charities to what Daniel Elazar has termed the "framing institution" of the contemporary Jewish polity. At times the Federated system has seen itself as the heir to the traditional *kehillah* and, indeed, no other institutional framework can claim to represent and serve *all* of the Jews residing in a given locality.

At a time when the amount of genuine community in Jewish life is not great, Federations' ability to embody at least one important dimension of Jewish communality—the sense of being connected to and responsible for Jews across time and space—should not be taken lightly. By bringing large numbers of Jews together for collective action that is linked to the worldwide community of *Klal Yisrael*, the Federated system (i.e., Federations, their associated local agencies, and the national and international organizations that are tied directly to them) constitutes a public, visible plausibility base for Jewishness that no institution or movement in Jewish life other than the State of Israel (with which it is closely linked) can match. As such, its potential as a skeleton around which to construct the "community of communities" we should be seeking is substantial.

But for this potential to be realized, Federations will need to rethink their fundamental character, commitments, and style of operation. On the one hand, they will need to take even more seriously than they have their role as mediators of Jewish community and meaning. What I described a decade ago as a Federation-centered and Federation-sponsored American Jewish civil religion—a set of beliefs, norms, myths, and rituals embodied in the Federated system's rhetoric and activities—has enabled a substantial number of American Jews to connect their personal life stories to the larger drama being played out on the world historical stage and to find a social reality, the Federated system itself, whose activity enacts this drama. But, as I argued in my work a decade ago, the meanings provided by this civil religion are at best partial, touching only selected spheres of personal existence, and the community that embodies and transmits these meanings is in many respects and for most Jews a fictive one (one that does not really engage them at a personal level). If Federations are to capitalize on the potential for building community and for communicating Jewish meaning that they have discovered in their work, they must link themselves to more encompassing forms of community and holistic frameworks of Jewish meaning. Their appropriation of Jewish language must become fuller, and their appreciation and support for the multiple dimensions of community life (learning, ritual, spiritual sharing, direct interpersonal contact, as well as activism) stronger.

This will not be easy for a system that has thought of itself as nonideological, if not altogether secular, and whose drive for consensus often seems to lead to "least common denominator" approaches to difficult issues. But the days are past when a Jewish activism rooted primarily in emotional responses to the Holocaust and Israel, explicated in a few catchphrases with little substantive Jewish content, and implemented through an organizational structure focused largely on financial concerns can by itself reproduce serious Jewish commitment. Many Federations and the national leadership of the Federation system have recognized this. As a result, the embrace of the Jewish continuity agenda by Federations has begun to lead to a serious soul-searching within the system itself.

This reassessment, however, must extend beyond efforts to communalize and Judaize the Federation or to strengthen its own potential as a plausibility structure. The critical role for Federations in the continuity agenda remains the classical one of community organization, although now in a new key. No other agency in American Jewish life can undertake the capacity and coalition building – the orchestration of the interplay of various institutional actors so that the whole is indeed greater than the sum of its parts – that is central to forging a "community of communities." Many Federations have already made this the hallmark of their continuity efforts.

The question is whether Federations will explore the implications of taking on this demanding role to the end. Traditional Federation community organization activity has (only occasionally and tentatively) reached beyond the immediate boundaries of the Federated system. Rarely has it embraced an explicit agenda of institutional transformation. The traditional assumptions and modalities of Federation planning strike many as ill-suited to an endeavor that will require decades, cannot be focused on a single problem or target population, will involve multiple actors with diverse cultures and ideological commitments, will require a massive investment of resources, and challenges some of the very achievements of the American institutional system itself. Those Federations that approach the continuity agenda in terms of seeding a handful of new programs aimed at promoting identification or affiliation—no matter how sound the programs themselves—are doomed to frustration and disappointment. Unfortunately, those that do see the implications in their full dimensions may well encounter even greater discouragement as they contemplate the magnitude and complexity of the task they have set themselves.[26]

Some Federations, faced with this challenge, may try to do too much themselves; others may shy away from the toughest issues (how do we get institutions to change themselves, not simply add new programs?). The best counsel I can muster is that Federations must develop a clear vision of the desired end, an understanding of the paths that are likely to lead toward it, and a readiness to invest the time and energy (and eventually money) required to pursue the difficult path of capacity building and systemic transformation. Federations will have to model this process on themselves and use their technical skills, moral influence, and what leverage their financial resources can provide to guide other institutions subtly and respectfully to join the endeavor. Some institutions will be more than ready, possibly way ahead of the Federations; others may never be prepared to join the effort wholeheartedly. But if Federations focus consistently on the theme of building living Jewish communities and building mutually supportive relationships among these communities, they will at least be pointing themselves and others in the right direction.

Once more, there are Federations that have sought to embody some or all of these principles in their continuity initiatives.[27] Their progress should be monitored closely because evidence of success on their part in promoting fundamental transformations will inspire and buttress other efforts for change.

And in the End, the Question "Why?"

As I said at the outset, the framework that I have laid out above is not and is not intended to be dramatically new. Rather I have tried, necessarily in a somewhat superficial way, to restate what we are about in today's Jewish continuity endeavor. I have argued it is important that we set our work in the context of an historical, social scientific understanding of the dynamics of Jewish identity development and of a model of institutional and cultural change. The theory I offer is straightforward: The transformation of Jewish individuals will require the transformation of Jewish institutions, which will, in turn, require transformations in the relationships among institutions, all aimed at creating a "community of communities."

I have dealt cursorily or not at all with some elements that will need to be part of an eventual "unified field theory." The psychodynamics of Jewish identity and identity development; the complex role of the family in relation to the individual and the community; the challenges of engaging marginal Jews in the lives of the communities that we are struggling to create; the details of capacity building; the question of how to pay for all this—all of these issues will need to be addressed far more fully and adequately, not primarily, of course, for the sake of a theory but because they are critical to any successful implementation of a continuity agenda.

Despite these obvious lacunae, I am prepared to argue that the direction for what must be done *is* clear and that if it is not precisely as I have described it, it cannot be dramatically different.

There is one final issue that I wish to address, although it is of a different character. Why do we wish to make the effort at all? The continuity endeavor is being driven by those of us who are already on the inside, by Jews whose own Jewish identity is relatively secure and whose commitment to the future of the community is manifest. In urging action to promote Jewish identity and continuity, we insiders find ourselves in the somewhat odd position of telling a patient that (s)he is in dire need of medical intervention when the patient is not even complaining of a problem and may even respond that the difficulty must lie in our heads! The vast majority of Jews seem not to be concerned with what bothers us, which makes it all the more difficult to imagine how they will be induced to take the medicine we prescribe.

Why do we persist? Perhaps we do so out of a stubbornness (arrogance?) that simply will not accept that those Jews who are indifferent truly know what is best for them. Perhaps it is because we are sure we know what the others are missing. Or perhaps we simply cannot bear to see indifference to what we value so highly.

There is, of course, another way to look at this issue. Perhaps our concern is not really for our contemporaries but for our children and grandchildren. This, after all, is what continuity is about for many Jews. Certainly the question "Will our grandchildren be Jewish?" has proven to be a powerful rallying cry for continuity efforts not only in North America. But this concern only defers the question of why being Jewish matters and does not answer it. And frankly, there is some room for doubt as to whether posing the continuity issue in this fashion as a concern for the Jewishness of future generations does not subtly reinforce the sense that the whole issue is about others and not about ourselves. As a rallying cry, "Will our grandchildren be Jewish?" seems more likely to provoke policy prescriptions than personal change. Thus, although concern for the future is undoubtedly a powerful motivating force for today's efforts, it is not, I would argue, a sufficient basis on which to ground them and may, in fact, lead us somewhat astray.

I believe that there is another reason for our determination to take action whose more explicit acknowledgment may be critical to our ultimate success. I suggest that we care about the Jewishness of others, including that of our progeny, because we still believe that being Jewish makes a difference in some larger scheme and not just personally. We do connect our own life narratives in some way with the master story of the Jewish people's covenantal character and mission, with the belief that we have distinctive values and a responsibility in the world. And we intuit correctly not only, as Arthur Hertzberg has suggested we do, that the disappearance of the Jewish people would be an unutterable tragedy but also that only a community that is strong, self-confident, and reasonably populous—not a remnant community—can effect our mission today. It is not mere pride or perversity that drives our current anxiety and efforts. It is the conviction that Jewish continuity is *not* a self-interested conceit. It is a vital contribution to the welfare of humanity.

Only the conviction that what Jews do as Jews has ultimate significance can validate a readiness and willingness to struggle for our distinctiveness when external reasons for doing so have faded. If Jews are to be prepared to say no to some aspects of contemporary culture, without which it is hard to imagine Jewish identity enduring, they must have a very good reason to do so. We cannot compel or convince those who are unsure of their commitment to accept our reasons. We can only share these reasons and seek to open a dialogue—an honest dialogue in which we grapple openly with the compelling, often troubling implications of this kind of faith in the contemporary world.

Even a "unified field theory" of Jewish continuity will lead not to definitive answers about our fate but to a confrontation with the mystery of Jewish existence. Without facing this mystery, for ourselves first of all, the Jewish continuity agenda may be neither feasible nor worth pursuing. But this is not so different from what many physicists and cosmologists expect from their own "unified field theory": an appreciation of the unity of the universe that leads beyond knowledge to wonder and appreciation.

Notes

1   This paper owes much to many. Only at great risk do I list some of those who have influenced my thinking greatly both in conversations and in writing: first, because I will forget to thank some who deserve it; second, because I have undoubtedly distorted the ideas of these people in the course of appropriating them. Still, credit, but no blame, must be given to: Arnie Eisen, Barry Chazan, Deborah Lipstadt, Carl Sheingold, Norbert Fruehauf, Art Vernon, John Ruskay, Jack Ukeles, Jim Meier, David Elcott, Irwin Kula, Steven M. Cohen, Steven Bayme, Riv Ellen Prell, Isa Aron, Sara Lee, Adrianne Bank, Susan Shevitz, Bernie Reisman, Joe Reimer, Sherry Israel, Richard Joel, Barry Shrage, all my colleagues at JESNA, and others unremembered. Special thanks to Noam Elcott for correcting my physics.

2   If we wish to be more technical, we can distinguish between the "salience" and the "centrality" of Jewishness in one's identity. The former refers to the importance that one attributes to one's Jewishness; the latter to whether one's Jewishness occupies a significant portion of one's life-space. There are people who claim that being Jewish is very important to them, even though it does not impact many aspects of their lives. This may well be true. For example, one may view one's Jewishness as highly significant in shaping one's social and political consciousness and behavior, despite the fact that one engages in almost no explicitly Jewish activity. (Another example is that of a father and mother whose Jewish observance and involvement are minimal but who become highly distressed when one of their children chooses a non-Jewish spouse.) From the perspective of Jewish continuity, the question is whether salience alone, without centrality, is sufficient for a transmissible Jewish identity. I am doubtful, for reasons that will become apparent.

3   Although I follow the convention of speaking about identity as an individual phenomenon, identity is, as I understand it, constituted in large measure by the relationship one has to social and cultural realities outside the self, i.e., to groups and to bodies of knowledge, customs, norms, and symbols that provide the content that defines the self and its characteristic ways of appropriating, understanding, and responding to reality.

4   As Arnic Eisen has commented to me, we should not let individuals entirely off the hook for the choices they make. Some people do, after all, choose to struggle harder to carve out Jewish space in their lives while others are content to "go with the flow." Nevertheless, the point remains that berating people for not deciding to be more Jewish (what Steven M. Cohen calls the "language of reproach") is neither entirely fair nor likely to work.

5   In *The Sacred Canopy*, Peter Berger describes the operation of plausibility structures in the following way: "Worlds are socially constructed and socially maintained. Their continuing reality, both objective (as common, taken-for-granted facticity) and subjective (as facticity imposing itself on individual consciousness), depends upon *specific* social processes, namely those processes that ongoingly reconstruct and maintain the particular worlds in question. Conversely, the interruption of these social processes threatens the [objective and subjective] reality of the worlds in question. Thus each world requires a social `base' for its continuing existence as a world that is real to actual human beings. This `base' may be called its plausibility structure." (p. 45)

6   In placing primary emphasis on the role of collective social realities (plausibility structures) in shaping and sustaining individual identity, I do not mean to dismiss altogether the impact that a single important individual can have as a role model and mentor. Social worlds are mediated through specific individuals as well as institutions, and experience provides many examples of how a parent, teacher, youth leader or peer can, through an especially powerful primary relationship, have a profound influence on the course of an individual's Jewish development. Institutions whose professed ideals do *not* find expression in the behavior of real individuals lose their power to socialize and enculturate effectively. Nevertheless, the impact of particular role models and mentors rarely if ever takes place outside the context of social processes, plausibility structures, which they, in effect, embody and represent. In fact, it is often this capacity to exemplify a whole social world in their person, I would suggest, that accounts for their influence.

7   Actually I view the statistics less negatively than some others do. There are elements of real strength in North American Jewish life that we should not ignore, including a core of committed Jews constituting perhaps a fourth of the Jewish population, numerous pockets of energy and cultural creativity, a residual attachment to Jewishness even on the part of many whom we include among the "Jews at risk," and capable, resourceful institutions. Were this strength not present, no continuity strategy could hope to succeed, including the one that I propose in this paper.

8   In this regard, we have much to learn from the Orthodox. They have succeeded in creating communities rich in inducements and reinforcements at the practical and social levels that support the beliefs and behaviors they advocate. Creating similarly powerful social contexts for other modes of Jewish living is the great challenge that non-Orthodox varieties of Judaism face.

9   I'm suggesting that although most of us tend to move through a number of social worlds in the course of our activities, we can and do feel differently about our rootedness in these worlds. Some we visit. In others we feel more at home. A "home" community, I think, is one in which we feel especially comfortable, one that we care about deeply, and one that we look to for both nurturance and guidance. The "home" community does not have an exclusive hold on the minds and hearts of its members, but it is recognized as being special and closer to the individual in some important ways than other social contexts in which he/she lives and works.

10 The dynamics of competition in a pluralized context are complex. On the one hand, failure to tout one's wares and to differentiate oneself in the marketplace is crippling; on the other hand, unbridled competition ultimately undermines the credibility of all the competitors. Too much parochialism and denigration of other Jewish institutions, movements, etc., renders the claims of all of them suspect.

11 Clifford Geertz asserts that this linkage of ethos and worldview so that each supports the other is the unique, defining characteristic of religion as a cultural system.

12 I am particularly indebted to my friends at CLAL, especially Irwin Kula and David Elcott, for the ideas in this section.

13 Of course, institutions are not powerless to address this problem. Hillels that are reaching out to involve students who are beyond their committed core, synagogues that are instituting learners' *minyanim* to acculturate those who find regular services intimidating and exclusive, Federations that are designing human resource management systems to smooth the way for new leaders to ascend to positions of influence are all examples of institutions that are struggling to extend the communality experienced by a few to larger numbers who have frequently found these institutions alienating and uninviting.

14 Some would argue that there is already much more available in the public arena that could be employed to heighten Jewish consciousness than we recognize and take advantage of. Certainly on one level the disproportionate attention that the media give to Israel and to Jews and Jewish life in general (itself the product of many complex factors) creates great public presence for Jewishness, albeit not always an entirely positive one. Jews and Jewish issues often show up in unexpected places (e.g., the question of whether to sit *shivah* for one's estranged father was a central element of the plot in a recent TV science-fiction series set in the twenty-third century). The Revson Foundation's work to create the Jewish Heritage Video Collection using extensive commercial film and broadcast material illustrates graphically the potential for mobilizing the media for the purpose of building Jewish identity.

15 See the paper "A New Role for Israel in American Jewish Identity" by Arnold Eisen, published by the American Jewish Committee.

16 The problem is heightened by the fact that the language of Israel's social and cultural discourse is Hebrew, a language that most American Jews do not speak. In general, the fact that North American Jews do not by and large share a distinctive Jewish language weakens their ability to maintain an integral community. The way in which we speak to one another, including the language itself, helps to create the plausibility structure for the meanings we seek to express. Much of Judaism can be translated (although imperfectly). But from a social constructivist perspective, the generally poor state of the Hebrew language in America is a barrier both to creating a solid link to the Israeli plausibility structure and to erecting such a structure on this continent.

17 The challenge is whether we can create a sense of dynamic connectedness between our Jewishness and all of the aspects of our personal and collective experience through a process of inclusion and engagement with contemporary society, rather than exclusion and disengagement that leaves us in a psychosocial ghetto. Riv-Ellen Prell has stated this idea well in saying that what we need is a richer dialogue with modernity, not a more powerful monologue to push out modernity.

18 Issues of sexuality and politics present paradigmatic cases with respect to this dilemma. The challenge is both to have something unique and significant to say about AIDS, homosexuality, or conflict in the Balkans and to be able to say it in ways that will induce Jews to listen. Examples include the work of the Reform movement's Religious Action Center, the Jews who have associated themselves with *Tikkun*

magazine, local programs such as Boston's "Return to Passion" sponsored by its Jewish Community Relations Council, and a host of smaller, grass-roots groups such as the New York-based Alliance for Judaism and Social Justice. (There may be groups on the right as well, although these are less visible.)

19 Of course, programs are needed to create community. What I am arguing against is the tendency sometimes evident in recent years to view programs as ends in themselves rather than as means. I am also suggesting that the program goals should be framed not only in terms of their desired impact on individuals but also in terms of their potential for community building. By thinking about the latter, we will enhance the likelihood of achieving the former.

20 I think we have a better chance of getting significant numbers of Jews to accept the concept of *mitzvah*—of being "commanded" or "committed" to doing *specific acts*— than to accept *halachah* as a personally binding comprehensive *system* of obligations. Indeed, all Jewish religious movements today, even those that understand themselves as non- or post-halachic, are seeking to instill in their adherents the sense of *mitzvah* as a necessary component of their spiritual lives.

21 The interest in synagogue renewal is growing rapidly. The Reform and Reconstructionist movements have projects underway among the consortia of their synagogues that are aimed at fundamental tranformations. In January 1994, Avi Chai, a prominent Jewish foundation, sponsored a conference on "Creating an Environment That Transforms Jewish Lives," which highlighted a number of synagogue initiatives and explored the challenges of the change process.

22 I use "secular" here in the "soft" sense of not being explicitly tied to a particular religious ideology. Soft secularism is compatible with affirming much traditional Judaic religious content, even with using a language of spirituality, but shies away from explicit theological discourse, denominationalism, or dealing with issues of religious authority. The "civil Judaism" that I described in my book *Sacred Survival* embodies a soft secularism.

23 Examples include combined adult education programs, expert youth workers from Centers training synagogue youth group advisers, using Center arts facilities and staff to enrich congregational education programs, the operation of JCC programs in synagogues, and combined synagogue-JCC memberships for young singles and families.

24 By "nonrelativistic pluralism" I mean a situation in which alternative versions of Judaism recognize their familial resemblance and respect the authenticity of each version as a good-faith effort to interpret and apply the religio-cultural legacy they share, while still feeling free to assert their belief in the superior "truthfulness" of their own interpretation. This seems to me the only way to accommodate the variety of Jewish meaning systems in the contemporary world in a mutually respectful manner without asking each subcommunity to give up its own claims to primary validity. I recognize that establishing a universally persuasive philosophical grounding for this position may not in fact be possible, and I have (I will readily confess) not attempted to do so.

25 There are already de facto divisions of labor in Jewish life today, with different groups seeking to appeal to different constituencies with different messages. This is true, for example, with respect to the complex issues that surround the Jewish community's response to the rise in intermarriage. Different movements and organizations have focused on different dimensions of what together may constitute the only viable

collective response: intensified efforts at prevention, an increased emphasis on the desirability of conversion, *and* outreach aimed at building some kind of connection to intermarried families.

26 The apparently "simple" task of forging new relationships between Federation and synagogue, a sine qua non for any serious progress in building a "community of communities," is itself fraught with difficulties that can be overcome (if at all) only with enormous patience, flexibility, and perseverance on both sides.

27 Without seeking to elaborate or analyze these initiatives, I cite Cleveland, Boston, New York, and Hartford as communities that have sought explicitly to foster institutional and communal transformation through some of the strategies suggested in this article. The North American Commission on Jewish Identity and Continuity is seeking to incorporate this approach in its work at the continental level.

REFERENCES

Alexander, H. A., and Russ, Ian. "What We Know About Youth Programming." In *What We Know About Jewish Education*, edited by Stuart L. Kelman. Los Angeles: Torah Aura, 1992.

Aron, Isa. "Instruction and Enculturation in Jewish Education." Paper presented at the Conference on Research in Jewish Education, Los Angeles (May 1987).

Berger, Peter L. *The Sacred Canopy: Elements of a Sociological Theory of Religion*. Garden City, NY: Doubleday, 1967.

Buber, Martin. *I and Thou*, trans. by Walter Kaufmann. New York: Charles Scribner and Sons, 1970.

Cohen, Steven M. *American Assimilation or Jewish Revival*. Bloomington, IN: Indiana University Press, 1988.

Eisen, Arnold; Woocher, Jonathan; and Gal, Allon. "A New Role for Israel in American Jewish Identity." New York: American Jewish Committee, 1992.

Elazar, Daniel J. *Participation and Accountability in the Jewish Community*. New York: CJF and AJCOP, 1980.

Gans, Herbert J. "Symbolic Ethnicity: The Future of Ethnic Groups and Cultures in America." In *On the Making of Americans: Essays in Honor of David Riesman*, edited by Herbert J. Gans, Nathan Glazer, Joseph R. Gursfield, and Christopher Jencks. Philadelphia: University of Pennsylvania Press, 1979.

Geertz, Clifford. *The Interpretation of Cultures*. New York: Basic Books, 1973.

Hertzberg, Arthur. "Jewish Identification After the Six-Day War." *Jewish Social Studies* (1969): 271.

Kosmin, Barry A., et al. *Highlights of the CJF 1990 National Jewish Population Survey*. New York: Council of Jewish Federations, 1991.

Rheingold, H. *The Virtual Community: Homesteading on the Electronic Frontier*. New York: Addison-Wesley, 1990.

Woocher, Jonathan S. *Sacred Survival: The Civil Religion of American Jews*. Bloomington, IN: Indiana University Press, 1986.

FROM THE CONGREGATIONAL SCHOOL TO THE LEARNING CONGREGATION

Are We Ready for a Paradigm Shift?[1]

Isa Aron

riting in 1988, Barry Chazan offered the following assessment of the "state" of the Jewish supplementary school:

> Generally, a mood of frustration and malaise has gripped the various participants in part-time Jewish education. Principals and teachers feel they do not have enough time or support to do their job well. Parents do not see many positive results from "Hebrew school," and they seem to spend much of their time forcing their children to attend.... The part-time school is a uniquely American Jewish educational form now faced with the challenge of reformulation and adaptation. (Chazan 1988, p. 5)

Other observers might challenge Chazan's sweeping generalizations or the bleakness of his tone, but few would quarrel with his last sentence about the need for new forms. Calls for restructuring the congregational school have been heard regularly over the past two decades. In this paper I review the evolution of the current paradigm of the congregational school and sketch the outlines of a paradigm that is very different.

The foundations of our current system of congregational education were laid in two stages under the inspiration of two different types of leaders. The groundwork was laid in the 1910s and 1920s with the establishment of the communal Talmud Torah, rooted in the nationalist and Hebraist ideology of Mordecai Kaplan and Samson Benderly. Later, in the 1940s and 1950s, communal Talmud Torahs gave way to congregational schools in which a more pragmatic generation of educators sought to increase enrollments and set a higher standard by making school attendance a prerequisite for Bar Mitzvah. The congregational school of today is the inheritor of this dual legacy. As we approach the end of the century, it seems appropriate, indeed essential, that this legacy be reexamined.

My argument in this paper is twofold: First, that the seeds of today's discontent lie in the rarely acknowledged dissonance between the educational vision of the 1910s and that of the 1950s. Second, and more important, that the 1990s present us with a radically different set of circumstances, calling for a radically different educational vision.

I begin this paper with a history of supplementary Jewish education, tracing the problems of today's schools to some of the conflicts that were never resolved by the grafting of the curriculum of the Talmud Torah onto the congregational setting and by the doubling of the number of students, most of whom were from rapidly assimilating families. I review the various innovations that were instituted over the years in an attempt to address the problems that today's schools face. Finally, I argue that the circumstances of American Jews today call for a radically new paradigm—a paradigm of congregational education over and above the congregational school. Partial exemplars of the paradigm I propose can presently be glimpsed in action in congregations throughout North America. I attempt to show how these partial exemplars might be brought together to create a new model of Jewish education in the congregational setting.

The Communal Talmud Torah

A 1908 survey of the Jewish population of greater New York (Friedlander 1913/1969, p. 136) estimated the number of school-aged children at 360,000. Of these only 100,000 (the vast majority of them boys) were recipients of some sort of formal Jewish education. A 1909 study by Mordecai Kaplan and Bernard Cronson listed six different venues for Jewish education (in order of decreasing popularity): privately run *chadarim*, Talmud Torahs, institutional schools (run by orphanages and settlement houses), Sunday schools, congregational schools (operating more than one day a week), and private tutors. Although Kaplan and Cronson had scarcely a nice word to say about any of these institutions, they concluded that the Talmud Torahs, "in spite of all [their] defects, ... instill more Jewishness into the lives of the children than any of the [other] agencies." (Kaplan and Cronson 1909/1969, p. 120)

Since a book-length history of Jewish education in this fascinating period has yet to be written, it is hard to know whether Kaplan and Cronson's assessment prompted the actions of the soon-to-be established New York Bureau of Jewish Education or simply served as a post-hoc justification. In any case, readers of this 1909 document by the Bureau would not be surprised to find that Samson Benderly, the Bureau's first director, put the bulk of his energies into "modernizing" the Talmud Torah. He called the principals of the Talmud Torah together, persuaded them to standardize their curricula, and began work on a series of textbooks. To set these institutions on a secure financial basis, a new schedule for tuition was developed, coupled with a novel method for collecting it. A cadre of young college students went door-to-door, assessing families' ability to pay and collecting the fees. A convenient by-product of this arrangement was that the process of collecting tuition also served as a method of recruiting new students. Model schools were established especially for girls. Teachers' salaries were raised, and a licensing system was instituted. Firsthand accounts from this period (Freidlander 1913/1969; Berkson 1920/1969) have a breathless quality, as though a cadre of *wunderkinds* had swooped down and waved a set of magic wands. Within a decade communal Talmud Torahs modeled after those in New York existed in most major cities.

Behind the sweeping reforms instituted by Benderly and his "boys" (as his disciples were called) lay three simple but powerful and far-reaching assumptions: (1) the public school was the most appropriate model for the renovated Talmud Torah to emulate; (2) Jewish education ought to be a communal endeavor; and (3) nationalism and Hebraism could provide the unifying force for this undertaking. The reformers of the 1910s and 1920s considered the establishment of "parochial" schools both impractical and "undesirable for the Jews from the civic point of view." (Friedlander 1913/1969, p. 138) They saw the public schools as both an essential instrument for the preparation of American citizens and a perfect model for Jewish education. They assumed that good Jewish education required orderly classrooms and that "a regular curriculum is impossible without textbooks." (Ibid., p. 144)

A number of historians have traced the influence of John Dewey, then president of Teachers College, on the Benderly Boys (Kronish 1976; Olitzky 1986), many of whom went on to pursue doctorates at Teachers College. But while these educators embraced the Deweyan ideals of democracy and cultural pluralism, they seem to have been unmoved by the "progressive" notion of adapting the curriculum to suit the needs and interests of the children.[2] They saw centralized authority and the setting of standards for both students and teachers as the hallmarks of a good education.

The notion of a communal educational system with a standardized curriculum was predicated on a view of Judaism as "a religious civilization" (to use Kaplan's later formulation). The aim of Jewish education was seen as "the preservation of the Jews as a distinct people, existing and developing in the spirit of the Jewish religion." (Friedlander 1913/1969, p. 138) For these educators, as for their counterparts in the public schools, the guiding metaphor was the melting pot, not the salad bowl. In their view, religious differences were irrelevant because the essential ingredients of a good Jewish education were the same for all:

> A sufficient knowledge of Hebrew, which should enable the children to understand the [siddur, Bible, and other texts],... Jewish history, ancient and modern, and *an acquaintance with religious observance.* (Ibid., emphasis mine)

The concept of Judaism as a religious civilization was dissonant from, if not antithetical to, the prevailing ideology of the Reform movement, which had declared (in an 1885 statement of principles, which came to be known as the Pittsburgh Platform): "We consider ourselves no longer a nation, but a religious community, and therefore [do not] expect... a return to Palestine." Thus it is not surprising that Reform Jews, whose members were of Western European extraction and were greatly outnumbered by the more recent Eastern European immigrants, shunned the Talmud Torahs and continued to send their children to Sunday schools. Nonetheless, it is interesting to note that one of the most gifted of the Benderly Boys, Emanuel Gamoran, was recruited to become the head of the Union of American Hebrew Congregations' Commission on Jewish Education in 1923. Gamoran campaigned actively for the expansion of supplementary education from one to two days a week, and for the inclusion of Hebrew in the curriculum. (Olitzky 1984, pp. 65-110) Although he met with much opposition, his proposals for change were endorsed by the UAHC and gradually took hold.

To those familiar with the history of educational reform in America, the mixed outcomes of this attempt at reforming Jewish education are not surprising. The only durable and unequivocal successes of Benderly and his disciples were the creation of the profession of Jewish education and the establishment of Bureaus of Jewish Education in cities nationwide. Attempts to create a cadre of professional Jewish teachers were relatively short-lived, falling victim to the economic hardships of the Depression and the breakup of the Talmud Torahs as Jews moved farther away from "the old neighborhood." Despite their rhetoric, neither Benderly nor his followers were able to turn Jewish education into a truly communal endeavor. Their vision of a unified educational system in New York turned out to be utopian. Within a few years the more Orthodox of the Eastern European immigrants withdrew their children from the New York Talmud Torahs, and the German Reform Jews (who had never enrolled their children in the first place) withdrew much of their financial support. (Winter 1966, Goren 1970)

Though it never fulfilled Benderly's full vision, the Talmud Torah left an indelible impression on Jewish education throughout the United States, setting it on a course from which it has never fully strayed. From this period on, Jewish education was seen as synonymous with school-based instruction. Its model was the public school. Throughout the Conservative movement, and in large sectors of the Reform movement, its curriculum was centered around Hebrew.[3]

The Rise of the Congregational School

The centralized Talmud Torah, whose fiscal viability and professional teaching staff were dependent upon large enrollments, was doomed to extinction by the upward mobility of its clientele. As Jews moved to new, less densely populated neighborhoods, they turned to synagogues to provide Jewish education for their children. Enrollment in congregational schools in the New York area increased 150% in the years between 1917 and 1927, (Ben-Horin 1969, p. 83) In 1918 only 23.6% of pupils in Jewish schools throughout the United States were enrolled in a congregational school; by 1948 the percentage had grown to 82.7%. (Pilch 1969, p. 123) Even in areas in which Talmud Torahs survived side by side with congregational schools, they were perceived as "schools for the poor." (Berkson and Rosen 1936/1969, p. 176)

Relatively little has been written about the goals and methods of the congregational schools of the '30s and '40s other than to describe them as "less intensive" than the Talmud Torahs in terms of both hours and quality of instruction. In 1942, Isaac Berkson offered the following assessment of the probable achievements of the average student in a congregational school:

> His major achievement would be the ability to read the prayer book with some facility, a little Bible, a smattering of Hebrew, some stories, some songs, some familiarity with the

ceremonies, a fragmentary knowledge of Jewish history. There would be little understanding of Jewish problems and probably little serious conviction about Jewish religious conceptions, or about the significance of Jewish cultural life generally. (Quoted in Pilch 1969, p. 115)

Even with the diminution in the number of hours, these schools apparently had some difficulty attracting students, enrolling only 25-30% of children aged five to fourteen. (Ben-Horin 1969, p. 83)

But while Jewish parents of that generation (not unlike those of today) were relatively indifferent to formal Jewish education, they were keenly interested in Bar Mitzvah preparation. By banding together and changing their rhetoric, the educators of that era were able to capitalize on this interest and double the enrollments in Jewish schools.

Without a detailed history of this period we cannot be sure of the exact sequence of events, but this much is clear: Beginning in 1938 and extending through the 1950s, congregations began requiring candidates for Bar Mitzvah to have completed a minimum number of years of supplementary education (usually three for the Conservative movement and two for the Reform) and achieved a certain level of knowledge and Hebrew proficiency. During the same period, enrollment in congregational schools increased dramatically, from 25-30% of school-aged children before World War II to 40-45% in 1958. (Dushkin and Engelman 1959, p. 44)

Stuart Schoenfeld has written perceptively about the Bar Mitzvah as a cornerstone of the Jewish folk religion, despite its denigration by the religious elite.[4] The disapproval of rabbis, some of whom went so far as to abolish Bar Mitzvah ceremonies altogether, did nothing to stem the public's interest in the ceremony itself and in the often lavish celebration that accompanied it.[5] As Schoenfeld describes it, the *shidduch* between Bar Mitzvah preparation and the congregational school is a classic example of folk-elite accommodation. Serving as matchmakers were local Bureaus of Jewish Education, the American Association for Jewish Education, the United Synagogue's Commission on Jewish Education, and the New York Federation of Reform Synagogues.[6]

Walter Ackerman describes the work of this generation of educational leaders in the following way:

[Its work] is marked more by administrative finesse than by intellectual sophistication. Its efforts have been directed more towards consolidating, firming up and smoothing out the rough edges of the plans and programs of its predecessors than toward innovation and change. Its dominant stance has been how rather than why. (Ackerman 1972, p. 5)

Ackerman's assessment helps us understand how the linkage of Bar Mitzvah preparation, which was so important to the folk, to formal education, which was so important to the elite, was accomplished. The maneuver was a classic example of administrative finesse, assuring the future of formal Jewish education at the expense of obscuring its goals. The architects of this "merger" saw it as a wonderful opportunity to increase enrollments and hours of instruction at the same time. They fought the battle to increase the hours of instruction in the congregational school to six hours per week and, in the Orthodox and Conservative movements, they largely prevailed. They strove, although less successfully, to establish Jewish teaching as a profession, despite the fact that teaching in a congregational school was rarely more than part-time work. They attempted to raise the level of instruction by advocating the use of a standard curriculum modeled after that of the Talmud Torah, whatever the particular setting. (Dushkin 1945, p. 5) Perhaps they thought that the momentous events surrounding the creation of the State of Israel would make a nationalistic and Hebraist course of study more appealing to parents, despite their ostensible interest only in Bar Mitzvah preparation. Perhaps they assumed that no one would notice that a curriculum centered on modern Hebrew had little to do with the Bar Mitzvah ceremony itself.[7] Whatever they thought, they were probably unable to foresee the dissonance and blurring of vision that would result from the promulgation of a nationalist curriculum in a religious institution, especially for students who were neither particularly nationalist nor particularly religious.

The 1950s and 1960s are generally considered the heyday of the congregational school, "an era of growth, expansion and legitimization" in which "synagogue schools became respectable institutions, which engendered excitement, dynamism and hope." (Chazan 1987, p. 170) Whether or not most congregational schools were really as successful as this statement suggests, a significant portion are remembered as being so. A number of factors accounted for the success of these institutions, especially in comparison with their counterparts of today: The newness and excitement of the founding of the State of Israel validated the teaching of modern Hebrew. A cadre of American-born teachers, mostly women, existed; these teachers approached their work – part-time though it was – with a strong sense of professionalism. Because day schools were still a relatively new phenomenon, congregational schools retained a core of committed, knowledgeable parents. The rates of intermarriage and divorce were lower, as were the number of working mothers. Perhaps most important, American society valued attendance at "Sunday" school as part of wholesome, middle-class life. (Gans 1951, p. 333)

Beneath the placid and prosperous image, however, lay a problematic fissure. "Preoccupation with Bar Mitzvah... [and] recitation of some prayers... tended to divert attention from the study of subjects which were considered the core of the curriculum: Bible, History and the Hebrew Language." (Pilch 1969, p. 131) "The poor quality of the school program" was a major topic of discussion at the Second National Conference on Jewish Education, held in 1954:

> A great deal of dissatisfaction with the attainments of the elementary school was voiced by delegates, both lay and professional. The various panels emphasized the need for improving the functioning of the Jewish school, the level of teaching, and the substantive content of the school program. (Ibid., p. 133)

Had those who promoted supplementary education as a vehicle for Bar Mitzvah preparation had the benefit of advice from a contemporary social scientist, they might have realized that in a conflict between folk and elite, folk almost always prevail. Just as *Kol Nidre* remains the focal point of the Yom Kippur liturgy (despite the ire of Maimonedes and countless other authorities), the Bar/Bat Mitzvah has remained the focal point of the congregational school, regardless of its official curriculum.

In his ethnography of a congregational school, Schoem characterizes the attitude of the parents in the following way:

> Parents believed that the realization of one's identification with the Jewish people came through the ritual of attendance at a Jewish school, culminating in the ritual ceremony of the Bar/Bat Mitzvah. (Schoem 1989, p. 53)

In the words of a "very influential member of the school board," "The goal is the Bar Mitzvah. And when they stand on the *bimah* you don't want them to embarrass you or themselves.... That's where it really is." (Ibid., p. 53)

Further evidence of the centrality of the Bar/Bat Mitzvah ceremony is the 60% dropout rate after the ceremony (Fishman

1987, pp. 20-21; Commission on Jewish Education in North America 1990, p. 37), despite the efforts of Reform congregations to emphasize the importance of Confirmation and of Conservative congregations to establish Confirmation as a new goal. Some congregations have succeeded in requiring candidates for Bar/Bat Mitzvah to commit to the continuation of their Jewish studies until Confirmation. Nonetheless, the overall dropout rate has stayed the same.

Other problems of the congregational school have also remained fairly constant over the ensuing decades: a chronic shortage of qualified teachers (Aron and Bank 1987; Shevitz 1988); seemingly intractable discipline problems (Schoem 1989; Heilman 1992); and a low level of student achievement (NYBJE 1989). A 1977 task force convened by the American Jewish Committee observed the following:

> Most Jewish schools produce graduates who are functionally illiterate in Judaism and not clearly positive in their attitudinal identification.... Graduates look back without joy on their educational experience. (AJC 1977, p. i)

In the same vein, a 1989 study of thirty-nine supplementary schools in the New York area, conducted by the Board of Jewish Education of Greater New York (NYBJE), concluded the following:

> Schools do a very poor job in increasing Jewish knowledge in all subject areas; they show no success in guiding children towards increased Jewish involvement; and they demonstrate an inability to influence positive growth in Jewish attitudes. (NYBJE 1989, p. 119)

While this study has been criticized as being both biased and flawed (Resnik 1993), it has been widely quoted by educators and communal leaders, probably because it reinforces their preexisting notions.

Over the past fifty years much has been written about the problems of the congregational school, and a variety of reforms have been urged. The attitudes of members of the Jewish educational establishment have fallen into two broad categories. The first perspective considers the current paradigm of congregational education salvageable if certain improvements can be made in the areas of curriculum, personnel, and programming. In contrast to this is a second perspective that has, in essence, given up on congregational schools, hoping to replace them with more intensive forms of education, such as day schools, camps, and Israel programs. In the following sections I examine each of these perspectives.

Tinkering with the Paradigm

At least through the 1970s, the dominant view of the Jewish educational establishment has been that the structure of supplementary schools is essentially sound but that improvements are needed in some aspects. Adherents to this view have taken as a given the notion that congregational schools ought to be modeled after public schools, complete with age-graded classes, certified teachers, standardized curricula, and up-to-date educational materials. These educators acknowledge that the time of day allotted to Jewish education is problematic; that the small number of hours available for instruction mitigate against the professionalization of teachers; and that the ambivalence of both parents and students serves as a powerful disincentive to learning. Nonetheless, they believe (or act as though they believe) that if only certain standards can be upheld, the enterprise can succeed. For example, the National Board of License and various Bureaus of Jewish Education around the country continued for many years to focus on maintaining rather stringent criteria for licensure, despite the fact that the number of applicants for certification had dwindled precipitously and the shortage of teachers had rendered certification largely irrelevant. (Aron and Bank 1987) Although there was much hand-wringing about the attitudes and ignorance of parents, little was done to reach out to parents until the late '70s. Similarly, little thought was given to different time frames or alternate use of certain time periods for purposes other than instruction.

Through the 1970s the primary thrust of the educational establishment was the creation of standardized curricula and the publication of educational materials. In 1963 the Melton Center began publishing curricular materials in Bible, followed in later years by a curriculum on Holidays and Mitzvot. Experimental editions of the UAHC's Shuster Curriculum began appearing in 1977; the United Synagogue produced its Menorah curriculum in 1978. Behrman House did a brisk business in textbooks at all levels for both the Conservative and Reform movements; their success encouraged younger entrepreneurs to start publishing concerns of their own. Every trend in public education seems to have found its way, five to seven years later, to the congregational schools: programmed instruction, values clarification, audiovisual technology, cooperative learning, and many others.

Beginning in the 1950s (Chazan, 1988) and accelerating in the 1970s a number of structural changes were introduced that altered the public school paradigm for the first time. Inspired by the success of Jewish camps, synagogue schools began incorporating elements of what is commonly called "informal" education into their programs, such as the weekend camp conclave or the in-house *Shabbaton*. In the 1980s the Jewish community discovered family education. The major recommendation emerging from the 1989 NYBJE study cited above, for example, was the "transform[ation of] the educational thrust of the synagogue from supplementary schooling for pupils to Jewish family education." (NYBJE 1989, p. 133) Family days and even parallel learning for parents were quickly incorporated into the programs of many schools.

Finally, the most recent effort at improving the basic paradigm has been that of the Council for Initiatives in Jewish Education (CIJE), through its "Best Practices" Project. The Council's first publication contains descriptions of eight "good enough"[8] supplementary schools (all but one located in a congregation). The CIJE hopes to use this report and others that follow as both "existence proofs" of success and "models that can be studied." (Holtz 1993, p. 10)

I want to be careful not to denigrate the efforts of the scores of talented educators responsible for many curricular and programmatic innovations over the years. While there has been virtually no research on the effects of these attempts at school improvement, one can only imagine what congregational schools would be like had these innovations not been implemented. Nonetheless, it is difficult not to conclude this historical survey on a note of discouragement. Despite countless attempts to modify and improve the paradigm, the basic problems have proven intractable. The failure of these efforts, contrasted with the dramatic successes of a number of other educational institutions, has given rise to a second group of community leaders who have adopted an attitude of "benign neglect" toward congregational schools.

Ignoring the Problems and Abandoning the Paradigm

The 1950s and 1960s were years of dramatic growth for four new and powerful educational agencies: the day school,[9] the Jewish preschool, the Jewish summer camp, and the Israel program. As the success of these enterprises became more apparent, two premises that date back to Benderly were called into question—that Jewish parents had a civic responsibility to send their children to public schools and that Jewish education should model itself on public education. By the 1970s members of the educational establishment, along with a growing number of Federation leaders, were beginning to ask themselves if the congregational schools were worth maintaining. Their doubts were fueled by the near simultaneous publication of two independent studies, one by Geoffrey Bock, the other by Harold Himmelfarb, which purported to demonstrate the existence of a threshold (1,000 hours, according to Bock, and 3,000 hours, according to Himmelfarb) below which formal Jewish education had no effect on one's identification and practice as an adult. The obvious conclusion, as numerous commentators were quick to point out, was that as far as one's Jewishness as an adult was concerned, supplementary schooling was the same as having received no schooling.

Even in the face of this "hard," seemingly incontrovertible evidence, few leaders of the organized Jewish community were willing to advocate the dismantling of the entire supplementary school "system," which accounts for more than two-thirds of the enrollment in Jewish schools. However difficult the task of improving these schools might be, the prospect of transferring even a significant percentage of their students to day schools seemed unlikely. Nonetheless, the clear implication of the Bock and Himmelfarb studies was that congregational schooling was not a good "investment," especially in comparison with alternative modes of education. These studies "tended to feed the rationale for the then new Federation funding of day schools, since day schools seemed to be the only institution which gave the kind of quality Jewish education which would make a difference." (Feldstein and Shrage 1987, p. 99) In the 1980s only 4% of communal funding for Jewish education went to congregational schools, compared to roughly 50% to a much smaller group of day schools. (Resnik 1988, p. iv)

In 1988 Steven M. Cohen published a critique of the Beck and Himmelfarb studies, pointing out a number of methodological problems common to both.[10] Drawing on data from the 1981 Greater New York Jewish Population Study, Cohen showed that even a small number of hours of formal Jewish education as a child correlated positively with one's Jewish identification and practice as an adult. By then, however, the damage to the reputation of the congregational school had been done. Federation executives, Bureau directors, and even researchers (Schoem 1992) continue to cite these studies as evidence of the failure of congregational schools.

A Third Option

Thus far I have described the two prevailing perspectives on congregational education: One adheres to the public school paradigm and models its reform efforts on comparable attempts in the public schools. The other has essentially given up on the congregational school and pins its hope on alternative institutions—primarily the day school—despite the unlikelihood of a large increase in day school enrollment. Are these the only options? If one were to judge from some of the most recent writings in the field and from the ideas and experiments of a younger generation of Jewish educators, it seems that a third possibility is emerging. A growing number of educators, rabbis, and communal leaders are questioning the suitability of using public education as the guiding paradigm for congregational education.

Some years ago (Aron 1989) I contrasted the paradigm of "instruction," as practiced in the public schools, with that of "enculturation," a term borrowed from the Christian educator John Westerhoff (1976). I argued then that the instructional paradigm is successful if and only if it is buttressed by a variety of external motivations: laws that compel children to attend school, societal expectations that schooling correlates positively with one's earning potential, and competition for college entrance. Lacking these sources of motivation, the Jewish school has suffered from the comparison with public school; Judaic studies, even in day schools, continue to be seen as less important than general studies. I suggested that rather than adhering to the instructional model, the congregational school ought to conceive of its educational task in different terms, as one of enculturation. In so doing, it could offer its students something that instruction alone cannot, a loving induction into the Jewish culture and the Jewish community.

In the ensuing years I have begun to see the issue in terms that are broader and more radical, involving the totality of congregational life, rather than being limited to the congregational school as a self-contained entity.[11] What would it look like if education were seen as the concern of the entire congregation rather than being relegated to its school(s)? Who would be the learner? Who would be the teacher? In what settings and through what modalities might synagogue members learn about being Jewish? These questions cannot be answered by an outsider looking in or by a theoretician or philosopher looking down. Each and every congregation must answer them for itself. These answers would best be arrived at through a series of conversations among congregants themselves and between congregants and professionals. If the conversations were to yield educational structures and programs that are both responsive to the needs of the "folk" and worthy of the highest aspirations of the "elite," they would have to be carefully orchestrated. Some of the other articles in this volume have much to suggest about the best ways in which these conversations can be structured.

In the remainder of this paper, I would like to raise some of the issues that would have to be considered in any attempt to create new paradigms of congregational education. While I have not hesitated to express my own opinions, I have tried to frame the questions in an open way, giving voice to opposing views and making it clear that many of these issues are far from being resolved, even in my own mind.

(1) *What is the function of Jewish education? Is it preparation for life or an integral part of the process of living?* One's answers to these question will have a direct bearing on one's conception of who the students are. The immigrant parents of the turn of the century were too preoccupied with learning what they needed to learn in order to succeed in America to worry much about *Jewish* learning for themselves. The "child-centered" parents of the '40s and '50s (Gans 1951) were too focused on their children to think much about their own religious needs or values. In our own time, however, the concept of lifelong learning has become commonplace. Given the rapid pace of technological and social change, continued occupational training (or, for a different class of workers, professional development) is considered a necessity. Given the increase in leisure time of many adults, "continuing education" has become the equivalent of skiing and theatergoing. In our society schooling may be limited to the first decades of one's life, but education is increasingly seen as continuing for the duration.

If we embrace the concept of lifelong learning, the obvious implication is that congregational education is for *everyone* at *every* age. But this raises a number of serious questions: Is lifelong *Jewish* learning qualitatively different from professional development and adult education? Can lifelong Jewish learning become an accepted norm? What modifications to current institutional arrangements will be required if congregational education is to become a lifelong process?

(2) *What constitutes lifelong Jewish learning?* How is lifelong Jewish learning different from its secular counterparts, professional development and adult education? For one thing, it

will never be as utilitarian as professional development. Should it consist of a series of optional programs on a wide range of topics?

Some argue that the adult education model is too individualistic to be an appropriate model. According to the tradition, Jewish learning is necessary not because it helps one perform better on the job or because it leads to self-improvement but because it engages one's spiritual and moral sensibilities. And the traditional mode of Jewish learning is, by definition, communal. In the process of learning, the Jewish community is re-created and reinvigorated.

On the other hand, the contemporary synagogue is far from a traditional community. And the ideology of Reform Judaism centers on informed *choice*. Do we value Jewish learning because it is a vehicle for self-awareness and growth, because it is a communal endeavor or—to state the case most extremely—because it is a communal obligation? Is it possible to promote both the individual and communal perspectives, or must we choose between them?

(3) *Are members of congregations ready to embrace Jewish learning as a lifelong endeavor?* The jargon of demographers has so permeated our discourse that we routinely speak of congregations as organizations with which one is affiliated, as though they were the equivalent of the Auto Club. One joins the Auto Club for convenience, drawing on its services as needed, but one's membership in that organization hardly impinges on one's sense of self. To the majority of its members, the synagogue is a similar service organization, essential for life-cycle events and major holidays but superfluous during times in between. Charles Liebman has argued that Judaism itself is viewed by many in similar terms. Citing a 1965 study of Jewish adolescents by Bernard Rosen, Liebman draws an analogy between their attitudes toward Judaism and their attitudes toward dental hygiene. "One has to do it, one might even enjoy it, and if one doesn't do it others may find out…. It is hardly an activity which engages one's mind, energy, or attention the rest of the day, however." (Liebman 1973, p. 129) Let's not forget that the adolescents of 1963 are the adults of today and the parents of the children in today's synagogue schools.

For those of us on whom the Jewish tradition has left a deeper and more powerful impression, the "affiliation" mentality poses a great challenge. How, we ask ourselves, can the tradition become a meaningful part of people's lives? We who have been moved by prayer and ritual and have resonated with the insights of the Bible and Midrash wonder how we might make these available to others.

How can we broker a meeting between the resources of the tradition and the average American Jew?

Following Kaplan, Arnold Eisen has argued that congregations must start their "in-reach" by catering to people's physical, psychological, and social needs—their needs for community, child care, and support groups of various sorts. The success of a number of synagogue centers and of the within-synagogue *chavurah* movement attests to the value of this approach.

Mixed in with these physical and psychological needs are spiritual ones—a need for prayer, for a sense of purpose, for an ethical touchstone. Eisen's suggestion presumes that members who initially come to a synagogue for child care or a support group will eventually get in touch with their spiritual needs and find an outlet for these needs in the synagogue. However, in attempting to infuse Jewish values and concepts into the lives of synagogue members, we face a great challenge. Alhough the Jewish tradition is rich in resources to meet these needs, its resources are too often alien and inaccessible. To feel comforted by rituals and prayers, one must feel comfortable with them. To find meaning in traditional sources, one must know how to find, decode, and interpret them. The question is, What kind of Jewish learning will help "affiliates" become active enthusiasts?

(4) *Is our goal knowledge or empowerment?* As it is currently constituted, Jewish learning, both for children or adults, focuses primarily on transmitting as much subject matter as possible. But Jews in America are a highly literate and accomplished group, accustomed to taking the initiative in a variety of social and political endeavors. This suggests that over and above any specific content, our goal might be to empower congregants to learn on their own.

In recent years the literature on reform and renewal in a range of fields has highlighted the importance of empowerment as both a proximal and ultimate goal. Workers who participate in decision making and who are knowledgeable about all aspects of their workplace have been found to be both more satisfied and more productive. Patients who are informed about and active in their medical treatment recover more quickly. By extension, many have argued, learners who are empowered to direct the course of their learning are more motivated to learn and are better able to integrate what they have learned into their daily life.

The goal of empowerment is not, however, unproblematic. Do congregants really want to be empowered? Perhaps only a minority will be willing or able to invest the time and energy required for active learning of a complicated and rarefied tradition. What happens when some congregants become empowered while others remain more passive and dependent? Does this polarization become divisive to the life of the community?

An entirely different set of problems arrives from a view of Jewish life that regards some subjects and/or content areas to be more essential than others. Is it not the role of experts to make these choices? And does focusing more on the tools of learning mean that we are focusing less on its content? [12]

(5) *What standards are appropriate for congregational education?* In modeling Jewish education on public education, earlier generations of Jewish educators believed in the importance of maintaining high standards, at least in theory, for teachers and for the curriculum. As I have tried to demonstrate, these standards were rarely achieved since they depended on a series of motivating factors that didn't exist.

The classical Jewish notion of *Torah Lishma* is based on an entirely different conception of motivation—that study is its own reward. [13] For halachic Jews who have a more explicit worldview (to borrow Rosenak's [1987] term), the study of Torah (both written and oral) is a *mitzvah*. For liberal Jews the rewards must be found in the domain of the implicit, the realm of personal meaning. If we accept the concept of *Torah Lishma*, our goal is for learners to value the study of Torah (construed more broadly) as a vital activity because it serves to enrich their spiritual and communal lives.

Can one devise a curriculum for *Torah Lishma*? Is the language of requirements and objectives appropriate to *liberal* Jewish education? If we find them inappropriate, can we devise alternative standards and alternative modes of evaluation that are more in keeping with our goals?

Congregational schools have already acknowledged *de facto* that accommodating people's problems and needs is more important than standardizing instruction. [14] Children who have scheduling conflicts of one kind or another (either because their parents are divorced or because their own outside activities are too numerous) are already accommodated, albeit begrudgingly. Can congregational education incorporate even greater and more purposeful flexibility? Can a synagogue become a place that facilitates learning whenever and wherever people are available, without polarizing its membership and without reducing a venerable tradition of serious learning to a laundry list of activities?

If congregational education is to diversify, becoming more responsive to people's interests and needs, the meaning of the Bar/Bat Mitzvah ceremony and its use as a motivating goal will have to be reconsidered. It would seem reasonable to require that becoming a Bar/Bat Mitzvah signifies the acquisition of knowledge and/or skills, both in preparation for the ceremony itself and in order to function as a full member of the Jewish community. But would the knowledge attained by one thirteen-year-old have to be the same as, or equivalent to, that of his or her peers?

(6) *What modalities will enable congregations to become more flexible in their educational offerings?* Good congregational schools already incorporate a range of old and new educational modalities, from learning in *chavrutah* (pairs) to learning through inquiry, and from the reading of traditional *midrashim* to the creation of one's own *midrashim* through art, drama, and storytelling. But if lifelong Jewish learning is to be adapted to suit the lives of contemporary children and adults, a range of new modalities will need to be explored, including interactive computer games, materials for group text study, and individualized learning packets. Experimentation with many of these has been going on in a number of congregations throughout North America, which raises certain questions: Which of these modalities work best with which learners under what conditions? Will it be possible to integrate what are now isolated programs into a coherent framework that is both flexible and thoughtful, acknowledging the priorities of traditional learning but allowing for individual choice?

Following this chapter are three vignettes that sketch three different ways in which a variety of learning modalities might be combined to form a program of congregational education that would meet divergent requirements. To some these vignettes may seem impossibly utopian. However, parts of them are already in operation in congregations throughout North America. In initiating the Experiment in Congregational Education, it is our hope that one innovation will lead to another as a different paradigm of congregational education takes hold.

The Experiment in Congregational Education represents a first step in the process of reconceptualizing congregational education and translating the new conceptions into working models. Each participating congregation has begun a process of asking itself the questions posed above and examining some alternative answers. This process will be long and arduous. We hope that it also will be invigorating and exciting. We don't expect that all the synagogues participating in the Experiment will come up with identical answers. Nor do we expect the Experiment to be an unqualified success. We have every expectation, however, that the new designs will be ingenious, the results surprising, and the process itself fulfilling.

Notes

1   I would like to thank Bill Aron, Bill Cutter, Sara Lee, John Watkins, and Michael Zeldin for their many helpful comments on earlier drafts of this paper.

2   To these educators accommodating the needs of children meant giving them fewer hours of instruction and, therefore, more free time after public school. (Berkson 1920/1969, p. 169)

3   Even today congregational schools are called "Hebrew schools" by both parents and students and by educators like Chazan (see the opening quote).

4   In the sociological literature these terms are descriptive not evaluative. The folk are the ordinary members of a religious group, not given to scrutinizing or justifying their practices. The elite, in contrast, are those who see themselves as the "keepers of the flame." To the elite, matters of canon, authority, and justification are of the utmost importance.

5   In the Reform movement the Bar Mitzvah ceremony was supposed to have been "replaced by Confirmation," according to the CCAR's 1923 *Rabbi's Manual*. Although this may have been the case in the 1920s and 1930s, a survey conducted by the UAHC in the late 1940s found a move toward "increased ritualism" and a reintroduction of the Bar Mitzvah ceremony "in virtually all temples." (Wertheimer 1993, p. 10) A survey of Reform congregations conducted in 1960 found that of the 336 congregations responding, only 12 did not conduct Bar Mitzvah ceremonies. (Efron and Rubin 1960)

6   It is worth noting that one group not mentioned in this list is the Union of American Hebrew Congregations or any other organization of Reform congregations located outside New York City. This comports with the official stance of the Reform movement, which was supposed to have given up Bar Mitzvah in favor of Confirmation. The history of actual Reform practice with regard to Bar Mitzvah remains to be written. As indicated in the previous footnote, by the late 1940s, Bar Mitzvah ceremonies were conducted in the vast majority of Reform congregations.

7   If so, they were largely correct. A 1959 study by Dushkin and Engelman found that one fourth of the parents of students in congregational schools could not name a single subject that their child was studying. "Even those parents who did name school subjects ... have a vague and inadequate knowledge." (Dushkin and Engelman 1959, p. 138)

8   This notion is derived from Bruno Bettleheim's concept of a "good enough" parent and Sara Lawrence Lightfoot's book *The Good High School* (1983). See Reimer (1990) for a discussion of this approach to research on schools.

9   Strictly speaking, the day schools that began to spring up in the 1940s were not a new phenomenon. Prior to the movement to exclude prayer from the public schools, Jews of German extraction had opened day schools in twenty-one American cities. The first of these schools opened in 1842 and the last closed in 1872 (Zeldin 1988).

10 Most problematic was the fact that both Beck and Himmelfarb failed to separate males and females in their analysis. Thus females who were traditional in their practice but who had until the 1950s received much less formal Jewish education than males made the entire group of adults with little or no education appear to be more Jewishly involved than the males alone were.

11 I am indebted to Sara Lee for this formulation.

12 A similar question has been raised by E. D. Hirsch in his book *Cultural Literacy* (1987). Hirsch argues that a shared cultural knowledge-base is essential to the preservation of an interdependent community. The recent interest in *Jewish* cultural literacy is related to this concern but raises some problems of its own (Aron 1993).

13 I am indebted to Michael Rosenak for this insight.

14 For an example of this see Joseph Reimer's paper in *Best Practices Project: The Supplementary School* (Holtz 1993).

REFERENCES

Ackerman, Walter. "The Present Moment in Jewish Education." In *Midstream*, December 1972.

American Jewish Committee. Preface to "Does Jewish Schooling Matter?" by Geoffrey Bock. New York: AJC, 1977.

Aron, Isa. "The Malaise of Jewish Education." *Tikkun 4* (1989), 32-34.

_____. "Uses and Misuses of Cultural Literacy." *Compass*, vol. 15, no. 3 (Spring/Summer, 1993), pp. 17-18.

Aron, Isa, and Bank, Adrianne. "The Shortage of Supplementary School Teachers: Has the Time for Concerted Action Finally Arrived?" *Journal of Jewish Communal Service* 63 (1987), 264-271.

Ben-Horin, Meir. "From the Turn of the Century to the Late Thirties." In *A History of Jewish Education in America*, edited by J. Pilch. New York: American Association for Jewish Education, 1969.

Berkson, Isaac. "Cultural Pluralism and the Community Theory of Jewish Education." In *Jewish Education in the United States: A Documentary History*, edited by Lloyd Gartner. New York: Teachers College Press, 1920/1969.

Berkson, Isaac, and Rosen, Bernard. "Social and Economic Change Reflected in Jewish School Enrollment." In *Jewish Education in the United States: A Documentary History*, edited by Lloyd Gartner. New York: Teachers College Press, 1936/1969.

Board of Jewish Education of Greater New York. *Jewish Supplementary Schooling: An Educational System in Need of Change*. New York: BJE, 1988.

Bock, Geoffrey. "The Functions of Jewish Schooling of American Jews." In *Studies in Jewish Education*, vol. 1, edited by Michael Rosenak. Jerusalem: Magnes Press, 1988.

Chazan, Barry. "Education in the Synagogue: The Transformation of the Supplementary School." In *The American Synagogue*, edited by J. Wertheimer. Cambridge: Cambridge University Press, 1987.

————. "The State of Jewish Education." New York: Jewish Educational Services of North America, 1988.

Cohen, Steven M. *American Assimilation or Jewish Revival?* Bloomington: Indiana University Press, 1988.

Commission on Jewish Education in North America. *A Time to Act*. Lanham, MD: University Press, 1990.

Dushkin, Alexander. "Common Elements in American Jewish Teaching." *Jewish Education* 17 (1945), 5-12.

Dushkin, Alexander, and Engelman, Uriah. *Jewish Education in the United States: Report for the Study of Jewish Education in the U.S.* New York: American Association for Jewish Education, 1959.

Efron, Benjamin, and Rubin, Alvan. "The Reality of Bar Mitzvah." *CCAR Journal* 8 (October 1960), 31-33.

Feldstein Donald, and Shrage, Barry. "Myths and Facts for Campaigners and Planners." *Journal of Jewish Communal Service* 63 (1987), 95-104.

Fishman, Sylvia. "Learning About Learning: Insights on Contemporary Jewish Education from Jewish Population Studies." Waltham, MA: Cohen Center for Modern Jewish Studies, 1987.

Freidlander, Israel. "The Problem of Jewish Education for the Children of Immigrants." In *Jewish Education in the United States: A Documentary History*, edited by Lloyd Gartner. New York: Teachers College Press, 1913/1969.

Gans, Herbert. "Park Forest: Birth of a Jewish Community." *Commentary* (April 1951).

Goren, Arthur. *New York Jews and the Quest for Community*. New York: Columbia University Press, 1970.

Heilman, Samuel. "Inside the Jewish School." In *What We Know About Jewish Education*, edited by Stuart Kelman. Los Angeles: Torah Aura, 1992.

Himmelfarb, Harold. "The Impact of Religious Schooling." In *Studies in Jewish Education*, vol. 1, edited by Michael Rosenak. Jerusalem: Magnes Press, 1988.

Hirsch, E. D. *Cultural Literacy: What Every American Needs to Know*. Boston: Houghton and Mifflin, 1987.

Holtz, Barry. *Best Practices Project: The Supplementary School*. Cleveland: Council for Initiatives in Jewish Education, 1993.

Kaplan, Mordecai, and Cronson, Bernard. "A Survey of Jewish Education in New York City." In *Jewish Education in the United States: A Documentary History*, edited by Lloyd Gartner. New York: Teachers College Press, 1909/1969.

Kronish, Ronald. "The Influence of John Dewey on Jewish Education." *Conservative Judaism* 30 (1976), 48-60.

Liebman, Charles. *The Ambivalent American Jew*. Philadelphia: Jewish Publication Society, 1973.

Lightfoot, Sara Lawrence. *The Good High School: Portraits of Character and Culture*. New York: Basic Books, 1983.

Olitzky, Kerry. "A History of Reform Jewish Education During Emanuel Gamoran's Tenure as Educational Director of the Commission on Jewish Education of the Union of American Hebrew Congregations, 1923-1958." Doctoral dissertation, Hebrew Union College-Jewish Institute of Religion, 1984.

_____. "The Impact of John Dewey on Jewish Education." *Religious Education* 81 (1986), 5-18.

Phillips, Bruce, and Zeldin, Michael. "Jewish Education as Communal Activity: Patterns of Enrollment in Three Growth Communities." *Journal of Jewish Communal Service*, 63 (1987), 123-136.

Pilch, Judah. "From the Early Forties to the Mid-Sixties." In *A History of Jewish Education in America*, edited by J. Pilch. New York: American Association for Jewish Education, 1969.

Reimer, Joseph. "The Synagogue as a Context for Jewish Education." Cleveland: Commission on Jewish Education in North America, 1990.

Resnik, David, editor. "Communal Support for Congregational Schools: Current Approaches." New York: Jewish Educational Services of North America, 1988.

_____. " 'Jewish Supplementary Schooling' in Perspective." *Contemporary Jewry* 13 (1993), 3-23.

Rosenak, Michael. *Commandments and Concerns: Jewish Religious Education in Secular Society*. Philadelphia: Jewish Publication Society, 1987.

Schoem, David. *Ethnic Survival in America: An Ethnography of a Jewish Afternoon School*. Atlanta: Scholars Press, 1989.

_____. "The Supplementary School." In *What We Know About Jewish Education*, edited by Stuart Kelman. Los Angeles: Torah Aura, 1992.

Schoenfeld, Stuart. "Folk Judaism, Elite Judaism and the Role of the Bar Mitzvah in the Development of the Synagogue and Jewish School in America." *Contemporary Jewry* 9 (1988), 67-85.

Shevitz, Susan. "Communal Responses to the Teacher Shortage in the North American Supplementary School." In *Studies in Jewish Education*, vol. 3, edited by Janet Aviad. Jerusalem: Magnes Press, 1988.

Wertheimer, Jack. *A People Divided*. New York: Basic Books, 1993.

Westerhoff, John. *Will Our Children Have Faith?* New York: Seabury Press, 1976.

Winter, Nathan. *Jewish Education in a Pluralist Society*. New York: NYU Press, 1966.

Zeldin, Michael. "The Promise of Historical Inquiry in Jewish Education: 19th Century Day Schools and 20th Century Policy." *Religious Education* 83 (1988).

VIGNETTE # 1

CONGREGATIONAL EDUCATION AT TEMPLE LOMDEI TORAH[1]

Isa Aron

t is mid-August and every member household of Temple Lomdei Torah receives the same letter from the congregational staff: "It's time for your annual Jewish checkup. Please come in for an appointment with one of the rabbis or educators so that we can draw up your educational plan for the new year." Over the course of the next eight weeks, members come in for their meetings, which may last over an hour. The members of each household have been given some questions to consider in advance:

- What aspects of the Jewish tradition are you already knowledgeable about and comfortable with? (A list of subject areas follows.)

- What would you like to learn more about? Are there any particular topics that you would like to focus on this year?

- Which of the following fit(s) best with the schedule and "learning styles" of each member of your household?

    A weekly (or biweekly) course in the daytime or evening

    An occasional all-day *Shabbaton* or teach-in

    Ongoing meetings with a *chavurah*

    Independent study at home, with or without your spouse and children

    A weekend retreat or a week-long family camp

- Are you interested in purchasing or borrowing any of the following?

    A set of books that you can read to your child

    Some Jewish historical novels

Articles on contemporary Jewish issues

Tapes of holiday songs, prayers, etc.

Interactive computer games that teach about Jewish history

- Are you interested in participating in any of the following committees? (A list follows, along with a description of the learning opportunities involved in belonging to each committee.)

Since this protocol has been in place for a number of years, both the congregants and advisers have learned how to prepare for their meetings. Members welcome the opportunity to reflect on their learning activities in previous years and to identify those they found the most successful. Many members come to their meeting with suggestions for new formats or topics; others come with complaints or problems that concern them. The advisers have learned how to encourage participation in new activities without giving a hard sell and how to advocate for subject matters that they consider more "canonical," while bearing in mind people's interests. Over the years advisers have developed a close rapport with many of their advisees and a fairly good sense of how to match individuals with learning opportunities.

Some of the members choose to attend fairly standard classes, such as Beginning Hebrew, Bible, or Introduction to Jewish History. The big difference that the development of the new educational plan has made has been the mixture of ages in these classes. While children and working parents are unable to avail themselves of certain daytime programs, a surprising number of adults have chosen to attend classes in the late afternoon and on Sunday. In the beginning teachers of these classes had some misgivings about the wide range of ages. But over the years they have developed some guidelines pertaining to the appropriateness of particular classes for particular age groups. Torah reading classes, for example, are open to everyone over the age of ten; history classes are limited to those over sixteen; holiday cooking classes are open to everyone; and Hebrew is offered at a number of age levels, including a class for parents and children. In general, teachers have found that the presence of adults makes the children behave better, while the presence of children encourages the adults to participate more.

The continued interest in formal classes notwithstanding, the educational hub of the synagogue has shifted from the classroom to the library, which has quadrupled in size and has been renamed the Educational Resource Center. The synagogue now has two full-time librarians/curriculum developers on staff. They are responsible for collecting and preparing the learning materials that form the backbone of the new educational program: *parashat hashavua* packets for family study; text study units for *chavurot*; study materials for the ritual and social action committees; interactive computer games that teach Hebrew and history; and so on. The librarian/curriculum developers are available every day of the week to assist committees, *chavurot*, and families in their choice and use of materials. A group of volunteers who assist in making games, assembling sets of materials, creating attractive displays, and keeping accurate records also work in the Resource Center.

A special area of the Resource Center is reserved for learning Hebrew. The rabbis, educators, and Education Committee all agree that increased Hebrew literacy is a goal for which they are striving. The synagogue has received a special grant for the creation of individualized units that allow both children and adults to work on their own through a carefully planned sequence of worksheets, games, books, and tapes. The Hebrew Center is staffed by a group of volunteers who are available to answer questions and check people's work. Large charts on the wall display the names of all current students and the number of units each student has completed. Upon the completion of ten units, a student receives a ribbon, a certificate, an announcement of his or her achievement at Friday night services, and a listing in the temple bulletin. The Hebrew Center also sponsors its own events, such as all-Hebrew dinners and softball games. An E-mail to Israel program has recently been started, and interest has been expressed in a special trip to Israel for all who have reached a determined level of Hebrew literacy.

Another section of the Resource Center houses four or five computers. It continues to draw many teenagers, who come in to borrow games (both Jewish and non-Jewish) and communicate on-line with Jewish teenagers throughout the country. In addition, there is a storytelling alcove. On regularly scheduled days volunteers come in to read books and tell stories to children and then help them select books to read at home. This is part of the synagogue's extensive after-school child care program, which also offers art, music, drama, and sports. This program has been so successful that parents have lobbied for it to be extended in the summer as a day camp.

Although the leaders of the temple are proud of the richness and diversity of their educational program, they sometimes worry that the "satellite" nature of most of the activities will fragment the community. As a response, they have staged a number of events in which the entire community is brought together. These include an art fair that features exhibitions and performances and an education fair that features the products of all the educational activities. In addition, the staff is constantly searching for opportunities to highlight the progress of one group or another, such as a service that features texts studied by the social action committee; the "Torah Times," which is produced by the *chavurot* engaged in Torah study and is a regular feature in the synagogue bulletin; and a yearbook filled with writing, artwork, queries, and puzzles that serves as a memento of the year's accomplishments.

So are the leaders of Temple Lomdei Torah satisfied? Not entirely. They are aware that a number of things are missing from their educational program. For example, the women's study group wants to educate the congregation about gender-inclusive liturgy; the social action committee wants to start a *tzedakah* collective; and the list goes on. Leaders of the temple think that in about ten years they will have fine-tuned the system to satisfy their own sense of perfection, just in time for a new generation of members to start agitating for a new set of changes.

Notes

[1] My ideas for this vignette were drawn from conversations with many people over the years. Among the most recent of those conversations are those I had with students and faculty at the Jewish Education Seminar at Stanford, members of the education task force at Leo Baeck Temple, and the students in the Masters Seminar at the Rhea Hirsch School of Education at HUC-JIR, LA. Some of the specific ideas came from Rabbis Ray Zwerin, Margaret Holub, and Peretz Prusan. The notion of an annual "educational checkup" is discussed in Blaser 1992, p. 3.

REFERENCES

Blaser, Elissa. "Batayl B'Shishim: Is What We Are Teaching Kosher?" Unpublished manuscript, 1992.

VIGNETTE #2

THE CHAVURAH SCHOOL[1]

Jonathan E. Kraus

hank you for your inquiry about membership at Temple Beth Torah. We are very proud of the dynamic Jewish religious community we are creating. We would love to share that community with you. This booklet explains a little about our history and describes our educational program. You will find that "Jewish learning for Jewish living" is at the heart of our congregation's identity. You will also find that we believe every Jew should be both a student and a teacher of Torah.

About seven years ago the temple's leadership made a courageous and visionary decision. They began transforming our religious school program into a Chavurah School. The goal of the new program was to reverse a disturbing trend that we had observed. Increasingly, like its secular counterparts, our religious school was assuming the traditional educative role of parents. In its attempt to help parents cope with the ever more challenging task of Jewish education, our school actually had disempowered and marginalized those parents as Jewish teachers. By contrast, the Chavurah School returns the primary responsibility for our children's Jewish education to the family and its support systems, where that task belongs both philosophically and in order to be truly effective.

During our initial transition from a more traditional school, members of the congregation were invited to participate in the process on a voluntary basis. After five years of experience and because of the growing popularity and appreciation of the program, the Board of Trustees approved its full implementation.

What is the Chavurah School? It is a program that provides every member of our congregation with a smaller social group within which they can learn and live a Jewish life. It is also a program that gives each of these groups primary responsibility for educating the children of that *chavurah*. The Chavurah School challenges and empowers every adult in the congregation to become not only a student of Torah but also a teacher. Finally, the Chavurah School does what all *chavurah* programs try to do. It provides powerful experiences of a supportive community, of interpersonal intimacy, and of the spiritual connectedness for which we all long. In this age of geographic mobility, the Chavurah School offers each of our congregants a nurturing, supportive group that can become a surrogate, extended family.

How does the Chavurah School work? When you decide to join us, we'll ask you to fill out an application and to schedule a meeting with the Va'ad Ha'Chavurot (Chavurah Steering Committee). After the interview you will be assigned to a *chavurah*—a small community group of approximately ten to twelve families and individuals. Since we believe that all Jewish adults should help to teach and raise the next generation, we assign all new members to a *chavurah*, whether or not they have young children of their own. Incidentally, we find that this requirement helps us to create a more integrated community. The inclusion of every person in our program insures a place of honor and importance for many members of our congregation (e.g., singles, seniors and empty nesters) who might otherwise feel marginalized and alienated by a family-centered program.

Some attempt is made to create homogenous groupings (e.g., families with young children, single parent families, and intermarried families are placed in a group that have some other similarly configured families). However, the Va'ad balances this concern against its desire to foster intergenerational relationships and to provide every congregant with exposure to a rich diversity of perspectives and experiences. Over the years, leaders of the Va'ad have become very skillful at choosing the right blend of people.

A professional team is assigned to each *chavurah*. This team consists of a Jewish educator and a social worker who are full-time employees of our congregation. Each team is assigned from three to five different *chavurot*. The Va'ad (which is composed of representatives from all the *chavurot*) has worked with the professional staff to develop an overall statement of goals. In addition, the Va'ad has identified Jewish culture and identity, Jewish holidays, life-cycle observances, ethics, history, Hebrew language, Jewish thought, prayer, and spirituality as mandated subject areas. However, each *chavurah* refines those goals and topics as it develops its own learning activities. In consultation with their professional team, each *chavurah* also chooses the time and location of their learning. Your team educator will help facilitate the adults' learning process as needed. She will also provide both moral support and educational resources that will help *chavurah* members teach more effectively. While the team educator may sometimes actually teach the children, all the adults in a *chavurah* are expected to participate fully in the learning experiences.

Your *chavurah* will meet with its professional team at least twice a month for purposes of planning, study, and group discussion. As might be anticipated, these meetings typically engage the adult members of the *chavurah* in a challenging and intense process of reflection about their own Jewishness. In fact, while the social worker may participate in some of the actual teaching sessions, she is much more involved in the planning/discussion stage. The social worker helps the group of parents and other adults work through such issues as the tensions experienced in intermarried or single parent families, the challenge of raising Jewish children in a non-Jewish society, and ambivalence about Jewish identity, religion, etc. He is also available for private counseling. When they are invited and at certain prearranged times, the rabbi, cantor, and director of education serve as additional resources for discussion and planning.

In one memorable example, a *chavurah* chose to do a unit on prayer. The topic evoked a wide range of responses from the adult members of the *chavurah*. In the course of planning that unit, the group engaged in intense dialogue with the rabbi and cantor about the history of Jewish worship and what praying means. The educational team facilitated a vigorous, passionate discussion about personal experiences relating to God and prayer as well as what we should teach our children about God and about prayer. The group attended services several times and discussed their positive and negative reactions to the experience. The professional team presented texts on prayer and spirituality written by a variety of Jewish teachers, both ancient and modern. Together with the director of education, the *chavurah* learned about the process of faith development in children and brainstormed age-appropriate, innovative activities.

Some activities included the entire group, like a hike to the mountains during which members looked for as many opportunities as possible to say blessings. Other activities were more age-specific. For instance, after the adults helped the children master a prayer appropriate to their particular developmental level, the children wrote their own interpretations of the prayer and led a service for the entire *chavurah*. The older children also discussed what they think about when they pray, what makes it hard for them to pray, and what they think about the concept that God hears prayers. Although they continued to view prayer in a variety of ways, every member of the *chavurah*, young and old, came away with a deeper understanding of Jewish worship, prayer, and their own spiritual lives.

Because we realize that this model could fragment our congregation into a collection of small, disconnected groups, all of our members participate in a variety of supplementary activities. These include congregation-wide holiday and Shabbat celebrations, as well as various retreats and workshops geared to specific demographic groups (e.g., young families, families about to celebrate a Bar Mitzvah, and seniors). In addition, two or three of our *chavurot* come together at various times for a shared program or outing.

The Chavurah School has produced many corollary benefits for our congregation. Since adopting this program, we have witnessed an increased sense of purpose, vitality, and community cohesion. In addition, our adult education program, which had been struggling, has experienced an explosion of interest. Congregants are asking for classes that will provide them with knowledge and resources they can share with their own children. Many of our congregants also now offer to teach classes in order to share with others what they have learned during their own preparation to teach.

While our synagogue did have some *chavurot* prior to the creation of the Chavurah School, the new program completely transformed and reinvigorated these groups. It seems that many of our *chavurot* had not found a focus around which to coalesce. Other groups had no Jewish focus at all and had served a purely social function. While many of the *chavurot* continue to engage in social activities, most also began to observe holidays and celebrate life-cycle events together and attend Jewish cultural and educational activities as a group. Some adult members even began to meet in order to study Jewish topics purely for their own benefit.

With the help of this program, we hope to send the following messages to every parent and every adult who decides to join us: You are our children's most important teachers of Judaism. You can teach competently and effectively. In fact, we at Temple Beth Torah are convinced that your active, intimate, and consistent involvement is essential to the success of our children's Jewish education. If you feel ignorant, we would love to help you become more educated about Judaism. If you are not sure how you feel about being Jewish or about religion, we'd like to help you clarify and deepen your understanding. You can develop your own answers to complex questions about how being Jewish meshes with your particular family or your life-style. You can play an active role in deciding what our children's formative Jewish educational experiences should be. Like all teachers, you can touch the future. And like all serious Jews, you can help to secure the Jewish future by bringing Torah alive in your own life and in the lives of our children. Come learn with us.

Notes

[1]   I first articulated many of the ideas contained in this paper in 1987 while I was a student at the Rhea Hirsch School of Education of the Hebrew Union College-Jewish Institute of Religion. The present paradigm expands on a model that was part of my master's project titled: "As Parents to Their Students: The Challenge of Parental Involvement in Jewish Education." I owe a great deal of my thinking on this subject to the gifted authors and educational leaders cited in the bibliography below. For more information, I refer you to those articles.

REFERENCES

Aft, Martha. "Parent Involvement." In *The Jewish Principal's Handbook*, edited by Audrey Friedman Marcus, and Raymond A. Zwerin. Denver, CO: Alternatives in Jewish Education Inc., 1983.

Aron, Isa; Greenspan, Jay; Rous, Janice; and Wolf, Michael. "Alternative Jewish Education: The Havurah Model." *Response* 30-31 (Summer/Fall 1976), 185-191.

Cowan, Paul. "World of Our Children." In *The New York Times* Magazine (April 3, 1977).

Debenham, Jerry, and Parsons, Michael J. "The Future of Schools and Families: Three Scenarios and a Recommendation." *Phi Delta Kappan* 59 (March 1978), 442-446.

Grad, Eli. "Issues of Quality in Jewish Education: A Critical Focus." *Jewish Education* 46:3 (1978), 10-15.

Raik, Jerome. "Maximizing Parent Participation." *Shema* 8:156 (September 1, 1978), 146-149.

Schoem, David. "Ethnic Survival in America: An Ethnography of a Jewish Afternoon School." Unpublished dissertation. University of California, Berkeley, 1979.

VIGNETTE #3

HIGHER AND HIGHER

REFLECTIONS ON THE SEFIROT PROGRAM

Richard Abrams, Kenneth Carr, and Susan Cosden[1]

hen Temple Ahavat Torah began reconceptualizing its educational program, we at the school also needed to rethink our goals, methods, and expectations. For the most part, the newly designed program has been a success. However, as in any situation, there are still "dark days." On those days when nothing seems to go right, I take out my letter file and cheer myself up by reading some of the letters that I have received.

From a Parent

When the rabbi spoke on Rosh Hashanah about acknowledging those people who had contributed to our lives in recent days, I knew that I had to write this letter because you have certainly contributed to our lives! When our family moved here and joined the synagogue, we were rather surprised to learn that we were all required to register for classes! Required? Sure, we wanted our kids to be educated, but we didn't want to be forced to study ourselves. It was enough to make us consider not joining the temple! But when member after member spoke with us about lifelong Jewish learning and living Judaism as a family, we thought we might give it a try—at least for one year.

From the beginning it was different from any Jewish school we had ever attended. First of all, our whole family got an opportunity to study together. We decided to try a Bible class, figuring that we could all learn some more about the Bible and the class would give us a chance to spend some time together. The second shock was the way the class was run. I had been expecting to be talked at, but the teacher—I mean facilitator—asked us instead what we wanted to learn. Each of us picked a topic that interested us. The facilitator pointed us in the direction of resources that would help us learn on our own so that we could present what we had learned to the rest of the class. It was quite a kick to hear my nine-year-old son explaining Noah's ark to both kids and adults. And I will admit that I remember more about the burning bush (my topic) even now than I remember about any Jewish topic I had been *taught* because I had to research it myself. Not only that, but if I ever want to learn anything else in the Bible, I now possess the skills to study the Bible on my own.

When the first series of classes ended, we were ready to sign up for new ones. This time our interests diverged, and we each picked a different subject. I took a second Bible class, while my wife studied Hebrew literature. Our fourteen-year-old daughter chose Israeli music, and our son discovered Jewish heroes. Once again, we had a fantastic time. The temple had achieved something I thought was impossible: It had gotten my children (and my wife and me) excited about Jewish education. Some evenings, dinner at our house even *sounded* like a school, resounding with arguments about issues that had come up in class.

We have benefited so much from the learning we have done in the Sefirot program. Not only has the program helped us become more knowledgeable, it has also influenced our religious life. After my wife and daughter took a course on home rituals and I took a class on modern views of God, we were able to make some conscious and deliberate decisions about what rituals to perform and how to perform them. We have met so many people through these classes, which has made it so much easier to make friends.

We hope to give back some of what we have received: My wife will soon finish her training as a facilitator. We are so appreciative of this opportunity to rediscover a vibrant, dynamic Judaism.

From a Teacher Turned Facilitator

As the Kindergarten teacher in the temple's supplementary school for sixteen years, I was quite rattled by the introduction of the Sefirot program. I had been fairly happy with our religious school, which had consistently introduced the newest and most interesting curricular programs we heard about at CAJE and NATE. And we had always run a highly successful Family Education weekend. We *thought* that what we were doing was very effective.

We had been hearing for several years that big changes were brewing at the temple. Two of the teachers had been on the educational task force, and all of us had been involved in various discussions. We liked the early changes that had been made, but we weren't fully prepared for the radical changes that were to come.

The changes began with a week of intensive staff training late in the spring. When we entered the packed room, the veteran teachers looked at all the newcomers with dismay. Unlike in previous years, no textbooks or curriculum guides were distributed. Instead, each of us received a loose-leaf binder filled with articles on independent learning and group facilitation. Most of us were shocked! Were we expected to learn something new this year? We were the teachers, not the students.

Our students in the coming year, we were informed, would include *all* members of the congregation. All, regardless of their age, would be given the ability and responsibility to choose their own classes. Classes would become six-week study groups. Finally, we were no longer considered teachers but facilitators.

Looking back, I don't know why I stayed in the room and did not walk out with three other veteran teachers. But I did stay. I stayed in the room the entire first day and learned about group facilitation. I returned for the second day and learned about family and parent education. I returned for the remaining days and became fascinated by the concepts of multi-age/level education, student empowerment through choice, and group dynamics. I learned how to guide a group of students in using resources to pursue their own learning. The temple staff had worked to develop an incredible resource center that included a vastly expanded library, with books and magazines on every topic of Jewish interest; a computer linkup with Judaic studies departments all over the world; Hebrew programs and other materials on CD-ROM; new equipment like a copier, a copy stand, and a laminating machine; a media center in which one could listen to Jewish music, watch videotapes, or practice speaking Hebrew; and a construction corner in which one could make ritual objects, games, and posters.

That week we explored the power that we, the facilitators, had to learn on our own, and we learned how to empower our students to do the same. When the staff workshop was over, I was both excited and scared. Although my years of experience were an asset, I knew that I would need much more than that in the coming year.

Very tentatively I offered to be the facilitator of a Bible class.

The class was made up of five families, three independent sixth graders (I mean, twelve-year-olds), and three post Bar/Bat Mitzvah students. Despite my anxiety the first six-week module went very well. The students were quick to decide exactly what and how they wanted to learn, and I supported them by showing them their options and helping them find resources. The different ages of the group worked very well, with everyone brainstorming ideas and helping everyone else. Each student presentation was impressive. Both the students and I were struck by how much everyone had learned.

Now, several years into the program, I feel much more comfortable with my role as a facilitator. I really enjoy working with multi-age groups, and my interactions with whole families have been wonderful. In becoming interested and involved in facilitating groups on different subjects, I myself have learned a great deal. Thanks for your perseverance in helping make this transition happen!

From a Former Student

I was in the sixth grade when the Sefirot program began. My first reaction to it was outrage. I had been looking forward to having only one year of religious school left. Now I was supposed to be in school forever!

Three things kept me from having a totally bad attitude and refusing to give the new system a chance. The first thing was that everyone was *supposed* to do it, including my older brother, my parents, my friends, and their parents. The second thing was that the school gave us a lot of choices, and each "semester" was only six weeks long. The third thing was that we got to pick our own topics in the classes and were asked to teach one another. In my very first class, which was on Jewish feminism, I was able to work with my best friend on a project on feminine images of God. By the time we were done, we knew more about that topic than almost anyone in the synagogue and were even asked to make a presentation to the Liturgy Committee! It's not surprising that my friends and I got hooked on the program.

One of the changes you made was really hard to believe: You made becoming a Bar/Bat Mitzvah an option rather than an expectation. In the past, it had always been a requirement, and then you told us it was a choice! At first I did not really want to become a Bat Mitzvah, but I decided to go through with it anyway for my family's sake. Eventually I came to my own rationale for becoming a Bat Mitzvah.

The Bat Mitzvah experience helped me synthesize the different classes I had taken into the beginning of a whole Jewish ideology. The concept of the *Sefirot* was a big motivator. According to the Kabbalah, the *Sefirot* are the ten levels of human awareness of the Divine Presence. Our synagogue adapted this idea to signify ten milestones of committed lifelong learning. For every thirty-six classes a person takes or facilitates, he or she moves up another level and is honored at a ceremony in front of the whole congregation.

At first the thought of taking thirty-six classes seemed impossible. But lots of things I was doing anyway counted as a "class," like learning to chant the Torah for my Bat Mitzvah, going to a Jewish summer camp, and working with the youth group on a year-long *tzedakah* project. Within five years I had accumulated enough credit to reach the first level, *Malchut*. It was thrilling to be honored together with people of all ages and to beat out my mom and dad, who were a few credits behind. Our group worked together to create our own service and our own special presentation, in which we shared with the rest of the congregation what we had learned.

This program helped instill in me a real love of Jewish learning for its own sake. Having to choose my own courses made me aware of how *I* learn best. When I go off to college next year, I'll be taking some Jewish studies courses there, too. The facilitators at the temple think I'll be pretty well prepared. And I'm already negotiating the number of credits I will get toward my next *Sefirah*!

Notes

1   This vignette was first developed as a final project for the Philosophy of Jewish Education Seminar at the Rhea Hirsch School of Education at HUC-JIR.

2

THE CONTEXT
FOR TRANSFORMATION

WHEN SCHOOL AND SYNAGOGUE ARE JOINED

Joseph Reimer

Introduction

To make descriptive statements about the space in which Jewish education takes place is to talk about an overlapping space where school and synagogue are joined. It is that joining that needs to be described before we can understand more about Jewish supplementary education.

This was the first paragraph of a paper I wrote in 1990 for the Commission on Jewish Education in North America titled "The Synagogue As a Context for Jewish Education." The paper was a plea to the leaders of the organized North American Jewish community not to give up on establishing quality Jewish education within the supplementary school. It was also a call to them to realize that until supplementary schools are seen within their proper context and understood more deeply in relationship to their host synagogue, there will be little chance of broadly enhancing their educational potential.

In this paper, I review some of the assumptions about the relationship between synagogue and school that I laid out in the 1990 paper. I do so because my thinking about this relationship has grown more complex as a result of the additional ethnographic research I have done since 1990.

That research was conducted in the academic year 1990-1991 at two Reform synagogues that I will call Temple Akiba and Temple Hillel.[1] Although both are located in the same metropolitan area, the former is a large, historic urban center while the latter is a postwar, mid-sized suburban congregation. I chose these temples because they were suggested by knowledgeable professionals as examples of synagogues with especially good educational programs. I spent the year as a participant/observer, dividing my time between the two congregations. My research involved sitting in on classes, participating in services and adult educational programs, and observing informal and family educational activities as well as the deliberations of religious school committees and board meetings. I also interviewed the principals, teachers, rabbis, and officers of each congregation.

I have begun to report on this research in other articles and am in the process of writing a book on my findings.[2] In this paper I will concentrate on questions that I partially addressed in 1990 but will explore more fully at this time.

They include:

(1) What is it about the history and culture of a synagogue that leads its congregants to place special emphasis on the quality of the Jewish education that it provides for its members?

(2) How do the rabbi and educational director work together to transmit a vision of quality Jewish education and translate that vision into workable educational programs?

In addition, I will focus on the following two questions that I did not previously address:

(3) What conceptions of leadership and change do the leaders of a congregation tacitly employ in thinking about how to improve the educational program of their synagogue school?

(4) What happens when a segment of the membership does not accept the educational vision advocated by the congregational leadership? How is dissent handled in this context?

In answering these questions, I will draw upon my observations of and interviews with members of two Reform congregations. I will cite in particular a case study from Temple Akiba, the large urban congregation, in which the educational director, together with the rabbi and certain lay leaders, introduced over a number of years changes in the school curriculum that galvanized a strong reaction from both supporters and opponents of the changes. I hope this case study will illuminate how complex the process of change in education within a synagogue context can be. This is due to the fact that change in one area (the school) reverberates throughout the whole system (the synagogue) and elicits reactions from players who may be responding to the proposed change on the basis of issues that have little to do with the educational issues being discussed.

The History and Culture of the Congregation

An observer only has to drive by Temple Akiba and Temple

Hillel to note how very different these two institutions are. Temple Akiba is located in a dense urban area but is housed in a building that denotes architectural grandeur and announces that it has a well-established community of Jews who see themselves as being an essential part of the city's urban landscape.

In contrast, one could drive by the suburban location of Temple Hillel and, except for the modest sign, never know a synagogue was located on the street. Set back from the road behind a parking area and a grove of trees, Temple Hillel is housed in a building that communicates modesty and a hesitancy to draw too much attention to itself. A closer look reveals a structure that has been expanded several times and includes a simple sanctuary joined to a school wing that contains a string of classrooms.

Yet despite the striking contrasts between these two synagogues, they both house congregations that, each in its own way, have made Jewish education a high priority on their agenda. How can we explain that two very different congregations each made education a high priority? A year of fieldwork in these synagogues did not yield easy or direct answers. Listening for hints as to why these congregations see it as their mission to provide quality Jewish education led me to the overgeneralized conclusion that this value is embedded in the history and culture of these organizations.[3] I will return to the question of whether or not the concept of education as a priority is shared by the majority of the members of these congregations, but I can say that for the leaders of these congregations—both lay and professional—placing special value on quality education is almost synonymous with what their congregation is and has been in the past.

A short anecdote might help to illustrate my point. Once I was invited to a meeting sponsored by the Jewish Federation in that area to discuss how to improve the quality of youth programs that synagogues provide for their adolescent population. The question arose as to whether any congregations had hired full-time youth workers. There were two: Temple Akiba and a large Conservative congregation. As the conversation continued, someone turned to an active lay leader, a past president of Temple Hillel, and asked what arrangement it had. He answered that when the congregation first hired a full-time assistant rabbi several years ago, it decided to give that rabbi the youth portfolio. Thus the assistant rabbi is the youth leader of the high school youth group.

Up to this point the group's discussion made it clear that most congregations hire a part-time youth leader, who, for several thousand dollars a year, serves as the leader of the synagogue's high school youth group. Everyone acknowledged that part-time youth leaders are limited with regard to what they can do, but congregations face budgetary constraints. Thus the person who asked the question about Temple Hillel commented that its arrangement regarding youth activities was very expensive. The past president acknowledged that fact but simply added, "That is how we do it."

If pressed on this issue, I am sure the past president could have elaborated that the synagogue's decision was a way to bring adolescents into the congregation by giving them "their own rabbi." (Of course this rabbi also has other responsibilities besides youth work.) I heard much about this point in my fieldwork at Temple Hillel. As a result of its investment in this program, the synagogue has a very fine youth group that contributes vitally to congregational life.

At this meeting I was struck not only by the modesty of the past president's remarks but also by his not suggesting that the arrangement of Temple Hillel might serve as a model for other congregations. He seemed to feel that putting the youth portfolio in the hands of a rabbi was simply the way they "do it" and, therefore, not necessarily applicable to other congregations. Indeed the participants at this meeting went on to consider the possibility of adopting for their congregations the Temple Akiba model of hiring a young adult (who is not a rabbi) as a full-time youth professional. But none of the leaders of Temple Akiba was present to advocate that others follow their example.

Although attending this meeting was not intended to be part of my fieldwork, it provided me with a perspective that was helpful in formulating a response to the first question posed on page 94. It helped confirm and exemplify the observation that these two congregations (among others) stand out because they provide unusually high-quality educational service. (I believe this is true with regard to both formal and informal education.) It also reinforced my sense that it is not easy to explain why they do so. The past president's comment underscored that his congregation's decisions are based on a shared sense of what the congregation is and what it values. I might say that the congregation's decisions stem from the members' collective identity as an organization and that they, feeling the uniqueness of this identity, are hesitant to offer their way as a model for others to emulate.

An organization's collective identity is connected to its sense of its own history. When I first interviewed the senior rabbi at Temple Hillel, we spoke about the special educational focus of that synagogue. He refused to take personal credit for that focus since he had found it in place when he arrived. When I was invited to share some of my observations derived from my research at a meeting with the board of trustees of Temple Akiba, one of the veteran members told me that the positive impressions I was conveying reminded her of the work of a former educational director who had served in the 1950s and 1960s. In their view, the present is continuous with the past. What makes the members most proud is that this special focus on education has been part of their congregation's tradition for as long as anyone can remember.

I see a "myth of continuity" operating, a created self-perception that the current level of educational excellence has always been part of this congregation's legacy.[4] While the myth conveniently overlooks the rough parts of the congregation's history, it protects the educational program when challenges to it are raised from within the congregation. Supporters of the current program can appeal to the congregation's mythic history to argue that reducing the scope of the educational program would betray the values that this congregation has long held dear.

But this myth of continuity also leaves an observer unable to explain why these congregations have developed this aspect of their identity. If they respond to my questions about their priorities by saying, "This is how it has always been," I gain little insight into the development of this identity. I would need more historical data than I have available to trace how this sense of identity developed over time. More to the point of this volume, I do not have a working hypothesis to explain why these congregations developed as they did or why other congregations developed in different directions. The best that I can conclude is that these congregations share a cluster of identifiable characteristics that make possible their maintaining high-quality educational programs in the present. I identified these characteristics in my 1990 paper as showing that a school has a favored status within the system of congregational values.

According to my definition, the statement that an educational program is favored means that all the major stakeholders in the congregation express through word and deed their support and recognition of the centrality of the program for the mission of the congregation.

This would include: (1) a community – membership and parent body – that highly values education for itself and its children; (2) a professional leadership that can articulate a clear vision of what the educational program of the congregation should be; (3) rabbis (and, where present, cantors) who are integrally involved in the educational work of the congregation; (4) a lay leadership that through its board and committee structure provides financial and organizational backing to the educational program; and (5) a congregation that integrates the children and teachers of the school into its communal and worship life.[5]

Congregational Ferment

Having made the claim that this commitment to providing quality Jewish education is embedded in the collective identity of these two congregations, I hasten to add a caution. It would be a mistake to view these commitments as permanently engraved on the stone tablets above each congregation's ark. Quite the contrary! My ethnographic data suggest that within these congregations there are on-going, dramatic debates about congregational life that at times challenge the leadership's notions about Jewish education.

The biggest surprise of my fieldwork was to find these synagogues in a period of ferment characterized by dramatic disagreements. While no one openly challenges the centrality of the educational mission of these synagogues, there are debates about the nature of that education that indicate that the vision of Jewish education that the rabbis and educators put forward and most of the lay leadership affirms is not universally accepted by the members of the congregation.

I will now present an account of a challenge to Temple Akiba's educational leadership that arose during the year I was doing my fieldwork. The purpose of the account is to show that even in a congregation that has a strong sense of itself as a leader in the field of congregational Jewish education, there is no easy or unchallenged route to reaching a consensus on what needs to be done to improve Jewish education. The challenge came from a group of congregation members who were experiencing difficulties accepting the educational direction endorsed by the rabbi, the educational director, and segments of the lay leadership. My focus will be on the nature of the challenge and how the leadership decided to respond to it.

Hebrew at Temple Akiba

Since the early decades of this century, Temple Akiba has prided itself on providing a quality Reform Jewish education for its children in a professionally run religious school. Until the 1940s the religious school met only on Sunday and did not include the teaching of Hebrew as a major part of the curriculum. Because religious services in those years were conducted primarily in English and because "classical Reform Judaism" was non-Zionist in orientation, there was little perceived need for teaching Hebrew to either children or adults.[6]

With a transition in rabbinic leadership in the 1940s came two significant changes in temple philosophy that affected the teaching of Hebrew in the congregation and the school. First, more traditional prayers and rituals (including Bar Mitzvah) were introduced into the liturgy. Second, the congregational leadership became more supportive of the Zionist cause to establish a Jewish homeland and to revive Hebrew as a spoken language. After World War II the temple for the first time began a Hebrew program for students.[7]

However, this new Hebrew program was neither mandatory nor fully integrated into the existing religious school. The religious school continued to meet on Sunday and those students who wished to learn Hebrew attended the voluntary Hebrew program during the week. The religious school education program culminated in the confirmation ceremony that was held after tenth grade. The Hebrew education program culminated in Bar Mitzvah at the age of thirteen.

Over the years, as more and more families in the congregation wanted their children to become Bar or Bat Mitzvah, the mid-week Hebrew program has grown in popularity because to become Bar or Bat Mitzvah a child has to know enough Hebrew to participate in the increasingly Hebraized Shabbat service. Many of these adolescents have continued on to the Confirmation program, where they are joined by some of the students who elected the classical Reform model of religious school education that does not include Hebrew or Bar Mitzvah.

In the late 1970s the current senior rabbi came to Temple Akiba with a serious interest in making Jewish and particularly Hebrew education even more central to the mission of the synagogue. A scholar in his own right, the rabbi has a passion for introducing textual study into the curriculum of both the religious school and adult education. He shares this text-oriented approach to Jewish learning with Rabbi Don Marcus who was his first assistant rabbi and who became the temple educator in the mid-1980s.

Since becoming the temple educator, Rabbi Don Marcus has been working in conjunction with Rabbi Davidman on implementing serious curricular reform in the way in which Hebrew and Bible are taught. They have chosen the Melton Hebrew Language Program, which places the learning of biblical Hebrew in the forefront of the curricular agenda. Recognizing that they could not expect the students in a part-time program to learn both modern spoken Hebrew and classical literary Hebrew, the rabbis agreed with the authors of the Melton Curriculum that the priority in synagogue schools should be given to learning the skills of reading and comprehending the classical Hebrew texts that are regularly used in Jewish rituals. The learning of modern Hebrew could be left for the higher grades once the students had mastered the elements of classical Hebrew. [8]

Working closely with the religious school committee, Rabbi Marcus was able to convince the temple's board of trustees to invest a considerable amount of money in implementing this and other key improvements in the synagogue's educational system.

Specifically, Rabbi Marcus initiated the measures that were needed to give a strong foundation to the Hebrew program by significantly increasing and improving the teaching staff.

I have reported elsewhere on my observations of the Hebrew program.[9] In summary, I would say that those students who have pursued the program seriously from grades three to seven emerge with the ability to read a biblical text in the original and can translate and read with comprehension with the help of a dictionary. They ask meaningful questions about the text and, in guided discussions, engage in a process of inquiry about the meaning of the biblical narrative. They also have a rudimentary ability to say simple sentences in modern Hebrew. Those students who have not pursued their studies as consistently have shown a capacity to read fluently but are less able to comprehend and translate the text. They usually cannot speak modern Hebrew.

As an observer, I have suggested that Temple Akiba has much to be proud of with regard to this Hebrew program. The majority of the students in the Hebrew program take it seriously, attend school regularly, pay attention in class, do homework at home, and show incremental progress in the mastery of the Hebrew they are taught.

The teachers and parents I spoke with are quite satisfied with the program and feel that serious learning is taking place. A vast majority of the students who attend the program three days a week continue their Jewish education beyond Bar Mitzvah and seventh grade.

Should Hebrew Be Mandatory?

The policy of the Hebrew program at Temple Akiba remained that attendance at the mid-week Hebrew program was optional for students. By 1989 only a very small percentage of the students in the religious school were choosing the non-Hebrew option. These students came for three hours on Sunday and took as one of their courses Synagogue Skills, whose purpose was to prepare them to participate in the temple's religious services. This involved their learning to read Hebrew. My observations of the sixth-grade level showed that the students' capacity to decode remained quite limited and stood in stark contrast to their peers in the Hebrew program.

In the spring of 1989, Rabbi Marcus proposed to the religious school committee that the time had come to consider whether or not "to make Hebrew mandatory." [10] As a standing lay committee within the congregation, the religious school committee (RSC) is responsible for setting educational policy for the school. If Rabbi Marcus's proposal were adopted by this committee and approved by the synagogue's board of trustees, it would eliminate the existing option of students from third grade on to attend religious school for only one day a week. It would require that every student study Hebrew in a mid-week program. Students would have the choice of attending the three-day-a-week Hebrew program that we have described or attending school on Sunday and arranging a Hebrew tutorial at home during the week. Although the school tried to discourage the tutorial arrangement, it was chosen at an extra cost by a sizable minority of families. [11]

This proposal also had symbolic implications for Temple Akiba. It would mean the synagogue's affirming the importance of learning Hebrew for all the children and, by implication, affirming that knowing Hebrew was an important element in being a "knowledgeable" Jew. For a Reform temple with a long and proud history, this change would reverse the vision of an earlier period of classical Reform when Hebrew played a minor role in the religious life of temples and worship services and study programs were conducted almost entirely in English.

Rabbi Marcus had a close relationship with the members of the current RSC. He had been working with them to develop a more informed and consistent lay leadership that could advise him on matters of educational policy. The question of whether to make Hebrew mandatory grew out of the work they had been doing together in reviewing and evaluating the religious school curriculum. They had come to realize that learning Hebrew should be a vital part of the school's curriculum. They wondered why, then, there was still the option available to receive a religious education at Temple Akiba without learning Hebrew beyond the minimal level.

Although Don Marcus must have favored this proposal, he did not press for its immediate approval because in the spring of 1989, the committee was quite divided over the wisdom of making Hebrew mandatory and eliminating the Sunday-only option. Those who were opposed had two reservations. Given the history of this temple, making Hebrew mandatory would be too much a reversal of the once dominant classical Reform ideology that still had some adherents in the congregation. In addition, eliminating the Sunday-only option might result in squeezing out certain groups of families who preferred that option.

The result of the RSC's first vote was so close that Rabbi Marcus suggested that a decision be postponed until there was time to carefully study the questions that had been raised. He was particularly concerned about whether the effect of this change would exclude certain groups of families. Along with the senior rabbi and others, he had been working hard to open Temple Akiba to more "marginal" Jewish populations, such as interfaith families, single-parent families, and New Americans, and he did not want to undo that work by unintentionally pushing them out of the religious school.

After carefully reviewing the data that showed why some families had chosen the Sunday-only option and discovering that no single type of family was overrepresented in that population, Don and Sherry Saunders, the committee chairperson, went back to the RSC to ask for it to reconsider. After deliberating again in the spring of 1990, the RSC voted by a wider majority to approve making Hebrew mandatory for all students in the religious school. In the words of the chairperson, they concluded that "the study of Hebrew is the lynchpin of making possible a richer understanding of the history, liturgy, and literature of the Jewish people." Therefore, "allowing even a small percentage of our population not to study Hebrew was inconsistent with our philosophy and goals." While "fully aware of the discomfort" that this decision would cause some families, the committee based its decision on the "long-standing tradition of excellence in our religious school education." [12]

I entered the picture as an observer after the decision had been made by the RSC and was about to be approved by the board of trustees. At its December 1990 meeting, the RSC was considering how to present this change in policy to the parent body of the religious school. In addition to notifying the parents in writing that this change would go into effect the next school year, the committee decided to call an open meeting for parents and interested temple members to discuss the change and other issues on the committee's agenda. The committee sensed that there would be some concern but did not fully anticipate what did occur. The open meeting became a forum for very heated disagreement by dissenting parents who felt that this change was a total reversal of the long-standing temple policy of offering members a choice as to how they wished to educate their children and, indeed, define themselves as Jews. The parental dissent, presented in very emotional terms, posed a major challenge to the RSC's proposed change in policy.

The RSC Reassesses

At their next scheduled meeting, which took place two weeks after the open meeting, the members of the RSC met to reassess where they stood in regard to the implementation of mandatory Hebrew. Everyone on the RSC realized that the decision the committee had made had run into a wall of parental opposition that had been expressed with great feeling by a few parents at the open meeting. Don Marcus opened the committee's discussion by reading the three letters he had received from parents who had spoken up in dissent at the meeting. They were thoughtful, emotional elaborations on the themes of the meetings.

Ben, a member of the RSC, picked up from where the open meeting had left off.

> We made a mistake in terms of process.... We lost touch with the constituency we represent. We see ourselves more as a committee relating to Don Marcus. We need to keep reminding ourselves of what are the ongoing issues for these parents.... In these letters there is a strong feeling among previous generations of Reform Jews that they are being attacked as Jews. They seem to need to prove that they are good Jews without Hebrew.

Three other board members quickly agreed with Ben that there were errors in process that needed to be rectified before this policy decision should be implemented. But Sherry disagreed.

> We are a private institution and not a school board. We are not elected. Analogies to school committees do not speak to me .... You don't just vote with the constituency but take a leadership role. We are charged with a responsibility to make a decision. In an open forum it's a given that you will hear from the dissatisfied. If we could poll the entire community, the vote might go with us.

Having once served on her town's school committee, Sherry has a different view from Ben of what the role of the RSC should be in the synagogue. While he sees it as a mistake that the RSC has "lost touch with the constituency we represent," Sherry does not believe the RSC represents a constituency. The committee members are not elected by the parents or temple members. They are appointed by the leadership. While Ben regards the fact that the RSC primarily sees itself "as relating to Don Marcus" as problematic, Sherry believes the committee should be taking "a leadership role" and has "a responsibility to make a decision." As she told me in a later interview: "This is a private institution... a community we have chosen to join. I have no claim on this seat. I asked and got the seat. Here I act more as an individual.... At the meeting I felt, "I can do this to you; if you don't like it, you can leave."

Ben responded by clarifying that he did not see the issue as primarily procedural but educational.

> In looking back at the process, we opted for change without realizing we had to catch them [the parents] up. Our decision was based on a lot of input. We didn't offer that educational process to the community, so they have been left behind. We need to educate them to the rightness of this decision or we will be in the terrible position of forcing them.

Don Marcus had his own perspective that was different from Ben's.

> At the meeting there was no opportunity for rational discussion or articulation of the Jewish educational issues. Emotion crowded reason out of the room.... I don't want to overreact to blackmail statements. I hear them in relation to almost every decision that I and we make.... We are not promising people "you can do anything you want to do." We get pounded on this. For example, with Bar Mitzvah, we cannot guarantee any

more a single Bar Mitzvah [as opposed to two on the same day]. All the emotional blackmail we get on that! Some of the criticism was valid. But I would hate to see us beat ourselves too hard.

From Don's perspective the emotional outcry of these parents sounded all too familiar, like those parents who are so upset to learn that they cannot have a solo Bar or Bat Mitzvah for their child that they are ready to quit the temple. He sees these threats as "blackmail statements" that must be resisted because it is impossible to run a temple properly if you allow people to do "anything [they] want to do."

Ben was not convinced and persisted in his argument. He insisted that "good process allows people to adjust to change" and the committee had not yet done that with regard to this issue. Don agrees in part.

> Finally, we need to accommodate people. We need to ask, "Are those the only two possibilities?" To deal with the emotional charge we have to consider other possibilities. Will the committee negotiate possibilities?

By "other possibilities" Don means arrangements other than the binary choice of either taking Hebrew or leaving the school. He is about to propose that the RSC should consider allowing the affected families who are already in the school flexibility and apply the new policy only to incoming families. But he is resistant to the suggestion by Ben and others to hold an educational forum for parents to discuss the reasons behind the change and to work through the emotional issues involved. He seems to believe that what is at issue cannot be dealt with through the channels of parent education.

Laura, whose views carry a lot of weight on the committee, agrees with Don and Sherry.

> If we hold another meeting, will it be only those with vested interests who will come? Will it give the range of opinions that really exist?... We have to separate the process from the decision. The decision is sound and forgive us for the process errors. That is the most honest approach unless the committee thinks the decision is a mistake.

No one present thinks the decision was a mistake. No one wants to change it because these members truly believe that Hebrew should be studied by all the children. What worries Ben is that "if we caused a lot of people to be incensed and alienated, it is no longer a curricular decision but a matter of preserving the community." Laura responds to Ben's concern in the following way:

> Say that we think that we made the right decision but to mitigate the impact on the individuals involved, we can put a process in place.... We could have educated people better, but still they would have been furious. With no challenge [in the RSC] to the decision, we should acknowledge our mistakes, correct what we can, but not by holding another open meeting.

Laura agrees with Don Marcus that education will not mitigate people's fury. The fury is a given of the situation. What the committee can do is to admit its procedural errors, offer a "process" to correct the errors, and stick by its decision. Don reinforces Laura's position by concluding, "People are not really interested in the principles they articulated but in their own situations." If those situations can be rectified by offering families already in the school the option of their children remaining in the school without taking Hebrew, the outcry will die down and the new policy could go into effect for families entering the school after the 1990-91 year.

The RSC adopted Laura's proposal, agreeing "not to reconsider their decision but to be responsive" to the needs of the families already in the school. Don Marcus assured them this could be done with those people already in the school being "grandfathered" into the old arrangement, that is, with their children continuing to take religious education on Sundays alone. Don concluded that the committee would thereby be sending a message to the affected people that "We want and care for you and your children, but we also want to give you the best we have to offer."

What Is at Stake?

I was fascinated by the debate at this RSC meeting because it captured much of what Jewish educators and synagogue lay leaders need to be thinking about when introducing change into a religious school curriculum. I will now restate the issues and consider what is at stake.

The debate between Ben and three of his fellow members on one side and Sherry, Laura, and Rabbi Don Marcus on the other was primarily about how the RSC should understand and hence respond to the dissenting voices that were raised about the decision to make Hebrew mandatory in the school. No one disputed that the committee had made procedural errors that had to be corrected.

Ben sees the RSC as being accountable to the parents in the school, who do not elect the members but are the committee's natural constituency. Accountable does not mean that the RSC should allow the parents to make this decision or that every family should be allowed to make policy for itself. Rather, the RSC has the responsibility to educate the parents about the rationale for these changes and encourage open debate in the community so that people will be given the opportunity to work through the emotional issues that distress them. Ben believes that teaching Hebrew is symbolic of deeper issues, including the attachment to the classical Reform tradition that some feel is under attack because of the changes that have taken place in the synagogue and are now taking place in the school. They think that the RSC is saying, "If you do not want to do it our way and have your child take Hebrew, we will exclude you from the temple community."

Sherry, Laura, and Don acknowledge that the RSC needs to be responsive to the parents. But even if the committee chooses to be more responsive, the voices of dissent hardly represent the entire parent body. A vast majority of parents have chosen to send their children to the school for a Hebrew education and the committee is hearing from the small minority of parents and their supporters. These parents have a legitimate procedural complaint, but they voice their complaint in such inflated terms that it is hard to take seriously the content of their remarks. Open meetings are invitations for such people to have a rhetorical festival. However, it is a mistake to allow the shrillness of their protest to distract the committee from the rightness of its decision. Let the decision stand and let the committee make accommodations for the individuals affected so that they will not feel that they are suddenly being excluded from the temple community.

On the surface, the facts of the case seem to support this second argument. Even at the open meeting, only ten of the thirty-five parents in attendance vocally dissented. I spoke with several others who told me they were surprised by the shrillness of the protest and did not agree with the protesters. Yet they felt that they could not express their views because the emotional temperature was so high. My sense is that had a vote been taken at the meeting itself, a majority of parents would have supported the change.

Nor could the members of the committee at that point have honestly said that they were looking for input with regard to how they should decide this issue. The RSC had followed standard synagogue procedure by voting in committee and sending its proposal to the Board of Trustees for approval. The board had already approved this change and hence the policy was already in effect by the time the open meeting took place. The meeting was, therefore, designed to explain the change in policy, not explore whether the change should take place.

Over a year's time I observed that Don Marcus's prediction proved accurate. Accommodations were made for the individual families that were affected by the change and the whole issue seemed to die down. With the exception of one parent, who raised this issue at a public meeting a year after this event, I never again heard reference made to the controversy pertaining to mandatory Hebrew. The change seemed to have been absorbed by the institution.

Then why is this debate of interest? It is because while on the surface the facts point in one direction, beneath the surface the two sides within the RSC represent dramatically different views of how educational change ought to be carried out and what role the leadership should play in the congregation. While in the short run the majority perspective on the RSC proved effective, the questions that Ben raised about its long-term effectiveness are important to consider because they get to the heart of our main concern: how to better understand how change in the educational realm affects and is affected by the culture of a congregation.

Leadership and Change in the Congregation[13]

To those familiar with conventional synagogue governance, the path that the mandatory Hebrew proposal took is not surprising. Most synagogues that have religious schools have a standing lay committee that oversees the operation of the school and works with the school's principal in setting policy for the school. The committee's members usually are appointed rather than elected and do their work without attracting much attention. It is only when the committee's work directly impacts the lives of families that it may attract congregational attention.

When the Mandatory Hebrew proposal attracted the attention of the dissenting parents, they raised four objections at the open meeting to how the RSC had done its work. First, the RSC had met behind closed doors without notifying the parent body that this change was being considered. Second, the RSC did not survey parent opinion to learn what was the broader spectrum of opinion on this issue. Third, they changed the rules in midyear and did not notify parents before the school year began. Fourth, they were reversing a long-standing principle of choice that has been a Temple Akiba tradition.

In response to these objections, all the members of the RSC agreed on two points. Proper process was not followed in notifying the parents of this change. Therefore, individual accommodations were to be made to rectify that error. But the call to survey parental opinion was foreign to the governance procedures of this synagogue. The bylaws of this congregation do not require the sampling of membership opinion about an issue like this one, and there was no reason to expect the RSC to do so.

What the two sides within the RSC disagreed on was the relation of the RSC as a leadership group to the larger parent body and the right of the RSC to institute an educational change that would affect the "principle of choice" within this congregation. I will now examine each of these questions separately.

No one on the RSC doubts that this committee is the appropriate body to make educational policy decisions. As active members of Temple Akiba, they have learned that this congregation relies on its leadership – professional and lay – to make the key policy decisions for the synagogue. The members of the committee consider the RSC to be a well-run committee that works closely with Rabbi Marcus and makes thoughtful decisions. They had carefully studied a variety of issues that are affected by mandatory Hebrew and, while they realized the imperfections in their process, they trusted their own judgment to make an educationally sound policy decision.

The question is what happens when that educationally sound decision comes into direct conflict with the views of some parents who believe that they, too, should have a voice in setting a policy that affects them and the whole congregation. The majority position of the RSC, as represented by Sherry, Laura, and Don Marcus, is that as long as the committee remains secure in its own judgment and the protesters remain a minority within the parent body, the RSC should proceed with its decision. In their view it is the RSC's responsibility to exercise educational leadership for this congregation.

In their view the task of leadership is to make the hard decisions and to take the heat for those decisions. A congregation that has until now offered its members a choice on whether or not to study Hebrew will find it difficult to take back that choice and say everyone has to study Hebrew. But if that is the way to improve the quality of education, the RSC is right to make this decision. If there is protest, it needs to stand firm. It should let the protesters have their say, make accommodations where necessary, but stick with the policy decision that it has made.

Ben's view of leadership is different. He feels that the RSC's leadership role extends to educating the parent body so that parents will better understand the rationale for why mandatory Hebrew makes sense as the congregation's educational policy. In an interview Ben told me of a meeting that he and his wife had with Don Marcus when they were first considering sending their child to this school.

> My wife came from a very Reform congregation and I came from a Conservative background where I learned to read [Hebrew].... Don was strongly recommending the Hebrew track. My wife, who had no Hebrew training, asked, "Why bother?"

> I always assumed you went to Hebrew school to learn Hebrew. That's part of a Jewish education. But I always felt ambivalent about it because it was just a matter of learning form, learning to read the prayers. Don talked about it and convinced my wife, who was leaning the other way, about the importance of it.

"Why bother?" is the question that needs to be addressed when it comes to studying Hebrew. Ben's wife grew up in a classical Reform congregation that taught her not to bother with Hebrew. Ben, who learned Hebrew as a child, has his own ambivalent memories with which to contend. But Don Marcus succeeded, in Ben's words, "to put us in touch with how much each of us had longed for a Jewish education that would be meaningful and tie together the ethnic, family, and cultural strands with some knowledge of what the customs are really about." Don was able to convince them that Hebrew was a key to understanding the Jewish life that they would want their child to have.

But Ben goes on to say, "As a committee we have not done a good job in publicizing the reasons for mandatory Hebrew and in that kind of vacuum, all kinds of misimpressions grow." If Don Marcus could explain to Ben and his wife why Hebrew is such an essential part of a Jewish education, why has neither he nor the RSC done the job of educating the other parents so they, too, grasp the rationale for this change?

Perhaps the answer lies in differing conceptions of leadership for different occasions. Don Marcus certainly sees that his role as educational director includes sitting with parents and explaining why they should send their children to the Hebrew program. But when the context shifts and Don is working with the RSC to implement a policy change, he may no longer view education as the appropriate response. Some of the protesting parents' oppositional behavior may lead him to believe that in this context, education will be of no avail because some of the "people are not really interested in the principles they articulated but in their own situations."

Ben is asking why this shift in context should determine the committee's view of these parents. In a sense these parents are only asking for the same treatment that the RSC grants its own members. When there was division within the ranks of the RSC, the committee members decided to postpone making a decision to give everyone more time to think about the issues involved. These parents are now asking – albeit in very emotional tones – that more time be devoted to talking about these issues in a public arena since they had been excluded from participating earlier in the process. Ben is suggesting that taking that next educational step is also part of the RSC's leadership role.

I think Ben's suggestion does not convince the majority because they view the process of change differently than he does. These members of the committee tacitly assume that there are three stages to the process of change. First is the deliberative process that takes place within the committee itself, in which the pros and cons of a decision are carefully weighed. This stage culminates in the RSC's making a policy decision. The second is the committee's presenting the decision it has made to the board for its approval and to the parent body for their acceptance. The third is implementing the change by making the necessary accommodations to allow the new policy to work. In this model, when opposition develops, there is no need to go back to the deliberative stage and discuss with the parents whether a decision is right or wrong. Rather, the RSC needs to stay in the implementation mode and try to find the appropriate accommodations that will allow them to deal with the opposition while putting the new policy in place.

Ben's concern is that accommodating the opposition is not the same as listening to their doubts and questions. Ben does not think that the majority of protesting parents are engaging in "emotional blackmail" to serve their own interests. While some may have been doing that, most are raising genuine questions that call for response. Many of these same questions arose within the RSC's own discussions and will not go away just because accommodations are made. Ben believes that rather than moving on to implementation, the committee may need to return for a second round of deliberation that includes the parents.

The majority of the committee members do not believe that these kinds of questions can effectively be addressed in a public forum because the discussion would again get very emotional and would not allow for explaining rational exchange. But what Ben is talking about is helping people work through their feelings about the proposal, which is an emotional process. Perhaps in talking about their feelings of exclusion and alienation, people would begin to separate those feelings from the issue of teaching Hebrew in the school. If they felt that their concerns were being heard and understood, they might feel less belligerent and better able to discuss these questions with detachment. The highly emotional tone of the open meeting may have had as much to do with how the RSC set up the process as with the strong feelings that these parents brought to the discussion.

Conceptions of leadership and the process of change are *tacitly* held assumptions that underlie people's thinking about decisions in a leadership capacity.[14] Rarely are these assumptions aired and discussed. But for the purpose of trying to understand leadership in the synagogue, it is helpful to articulate these tacit differences so that the choice points that the RSC members faced can be better understood.

Educating for Change

The majority of the RSC chose to pursue the mandatory Hebrew policy because they agreed with Rabbi Marcus that "without Hebrew, the universal Jewish language, it is not Jewish education." They hope to make learning Hebrew essential to Temple Akiba in a way that will *not* make this synagogue a less welcoming community to its diverse constituencies.

But could the members of the RSC have made this decision in a way that would have generated less social conflict than we witnessed in this case? This is a major question for this analysis. I believe they could have generated less dramatic conflict had they thought differently about their role as leaders in the congregation and about the process of change that they were spearheading. I am not suggesting they could have engineered a smooth change, but they could have avoided some of the harsher aspects of the conflict that were expressed at the open meeting.

How might that have worked? The key difference would have been the RSC's seeing itself as "educating for change" rather than "legislating change."[15] In legislating change a synagogue committee sees its role as carefully studying an issue and coming to a decision on what policy to adopt for the congregation. The committee presents its decision and rationale to the Board of Trustees, which either approves or disapproves the change. If approved, the change is then presented to the relevant members of the congregation as a fait accompli that they will have to live with. If there is dissatisfaction, certain adjustments can be made. If some members remain fundamentally unhappy, they have the choice of petitioning the board or leaving the synagogue. But they are never included as part of the actual decision process.

In educating for change, the first assumption is that the congregation is part of the change process. There is the realization that congregants will react to a proposed change from many perspectives, not just from the perspective that a committee has adopted. The congregants will see a proposal for making Hebrew mandatory not just in terms of what makes educational sense but also in terms of what makes personal sense for them as parents and members of the congregation. In educating for change there is a basic understanding that policy questions in a synagogue are often understood by congregants in very personal terms. A proposed change in curriculum can raise a lot of questions from congregants: Has the religion changed in one generation? Is what we were once taught to believe no longer true? If *I* don't know Hebrew, am I less of a Jew? If I *hated* studying Hebrew, do I have to impose that on my child in order for her to be a good Jew? If my non-Jewish spouse is uncomfortable with our child's learning Hebrew, do I have to insist upon it for him to be considered a Jew?

The task of a committee is to try to see its proposal for change through the eyes of those who will likely have problems with it. The committee can open its process to such people in the midst of its deliberations and learn what the concerns of these people are. While the concerns raised may not deter the committee from making the same decision it would have, it can give the members time to think how they might address the concerns and anxieties that will arise. If the majority of the members of the RSC wanted to change the curriculum of the school without making some members feel less welcome, how might they have made it clear that emphasizing Hebrew in the school need not make this a more closed community?

Once the committee has reached its decision, the real work of educating the congregation begins. This certainly can be time-consuming, but it assumes that those interested parents and congregants who will have objections to the proposed change are entitled to voice their objections and discuss the issues with the committee members. This means being open to wider feedback and more varied dissent than one would hear from within the committee. It also means slowing the pace of decision making in favor of making a more inclusive decision.

This does necessarily mean that a consensus will be reached. I doubt whether all the sides in this controversy would have agreed with one another no matter how much time they left for dialogue. But just by making the time, the congregation is saying that everyone still has a voice that counts.

Finally, educating for change means asking the rabbis and educators to address the difficult theological questions that the conflict has raised. How can the current rabbi disagree with his predecessors on basic issues of faith? What does it mean if a Jew does not know any Hebrew? Can and should an interfaith couple feel as welcome in a synagogue as an all-Jewish couple? These are questions that deserve responses over and again.

Conclusion

The irony of this case is that Temple Akiba is a synagogue in which many difficult issues concerning Jewish identity are regularly discussed. It is hardly the style of either the rabbi or the educator to bury issues under the rug because they are controversial. But in this case, I believe that it is precisely because the RSC was operating with a particular conception of change and leadership that the openness for discussion that one finds on other occasions in this congregation was not present.

Leadership is a thorny issue at Temple Akiba, which has often had strong rabbinic leadership without a comparably decisive leadership from the lay people. Rabbi Marcus has worked hard over these past years to make the RSC a lay committee that functions well. Mandatory Hebrew was the first controversial policy issue that this group of committee members worked through from beginning to end. Don Marcus was very invested in seeing that their work bears fruit. I assume the members were similarly invested.

Perhaps it was this particular investment that created the

incentive for action. Don Marcus commented in retrospect that he did not disagree with Ben's theoretical stance on change. He simply did not think that it would work within the Temple Akiba framework. What is ultimately of consequence is not this particular controversy but what we learn from it. By describing these tacit models for leadership and change, I hope that I have made it clearer how legislating change is not the same as educating for change. While educating for change is more time-consuming and difficult, I believe that in the long run it allows for greater acceptance by more of the community of the changes being proposed. As Ben reminded his colleagues on the RSC, "Good process allows people to adjust to change."

This is an especially important point to make at this time when rabbis, educators, and lay leaders are poised to fight for the cause of quality Jewish education in their synagogues. My 1990 paper may have left the impression that if they establish the right conditions within their congregations, positive change in Jewish education would be a step or two away.

As a result of this further research, I now feel a word of caution needs to be added. Temple Akiba may not be the only synagogue in which the "forces for good" will encounter opposition from within the congregation. There are many committed Jews who do not understand why more intensive Jewish education is needed. There are some who may feel that intensifying that education calls into question their own credentials as Jews. How to handle that opposition and respond to such questions is an important part of planning for educational change in synagogues.

Having a thoughtful ideological stance, a sound educational philosophy, and a well-established political base in the congregation are important requisites for educational change. But beyond these requisites stands the less obvious although equally decisive question of conceptions of leadership and change. *How* the leadership brings about change is as significant as *what* change they bring about.

When rabbis, educators, and school committees set out to improve the quality of Jewish education by making changes in their congregation's educational policies, they need to ask themselves two questions: How well do we understand what the symbolic implications of these changes will be for the diverse membership of the congregation? How prepared are we to educate the whole congregation to understand why these changes are both positive and necessary? By asking these questions and trying to see their proposal from the perspectives of the diverse constituencies within the congregation, they may move from a model of legislating change to a model of educating the congregation to understand and accept that change.

Notes

1   All the names used in this paper have been changed to protect the identities of the synagogues and the people who participated in the research.

2   The book, *When Synagogues Educate*, will be published by the Jewish Publication Society of America. See my article on Temple Hillel, "Between Parents and Principal: Social Drama in a Synagogue," *Contemporary Jewry*, vol. 13, 1992, 60-73.

3   My use of "culture of the congregation" is influenced by the writings of Sarason (1971) on the culture of schools, Myerhoff (1980) on the culture of a senior adult center, Schoem (1989) on the culture of a synagogue school, and Shevitz (1993) on the culture of organizations. I am contending that over time, synagogues as religious organizations develop a view of the world and their place in it that sets standards of appropriate thought and behavior in that context. Denominational affiliation plays but a part in establishing that culture. In moving from congregation to congregation, one can sense that for all their commonality, each is a world unto itself. My larger claim is that to understand how Jewish education functions within a synagogue, one first has to understand the culture of that congregation. For it is that culture that sets the parameters for its decisions about education.

4   "Myth of continuity" is based on Barbara Myerhoff's discussion of riuals of continuity in *Number of Days*, New York: Simon & Schuster, 1980. She writes, "It is their very nature for rituals to establish continuity" for "continuity is something not automatically given by experience. It must be achieved." (p. 108) My claim is that the members of these synagogues achieve a sense of collective continuity by creating myths or narratives about how good their programs of education have been over time. The myth allows them to feel pride in their congregation. Since it is based on a solid record of actual achievement, it is a source of collective self-esteem.

5   Joseph Reimer, *The Synagogue as a Context for Jewish Education*. Commission on Jewish Education in North America. Cleveland, May 1990.

6   The term "classical Reform Judaism" will be used in two ways in this paper. First, to describe a distinctive era within the development of American Reform Judaism. That era extended roughly from 1880 to 1920. Second, to refer to a set of ideas that characterized that era but still continue to exert their influence. These are ideas about how Judaism should be adapted or reformed to fit the major ideological paradigms of modern American society. For a historical introduction, see "Classical Reform Judaism" in Michael A. Meyer, *Response to Modernity: A History of the Reform Movement in Judaism,* New York: Oxford University Press, 1988, Chapter 7.

7   These changes were not limited to Temple Akiba but were sweeping broadly, although not universally, through American Reform Judaism in the years following World War II. These changes in religious and educational practice have progressed continually through the 1970s. See Sylvan D. Schwartzman, *Reform Judaism Then and Now*, New York: UAHC, 1971. Also Eugene B. Borowitz, *Reform Judaism Today,* New York: Behrman House, 1978.

8   For a more detailed description of the philosophy of the Melton Hebrew Language Program, see Ruth Raphaeli, "The Melton Curriculum and the Melton Hebrew Language Program for Afternoon Hebrew Schools" in *Studies in Jewish Education*, vol. 4, Jerusalem: Hebrew University Press, 1989.

9   Joseph Reimer, "Temple Akiba" in *Best Practices Project: The Supplementary School*, edited by Barry Holtz. Cleveland: Council for Initiatives in Jewish Education, 1993, 95-111.

10   This account of the RSC's handling of the issue of mandatory Hebrew over this two-year span was provided by Sherry Saunders, the chair, in an April 1991 interview.

11   The tutorial program was begun in recognition of the fact that Temple Akiba draws members from a wide geographic range around the metropolitan area. It would be very difficult for some families to get their children into the city for afternoon classes. Tutorials allow the Hebrew teacher, appointed by the Hebrew coordinator, to go to the family's house once a week. The cost is an extra $950 per child per year. The school does not encourage use of the tutorial for in one hour the teacher cannot cover the same amount of material as is covered in two afternoons of class instruction. In addition, the students spend less time getting to know the synagogue. Yet the program proved popular even with families living closer to the temple. In 1990-91, 85 students were enrolled in the tutorial program as compared to 126 in the regular Hebrew program.

12   These statements are quoted from the Report to the Board of Trustees of a Change in Policy Regarding the Study of Hebrew that Sherry Saunders wrote in December 1990, on behalf of the RSC.

13   In this section I am moving from the directly observable statements made by the members of the RSC at their meetings to the inferred tacit conceptions that underlie their thinking. The articulation of these conceptions is my own construction but is based on the literature about how people in positions of leadership think about leadership and the change process. I am most directly influenced by the work of my colleague Susan L. Shevitz (in this volume), who does a masterful job of showing how these assumptions of leadership and change play a crucial role in how educational change is carried out in a synagogue context. Her influence is evident in much of the rest of this paper. I am also drawing on the works of Argyris and Schon (1974) and Schein (1985).

14   "Tacit knowledge is what we display when we recognize one face from thousands without being able to say how we do so, when we demonstrate a skill for which we cannot state an explicit program, or when we experience the intimation of a discovery we cannot put into words." (Argyris and Schon, p. 10) The members of the RSC do not discuss these tacit conceptions, but I am claiming they are displaying them in their arguments for why to make one choice or another in how to respond to the protesting parents.

15   The terms "legislating change" and "educating for change" are my own version of the two differing conceptions of the change process operating in the RSC. The ideas behind these terms are borrowed from Shevitz (1993), who distinguishes between a "rationalist" and a "non-rationalist" approach to change. In brief, the rationalist approach expects that change can be brought about by the leadership's taking a number of clear steps that will bring that change into place. The non-rationalist approach believes that change is complex precisely because in organizations like synagogues so many different subgroups get drawn into the process. Change

becomes more a matter of negotiating, educating, and including a lot of different per-spectives into the process. Change moves ahead slowly. The outcome is not a lin-ear leap from here to there but a circular sweep of many perspectives that allows more parties to buy into a slower-paced and less linear set of changes.

REFERENCES

Argyris, Chris, and Schon, Donald. *Theory in Practice: Increasing Professional Effectiveness*. San Francisco: Jossey-Bass, 1974.

Borowitz, Eugene B. *Reform Judaism Today*. New York: Behrman House, 1978.

Meyer, Michael A. *Response to Modernity: A History of the Reform Movement in Judaism*. New York: Oxford University Press, 1988.

Myerhoff, Barbara. *Number Our Days*. New York: Simon & Schuster, 1980.

Raphaeli, Ruth. "The Melton Curriculum and the Melton Hebrew Language Program for Afternoon Hebrew Schools." In *Studies in Jewish Education*, vol. 4, Jerusalem: Hebrew University Press, 1989.

Reimer, Joseph. "The Synagogue as a Context for Jewish Education." Commission on Jewish Education in North America. Cleveland: May 1990.

_____. "Between Parents and Principal: Social Drama in a Synagogue." *Contemporary Jewry*, vol. 13 (1992), 60-73.

Sarason, Seymour B. *The Culture of the School and the Problem of Change*. Boston: Allyn and Bacon, 1971.

Schein, Edgar. *Organizational Culture and Leadership*. San Francisco: Jossey-Bass, 1985.

Schoem, David. *Ethnic Survival in America: An Ethnography of a Jewish Afternoon School*. Atlanta: Scholars Press, 1989.

Schwartzman, Sylvan D. *Reform Judaism Then and Now*. New York: UAHC Press, 1971.

Shevitz, Susan, L. "Receptive Contexts and Enabling Traits for Changing Congregational Education." Paper presented to the Consultation for the Experiment in Congregational Education, Rhea Hirsch School of Education. Los Angeles, May 1993.

CHANGING PUBLIC SCHOOLS AND CHANGING CONGREGATIONAL SCHOOLS[1]

Larry Cuban

ince the end of World War II, American public schools have endured unrelenting criticism. From inadequate space to house students to the quality of teachers to undemanding curriculum and unimaginative instruction, school boards, administrators, and teachers have been chided continually for failing to live up to parental and taxpayers' expectations.

Criticism spawned reform again and again. From enthusiasm for science, math, and newly invented Advanced Placement programs to the brief flowering of open classrooms and alternative schools in the mid-1960s to the back-to-basics movement in the mid-1970s and, finally, to the state and national efforts to revitalize public schooling through mandates and reorganization in the 1980s, the message has been the same: Schools must improve. Notwithstanding all of these efforts at reform, the criticism continues today.

For the last three decades congregational (or supplementary) schooling[2] has similarly endured unremitting criticism. David Schoem flatly says that "thirty years of research on the Jewish supplementary school has documented that these schools are failing." (Schoem 1992, p. 163) According to the critics, large numbers of adult Jews who went to these schools as children seldom identify themselves with the Jewish community, lose themselves in the larger culture, and, worst of all, are illiterate about Judaism. (Sklare 1983, pp. 367-368)

Indeed, like their secular counterparts, Jewish bureaus of education, private foundations, and individual synagogues have responded to these enduring if not scorching critiques by designing reforms to improve the school experiences of Jewish boys and girls. For well over a quarter century, major efforts have been undertaken to recruit better teachers, modernize the curriculum, tie formal and informal instruction together, and make dozens of other reforms. Nonetheless, the criticism persists. (Aron in this volume, Chazan 1987)

So after almost a half century of criticism and reform in secular schools and three decades of the same for congregational schools, what can be learned both about the content of these changes and the process itself?

To begin to answer that question, I need to make clear what I mean by change. Critics anxious to reform schools err in assuming that this common word has a shared meaning. It does not. During the last presidential campaign Governor Clinton's presentation of himself as the candidate who would "change" America prompted President Bush—who presided over the very conditions that the Democratic candidate proposed to improve—to state that he was the leader who could better bring "change" to the nation. So it is best to define what I mean by change and to make a few distinctions. After doing this, I will argue that while there are many similarities between secular and congregational schooling, there are crucial differences in their essential features that make fundamental Jewish school reform a far more difficult—perhaps the better word might be challenging—enterprise.

Second, I will argue that congregational school reformers can learn from the experiences of their secular counterparts, but the direction that these part-time schools pursue and the models of change they use will need to differ fundamentally from those of the public schools. In short, I argue that pursuing the content of secular reforms, such as reorganizing governance of the schools, empowering teachers, reshaping curriculum, focusing on pedagogy, building effective schools, etc., may well lead to further disillusion and is, ultimately, a dead end. What is needed is an appreciation of the singular goals of congregational schooling and reforms that are tailored to the dimensions of that unique invention.

Understanding Change: Paradox and Beliefs

I begin with the central paradox of change in secular schooling in America: Why do schools perennially adopt trendy innovations yet they are persistently accused of being as hard to change as moving a cemetery without shovels? To unlock this paradox, I need to examine, albeit briefly, some common beliefs about change.

The first is that planned change is positive. It is growth, progress, and improvement wrapped into a shiny package.

Anchored in evolutionary ideas that can be traced back to the Greeks and wedded to the historic values of the American culture, the idea of progress has been honed to sharpness by generations of theorists, policymakers, and publicists. (Nisbet 1980)

Yet deliberate change may or may not be progress. The divorce that devastates one spouse finds the other relishing a newfound freedom. Similarly, among the four groups of affiliated Jews, the idea of intentional change with its accompanying emotional electricity varies considerably. For example, national organizations of Orthodox and Reform Jews approach changes in liturgical ritual in profoundly different ways. What each national group does (and remember that congregations within each movement vary among themselves) may be considered consistent with tradition, opposed to it, or even irrelevant. Hence change in of itself may or may not be viewed as progress. Much depends on from whose vantage point the determination is being made.

A second common belief is that you can't have both change and stability at the same time. but continuity and change do coexist in an individual, group, organization, and culture. Psychologists point to the durability of personality traits over time even when a child matures into a youth and adult. Sociologists stress the persistent features that mark organizations as they evolve from infancy to maturity. Anthropologists record how both distant and near cultures adapted traditions. Political scientists underscore the continuity of national impulses that endure through centuries of revolutionary changes in regimes. Stability and change are entangled in individuals, families, institutions, and nations. So schools as a central institution of modern societies are expected to conserve traditions and simultaneously prepare children to become adults in a world undergoing constant change. However, it is not only secular schools that are pinched by competing goals. Anyone familiar with the histories of the Conservative and Reform movements in the United States since the mid-nineteenth century knows how intertwined change and constancy are in their ideologies, religious practices, and congregational schools. It is not wordplay to speak of stable forms of change or continuity amidst change. (Moore 1963; Meyer and Rowan 1978; March, 1981; Nisbet 1969; Gartner 1983)

Finally, not all planned changes are the same. I distinguish between two types. (Watzlawick, Weakland, and Fisch 1974) First-order or incremental changes are intentional efforts to enhance an existing system, for example, a congregational school, by correcting defects in policies and practices. Such changes try to make what exists more efficient and effective without disturbing the basic organizational features. Thus those who propose incremental changes assume that the existing goals and structures of schooling are both adequate and desirable. Such changes are aimed essentially at improving the core features of an organization.

Examples of incremental public school reform include raising salaries, selecting new texts, adding (or deleting) courses to (and from) the curriculum, lengthening the school day, and introducing more effective evaluation of teachers. The school effectiveness movement in the late 1970s and its swift spread into state-driven reforms in the 1980s, with its emphasis on instructional leadership from the principal, more student time spent on academic tasks, and tighter alignment with curricular goals, texts, and tests, is an instance of incremental change. Many innovations in congregational schools, such as raising teachers' hourly salaries, changing from a two- to a three-day school, introducing the Melton Hebrew curriculum in Conservative schools, and others, are incremental.

Second-order or fundamental changes seek to alter the essential ways in which organizations are put together because of major dissatisfaction with present arrangements and a vision of a better order. Fundamental changes question the taken-for-granted assumptions about purposes, structures, cultures, and roles. Such reforms often apply novel solutions to persistent problems and thereby transform routines.

For example, mid-nineteenth century U.S. school reformers imported from Prussia the innovation of the graded school. These reformers sought to restructure the then current one-room schools in towns and cities to fit a new vision of an efficient, democratic social order. Moving from the one-room schoolhouse in the 1840s with one untrained, unsupervised teacher responsible for children ranging in age from six to eighteen, where each child would get a few minutes a day of the teacher's attention, to a graded elementary school that had a principal, a separate classroom for each teacher, children grouped by age, a curriculum divided into grade-level pieces, and annual promotions was a fundamental change in schooling. (Kaestle 1973, Tyack 1974) Each of these innovations replaced the basic assumptions about knowledge, teaching, and learning that were embedded in the one-room school system with another set of assumptions that later generations of school reformers questioned.

Other more recent changes intended to alter secular schools and classrooms in fundamental ways include current efforts to reorganize the governance of schools so that principals share their authority to make schoolwide decisions with teachers, parents, and students; or converting conventional junior high schools into middle schools in which young teenagers can develop personal relationships with teachers while developing their intellectual and artistic talents in longer class periods with different subject-matter teachers who work together; or coping with the increasing cultural and socioeconomic diversity among students by reorganizing schools so that they have multi-age classes, learning through small groups, and expanded access to classroom computers.

There also have been efforts to change fundamentally Jewish education in this century. (Aron in this volume) The establishment and growth of community-funded Jewish day schools since the 1960s, for example, was a sharp departure in teaching Jewish children up to that time. Two basic assumptions about Jewish commitment to public schools and funding schools wholly within synagogue budgets were reexamined by the creation of these new schools. In addition, importing secular pedagogies such as open classrooms (informal education, in the lingo of mid-1960s reformers) and electronic technologies represented efforts to alter conventional forms of instruction in fundamental ways.

Yet with all of the changes in secular schools, criticism persists. Moreover, with all of these muscular reform efforts, schooling seems to remain pretty much as it has been. (Goodlad 1984; Boyer 1983; Cuban 1993) How do secular schools maintain their fundamental structures in the face of deliberate attempts to alter them?[3]

Part of an answer to this question can be found in the many innovations seeking fundamental change that, over time, lapse into incremental ones. A familiar example is the curricular reforms of the 1950s and 1960s in public schools that were guided in large part by academic specialists and funded by the federal government. Aimed at revolutionizing teaching and learning in math, science, and social studies, millions of dollars were spent to produce textbooks and classroom materials and to train teachers. By the end of the 1970s, when researchers reported on what had occurred in classrooms, they found little evidence of student involvement in critical thinking, although there was a different curricular residue left in textbooks. For the most part, conventional methods of imparting knowledge to passive students remained in place. (Atkin and House 1981; Stake and Easley 1978; Suydam and Osborne 1977; Weiss 1978)

A more complicated way in which fundamental reforms become incremental changes is through what George and Louise Spindler call "substitute change." They studied a small school in a southern German village called Schonhausen for over a decade. The villages in this once rural area were undergoing changes in land ownership and wine production. As a result, larger plots of land were being created and new machines to till and harvest grapes were introduced. In addition, shifts in population were urbanizing the area.

For decades, the area's school curriculum had emphasized the land, the village community, and family values. The federal and provincial ministries of education, however, mandated a new curriculum and textbooks based upon life in cities, the importance of modernization, and high technology. The Spindlers first studied the village and its school in 1968 and then returned there in 1977 after almost a decade of reform.

What surprised the Spindlers was that in spite of the clear attempt by ministry officials to make the village school more modern and responsive to urban and cultural differences, children, teachers, and parents continued to make tradition-based and village-oriented choices. In the school, trips that once took classes for day-long strolls in the countryside gave way to role-playing a petition to the village council. Much of the earlier content about the beauty of the land was lost but the cultural goals and values nourishing the traditions of the village were maintained. How?

The Spindlers found that the way in which the teachers taught the new content and maintained classroom order sustained village traditions in the face of curricular reforms. Although teachers substituted a play about the village political process—recommended in the new curriculum—for a romantic folktale that was in the previous curriculum, the way in which the play transpired in the class conveyed the same core meaning of the importance of living in the village as the folktale did. The effort to alter the values of villagers in that part of Germany in order to make them more responsive to urban life was transformed into a reaffirmation of village values. (Spindler and Spindler, 1982)

Do these patterns of incrementalizing fundamental changes occur in congregational schools? Importing child-centered ways of teaching into part-time schools—such as open classrooms with multiple learning centers or sociodrama or cooperative learning (actually a traditional form of Jewish pedagogy)—to get away from frontal teaching have been tried in various congregational schools over the last quarter of a century. Invariably, these methods ended up working for those individual teachers who had the expertise and inclination to use them in their classrooms, but these methods seldom became a schoolwide practice. (Aron in this volume)

The current interest in Jewish Family Education, an attempt to make the supplementary school and family work and learn together to become more of a Jewish community, depends upon the synagogue's reconceptualizing itself from a narrowly conceived house of prayer into an educational institution for both adults and children. When synagogues eager for change adopt such a program and place it under the wing of the school principal without examining the consequences for changes elsewhere in the congregation, Jewish Family Education becomes just another instance of an intended fundamental change's becoming an addition to the existing program. (See Reimer 1992 for definitions and descriptions of JFE programs.)

This pattern of incrementalizing fundamental reforms is seldom conspiratorial or even the result of conscious acts on the part of individual school district leaders or, in the case of congregational schools, rabbis or educational directors. Such mutations occur as a consequence of bureaucratic and political processes that are deeply embedded in organizations as they interact with external forces in the larger society. For example, organizations have a strong impulse to survive. To survive, an organization must appear to be legitimate, that is, it must conform to what people expect and to what is generally accepted. (Meyer and Rowan 1978) In the case of schools, politically they must appear "real" to their patrons, who provide children and dollars, in order to convince the latter that what happens in these schools is what they think is supposed to occur in a place called a school. If schools do not appear "real," their political (and financial) support will diminish. Part of being "real" is to change as conditions change. If other schools are buying computers for their students to keep pace with changing workplace technologies, then "our" school must do the same. That is also part of being a "real" school. This is especially true for synagogue schools since the standard for judging the worth of a school that has been in place for decades is the standard that is used for the secular public school.[4]

To sum up, then, contrary to common beliefs, change is not necessarily progress. Change is not inherently good. Nor can change and stability be divorced. They are bound together within organizations. Finally, distinguishing between incremental and fundamental change makes the contradictory phenomena of schools' continually adopting innovations yet remaining largely unchanged in their fundamental structures and practices less puzzling. Using these definitions and distinctions, I now turn to an analysis of the major differences between secular and congregational schools and how those differences can be incorporated into planning for changes in congregational schooling. To do this, I think that it may help to discuss the lessons that have been learned from deliberate efforts to alter secular schools and which of these lessons, if any, may apply to congregational schools.

Differences between Secular and Congregational Schools

The most obvious and telling difference between these schools is that secular schools are public and congregational schools are private. No great revelation. But this commonplace observation needs to be stated bluntly because the historic pattern of Jewish supplementary schools unrelentingly copying secular practices and innovations has been, in my judgment, ultimately harmful. For example, emphasizing that a congregational school has self-contained graded classes and schedules with forty-five minute periods just as public schools do certainly makes sense in terms of trying to convince patrons that a part-time congregational school is as "real" as the public school that their children attend. This is an understandable strategy for increasing support for the religious school. But it fails to consider the deeper implications of the fundamental differences in aims that secular and Jewish schools have.

Tax-supported public schools primarily strive to achieve multiple and competing goals. These include helping students, (1) acquire basic academic skills that will equip them for the job market or further education; (2) become active citizens; and (3) acquire a sound moral character, in that order. More recently much effort has been expended to make inculcating a common culture through a core of subjects that all students must take the goal of public schooling. Moreover, the schools are also expected to evaluate students to make sure that those who can profit from further education are selected and separated from those who will end up in the job market immediately after high school. Trying to achieve all of these goals creates enormous tensions since resources are limited and ideas of what is best for children change over time.

Finessing the goal-conflict of providing equal services with limited funds to children who come from varied socioeconomic and cultural backgrounds and have different interests and abilities while at the same time selecting their different paths to future careers has been the historic challenge of American public schools. Private religious schools have different goals and in many respects far more flexibility for achieving them, although they share the secular schools' uncertainty about which goals ought to be primary.

In the literature produced by laity and professionals on what the main goal of Jewish schooling is, most writers stress survival or "the affirmation of Jewish identity." As Yehuda Rosenman explained, "...we wish to assure that as many as possible of our next generation will remain proud and active Jews." (foreword to Heilman 1984, p. 1) In previous generations Jewish identity had been the province of interconnected daily practices in the home, at work, and in the synagogue. Since World War II, however, potent assimilationist trends, agonizing memories of the Holocaust, and the growing awareness that many Jewish families are loosely attached to Judaism elevated the goal of strengthening Jewish identity in the minds of many religious and lay leaders. The school, then, became viewed as the institutional mortar that would bond the family to the synagogue, religious practice, and the larger Jewish community.

Connected to the goal of strengthening Jewish identity is the objective of gaining essential knowledge, skills, and attitudes that contribute to becoming "proud and active Jews." Knowledge of the Bible, liturgy, history, Jewish holiday and life-cycle events, Hebrew, and dozens of other subjects have competed for the attention of teachers and students in these part-time schools. The absorption of the Bar/Bat Mitzvah into congregational schooling has brought together Jewish knowledge and identity into a public ritual that now demands years of religious school attendance. (Schoenfeld 1988)[5]

As I interpret them, these goals differ substantially from those of secular schools, although there is much in common between the two institutions in having goals that conflict. While there is talk in public schools about the importance of self-esteem and a common American culture, none of these approach the primary goal of a religious school— as expressed repeatedly by Jewish sources—of seeking a strong Jewish identity. The goals of congregational education not only differ from those of a secular education but compete with them. The larger issues are whether congregational rabbis, educators, and lay leaders acknowledge the differences in goals, feel the tensions, or are even clear as to what their school's mission is.

Other demographic and systemic differences between congregational and secular schools suggest even further that copying secular schools is strategically unwise. Consider first the facts of public school enrollments. Over 98 percent of American children attend elementary public school during seven years of formal schooling; the percentage of students attending secondary schools is between 75 to 100 percent and varies by socioeconomic group. These students attend school on the average of about 1,100 hours a year or a total of over 13,000 hours during their student careers.

The figures for Jewish schools are stark in comparison. First, fewer than half of all Jewish children attend *any* religious school. Supplementary schools enroll 28 percent of all Jewish school-aged children (18 percent of those children going to religious school attend day schools). Attendance in part-time schools varies with age. For six- and seven-year-olds it is 28 percent, but enrollment climbs to 55 percent for ten- to twelve-year-olds (just before Bar/Bat Mitzvah) and then drops to 8 percent for sixteen- to seventeen-year-olds. (JESNA 1992, p. 5).

The time students spend in Jewish schools is considerably less than the time they spend in public schools. Most Jewish children attend supplementary schools less than 200 hours a year.[6] So the total amount of time that Jewish children spend in congregational schools is less than one-fifth of the time their peers spend in public schools.

Another major difference between the two types of schools is organizational. Each tax-supported public school is part of a larger school district that has locally elected officials making policy. Each school in the district is expected to follow the policies laid down by the school board and its appointed superintendent (while following all relevant state and federal laws as well). If the district mandates that all schools give standardized achievement tests annually each spring, each school staff will administer those tests at that time. If state law requires, for example, that United States history be taught, an individual high school cannot decide on its own to drop the subject from the curriculum. But each school's principal and faculty can exercise certain amounts of discretion within limits in implementing district and state policies. Thus American history will be taught in each high school, but some teachers will teach some topics and not others and a few will use no textbooks. Nonetheless, each public school is part of a larger system of formal schooling.

Congregational schools do not operate on this system. Since the large-scale post-World War II shift of Jewish population to the suburbs, the supplementary school has been located in the synagogue. A Jewish family sending its children to a part-time religious school in most cases would have to join a congregation. Talmud Torahs and other independent part-time community schools have largely disappeared and have been replaced by schools nested within synagogues.

Thus most supplementary schools are organizationally dependent upon a principal or an educational director who is hired by the congregation's board of directors and who reports either to the rabbi, an executive director, or the president of the board. Most supplementary schools are fiscally dependent upon a portion of the congregation's budget requested by a lay subcommittee that often advocates for the school within the larger temple or synagogue community. Most congregational schools are philosophically dependent upon the rabbi's active or passive beliefs of what a "good" Jewish education is.

What makes these religious schools differ so greatly from secular ones in which the relationship is between an individual school and a district and state is their total dependence upon the congregation's organizational, fiscal, and philosophical resources. The system in this case is the individual temple or synagogue, not a larger group of religious institutions. It is true that Reform and Conservative synagogues belong to regional and national organizations that formulate policies for their constituent congregations. But the strong commitment to decentralized governance by American Jewish congregations places enormous discretion in the hands of each individual temple and synagogue. Thus congregational schooling is largely a function of what each temple and synagogue does. (Reimer 1990)

Altogether these demographic, systemic, public/private differences between secular and congregational schools produce substantial consequences for Jewish supplementary schools. Because the latter are part-time ventures located within the political economy of a congregation, a number of questions are continually being asked: What will the rabbi role's in the school be?

What is the relationship between the head of the school and the rabbi? Is congregational membership growing, on a plateau, or shrinking? Is school enrollment growing, remaining stable, or declining? How much will be allocated to finance part-time and full-time staff? What is the status of the members of the education committee vis-à-vis social action, liturgy, adult education, and other standing committees within the larger board of directors? Can we achieve our goals to be "proud and active Jews" when our children attend congregational schools only eight or less hours a week?

These questions are tough ones, and because each congregation is largely on its own, they are often answered one by one by each congregation. The thought of trying to make more than cosmetic changes in almost 2,000 independent congregational schools whose main goal is to create a cultural identity in Jewish children attending classes for eight hours a week for thirty-six weeks a year weakens any potential reformer's impulse to do so. (JESNA 1992, p. 2) The question is, Can any lessons about the content and process of change in secular schools apply to these intensely autonomous, part-time religious schools?

Recent Lessons about Change

Congregational school reformers can learn from the experiences of their secular counterparts, but the direction that religious part-time schools choose to pursue and the models of change they might use depend greatly upon what kinds of changes religious school reformers are seeking. If rabbis, educators, and their congregations are largely satisfied with the quality of their students' attachment to Judaism and the direction of their schools, then seeking incremental changes would be reasonable. Since most supplementary schools have been engaged in such changes for decades, what they can learn from secular schools can be picked up easily enough. Most Jewish school educators already are familiar with both the content and process of such changes.

However, if rabbis, educators, and congregations are largely dissatisfied with the disjunctures between Jewish schooling and Jewish practices in the home and are concerned about continued illiteracy and assimilation among Jewish adults, then these congregational leaders might consider making fundamental changes in what they offer their children. If that is the case, imitating patterns of public school reform would be a mistake.

Pursuing the content of secular reforms—such as having teachers, principals, and parents share decision making; introducing an innovative curriculum; focusing on instructional practices;

and building "effective schools"—is a dead-end road for congregational reformers seeking fundamental changes because the central goal of religious schooling is so different from the goals of public schools. Adopting such innovations without carefully scrutinizing them to determine whether they will fit borders on the foolish. In short, goals matter.

Knowing what a religious school should strive for determines what kinds of changes should be sought. If the goal is to produce "proud and active Jews" and if congregation members are dissatisfied (a key point) with how their school works, then reconsidering the school's relationship to its rabbi, the school's status in how the congregation allocates resources, organization, staffing, and the weekly program become imperative in deciding upon incremental or fundamental changes.

Thus far I have argued that the very nature of the Jewish identity goal that most congregational schools seek and the time available to achieve it call for a serious reexamination of the strategy of copying secular schools. An uncritical examination of what is borrowed from public schools and, more important, why it should be borrowed has, I believe, put congregational schools into their present bind.

Suppose, then, that there are rabbis and congregations that seek a goal of producing in the next generation "proud and active Jews" and conclude that their current program, while up-to-date and meeting most standards laid down by their national organization, fails to close the gap between home and school and achieve their goal of a stronger attachment to Judaism. What might they consider doing, given the constraints of available time, money, and the political economy of the congregation?

For purposes of discussion, I argue that supplementary congregational schools seeking fundamental changes must be unschooled and converted into mini-communities.

I believe that there should be far less concern that these schools mimic "real" public schools and more concern for creating congregations that are full-time educational communities for adults and children and, in the case of once part-time schools, afternoon and weekend Jewish mini-communities. But what features would mark such a community?

First, each congregation would engage in a serious, ongoing discussion about its goals for a Jewish education and the content of that education. By serious I mean that the synagogue's goals would be linked to those of education for the entire synagogue community of adults and children. By ongoing I mean that there would be a standing committee that meets periodically throughout the year and has legitimacy and authority to act because it consists of the major leaders of the synagogue.

Second, the mini-community would be marked by much interaction and participation. By that I mean that there would be continuous planned activities involving Jewish holidays and the life cycle (birth, Bar/Bat Mitzvah, Confirmation, marriage, illnesses, death) that require children's active participation in joint projects inside and outside the congregation. Opportunities for Jewish performances and exhibitions would provide children with ways of playing different roles and experiencing collective responsibility. By working together on Jewish projects and deciding what has to be done, children would satisfy strong needs to act on behalf of a common good.

Third, interaction and participation would produce interdependence—another feature of community. Members would come to see that they need one another to achieve common goals. Moreover, children would form attachments and loyalty to the group as a whole. For example, a year-long project in which ten- to twelve-year-olds spend time at a Jewish home for the elderly being companions to the residents for a few hours, taking down their oral histories, returning to the synagogue where pairs and trios would work together tying those personal histories to turn-of-the-century American Jewish history or Eastern European communities, producing a book and a presentation for the elderly residents at the home and for the congregation suggests how interaction, participation, and interdependence intersect as features of a community.

Fourth, the above features would produce shared beliefs and interests. The very basis of a sustaining community is that a foundation of common understandings is shared by its members. Through the above mentioned experiences in the congregational mini-community and participation in other congregational activities, the enactment of Jewish beliefs and interests strengthens a core of commonality that marks those engaged in the above activities. (Bellah 1985)

There are also other features that can be drawn from secular and religious theorists and activists who believe in developing communities as ways of strengthening attachment to Judaism. I suggested only a few to illustrate what I meant. None of the above should strike readers as alien. Informed observers of congregational schools have seen instances of what I describe. In the very best of schools, parts of these features are already in place and activities elsewhere in the congregation and in the larger community are available. My argument is that given the constraints of part-time attendance and persistent mimicking of secular schools, the concept of school, while not foreign to the kind of mini-community that I sketch, is on the whole too formalistic and rigid in practice to accommodate—save for the unusual congregation—the notions of community offered here. (See Reimer 1993 for his descriptions and analysis of two Boston-area congregations.)

What might an after-school mini-community look like? There would be no bell schedules or groupings by grade level; some children would be in classrooms working together on projects and others would be outside the congregation working in the larger Jewish community. Adults of all ages in the congregation, youth leaders, former camp staffers, and also credentialed teachers from the congregation and elsewhere in the Jewish community would staff the mini-community. They would teach, help, advise, and coach the children. Activities would include short- and long-term academic and service projects, learning Hebrew and Hebrew texts, art, sports, study of fewer topics but in greater depth, handicrafts, and constant performances and exhibitions for themselves, the congregation, and the larger Jewish community. Elements of camp life, youth group activities, religious retreat work, and study group tasks in which adults and children mix often and freely would constitute these congregational-sponsored settings.[7]

No longer called schools, these mini-communities would become places in which individuals, families, and children would be constantly mixing, performing, and serving. The goal is to create small Jewish communities of adults and children in which living Judaism – as defined and continually revised by each congregation – is meaningful enough to create a far stronger attachment to it than currently exists.

If congregations wished to move in these directions, how might they go about making such fundamental changes? This question goes to the nature of the change process. Here are some answers from secular schools and other organizations. I briefly present three larger strategies that have emerged as critical in planning for and implementing deep changes in the formal structures, cultures, and individual behavior in schools and other settings.

Cultivate leadership. As much as technocratic solutions to complex organizational problems are prized in the larger society, again and again, initiating and sustaining change in a school, workplace, or large organization comes down to one person's or several people's providing leadership. In this case, I mean one or more people having a picture of what ought to be, taking risks (that is what the word "initiative" means) to launch a change, and figuring out how to mobilize resources to keep the change afloat as the reform adapts and readapts to the inevitable surprises that occur. For congregations that leadership may come from the rabbi, the laity, or religious school administrators and teachers. But as Reimer so aptly points out, the vision of a congregation as an educational community that has rabbis either building that view, endorsing it, or participating in it seems to be a necessary but not sufficient condition for such a reform to be born and to survive. (Sergiovanni 1989, Cuban 1988)

Ideas are important, but for ideas to survive in organizations, pay attention to implementation, assessment, and the inevitable adaptations that occur again and again. If there is a lyric to the siren song of school reform that has been a constant it is that the hard work of changing an institution begins after the change has been adopted by those in authority. And the chorus that repeats itself again and again is, Adapt, assess, adapt, and assess! Such lessons place a heavy premium on local leadership, deep understanding of the nature of the reform, the importance of those directly involved doing the work while tailoring the reform to local circumstances, and constant efforts to build and strengthen the skills of participants to carry out the changes (in educational jargon this is called "capacity building"). (David 1993; McLaughlin 1987; Elmore and McLaughlin 1988)

Assessment of the reform and of the learning that occurs needs to be built in at the very moment that the reforms are launched because the lack of data, inconclusive results, or stonewalling on what is happening has killed more attempts to change institutions than suicide has killed people. By assessment I mean, How can we learn about what we are doing so that we can improve it now rather than later? How will we know that what we wanted to do is occurring? Such questions have to be asked by every person who works for fundamental change. Assessment occurs all the time in the classroom and in the school and is essential for planning. Assessment includes daily teacher judgments, collections of student work reviewed by the teacher, and verbal and written displays of student work. It also includes tests (although the definition of tests can be expanded because a piece of paper with multiple-choice items on it and a science project submitted to an exhibition are both assessments). (Wiggins 1989, Stiggins et al 1986)

What all of this attention to implementation, adaptation, and assessment means is that the change process is unending. Continuous attention to problem finding, diagnosis, analysis, and evaluation needs to be built into both the process of organizational change and into the repertoires of those who are daily involved in making and sustaining reforms. (Elmore and McLaughlin 1988; Berman 1981)

Have patience. Fundamental reform takes a long time. Making deep changes in an institution's assumptions, structures, and culture is steady work that typically takes one to three years to develop a vision, mobilize support, and deal with the inevitable but crucially important resistance that will arise. Resistance is important because those less enthused about the changes will raise legitimate issues that need to be addressed and questions that true believers in the reform may not think of. It will take at least three to five years to establish revised versions of the original plan and begin to see barely the leading edges of some possible results. Not for at least five to seven years will desired results begin to appear clearly. (Miles and Huberman 1984, Louis and Miles 1990)

In Closing

This essay has explored the similarities and differences between changing secular and congregational schooling. While there is much that is similar in the content and processes of the two changes, I have argued that there are core differences in essential features between the two forms of schooling that make fundamental Jewish school reform a far more demanding task but one with much more promise than reform in secular schools because of fewer legal and organizational constraints.

Congregational school reformers can learn from the experiences of their secular counterparts, but the path that part-time schools follow and the models of change they use need to be fundamentally different from those of the public schools because of the profound difference in the congregational school's central goal. It is, I argued, a fool's errand to pursue such trendy secular reforms as restructuring school governance, shared decision making, the latest pedagogical fad, or whatever because such unexamined borrowing may well lead to further disillusionment and is ultimately a cul-de-sac. What is needed is an appreciation of the singular goals of congregational schooling and reforms that are tailored to the dimensions of that unique institution.

Notes

1   The final version of this paper profited greatly from the suggestions of Dr. Debby Kerdeman, University of Washington.

2   I use the adjectives "supplementary" and "congregational" interchangeably in referring to part-time synagogue schools, not camps, youth organizations, or Jewish day schools.

3   Often when eager reformers discuss incremental and fundamental changes, they tend to show a bias toward fundamental changes, declaring them to be superior to incremental ones. I want to avoid such dichotomies and value judgments. There is nothing intrinsically superior about one or the other. It all depends upon what the overall goals for improvement are. Moreover, by thinking strategically, reformers can seek fundamental changes and approach them in an incremental manner.

4   One example from congregational and day schools might help. Advertisements from a recent supplement (February 19, 1993) of the *Jewish Bulletin of Northern California* promote those items that parents seek in a Jewish day school. One ad for a Conservative synagogue school asks, "How will your Jewish child learn to be Jewish?" Another ad for a day school includes in its listing of attractions:

   •   Stresses cooperative learning, team-building skills, personal decision making, critical thinking.

   •   Warm, nurturing environment that strengthens Jewish values, pride, and identity.

   •   Innovations in Education.

   •   PE, Music, Computer, Science, and Art.

5   A discussion with graduate students of an earlier draft of this article revealed to me that lay and professional Jewish educators may see the connection between the cultural identity goal that I view as the primary aim of most Jewish formal education and the acquisition of Judaic knowledge (historical, ritual, cultural, etc.) as a dichotomy. In other words, their position is that we need to give our children one or the other. I do understand that for formal congregational schools, the knowledge aim often takes precedence: What teachers and schools can do reasonably well is convey knowledge to learners. The argument that I make here is that although both cultural identity and knowledge are important, it is the identity—the feeling of attachment—and the survival of the religion that drive the hopes and fears of most parents, rabbis, lay leaders, and educators. Subsumed within the goal of identity is the acquisition of Judaic knowledge. The two work in tandem. My hunch is that rabbinical and lay congregational leadership let professionals run the school, thinking that is an important but separate operation, while educators stressed knowledge acquisition, assuming that such information would lead to stronger attachments to Judaism. But lay critics in the larger Jewish community, rabbis, and some educators realized that stressing knowledge/language/etc., did not necessarily produce strong feelings of Jewishness that continue into adulthood and thus have questioned this arrangement.

   A better way for me to convey what I mean is by using the image of an umbrella where survival of Jewish identity covers the acquisition of knowledge. The point that I want to underscore is that absorbing knowledge has, I believe, been overemphasized as a primary goal—the assumption being that to know is to believe—because that is what schools do best. Think "school" and you think information and organized knowledge. You don't think Jewish identity because schools don't do that stuff well. I argue that the two are intimately related and need to be brought together more imaginatively than they have been thus far. As I interpret the criticism of supplementary schools, the primary purpose of congregational schooling is to strengthen and to affirm people's attachment to Judaism. Conveying knowledge is crucial for this goal and cannot be separated from it. Understanding both dimensions of the quest is crucial.

6   I estimated six hours a week for the average congregational school meeting three times and thirty weeks to the school year, since virtually all supplementary schools follow the secular school calendar.

7   I present broad themes that would characterize such settings. Practical questions about who is in charge, who makes decisions, how assessment gets done and what gets measured, and how the few hours of available time get scheduled are very important. I am not offering a blueprint, only a sketch. These crucial questions need attention but are beyond the scope of this paper.

REFERENCES

Aron, Isa. "From the Congregational School to the Learning Congregation: Are We Ready for a Paradigm Shift?" Paper prepared for the Rhea Hirsch School of Education Consultation on the Experiment in Congregational Education, 1993. (See this volume.)

Atkin, J. M., and House, E. "The Federal Role in Curriculum Development." *Educational Evaluation and Policy Analysis* 3:5 (1981), 5-36.

Bellah, R.; Madsen, R.; Sullivan; W. M.; Swidler, A.; and Tipton, S. M. *Habits of the Heart: Individualism and Commitment in American Life.* Berkeley: University of California Press, 1985.

Berman, P. "Toward an Implementation Paradigm." In *Improving Schools: Using What We Know*, edited by R. Lehming and M. Kane. Beverly Hills, CA: Sage, 1981.

Boyer, E. *High School.* New York: Harper and Sons, 1983.

Chazan, Barry. "Education in the Synagogue: The Transformation of the Supplementary School." In *The American Synagogue*, edited by J. Wertheimer. Cambridge: Cambridge University Press, 1987.

Cuban, L. *The Managerial Imperative: The Practice of Leadership in Schools.* Albany, NY: State University Press of New York, 1988.

_____. *How Teachers Taught.* 2d ed. New York: Teachers College Press, 1993.

David, J. *Redesigning an Education System: Early Observations from Kentucky.* Washington, DC: National Governors Association, 1993.

Elmore, R., and McLaughlin, M. *Steady Work.* Santa Monica, CA: RAND Corporation, 1988.

Gartner, L. "Jewish Education in the United States. In *American Jews: A Reader*, edited by M. Sklare. New York: Behrman House, 1983.

Goodlad, J. *A Place Called School.* New York: McGraw-Hill, 1984.

Heilman, S. *Inside the Jewish School.* New York: American Jewish Committee, 1984.

Jewish Education Service of North America. *Trends* 16 (Fall 1992).

Kaestle, C. *Pillars of the Republic.* New York: Hill and Wang, 1973.

Louis, K., and Miles, M. *Improving the Urban High School.* New York: Teachers College Press, 1990.

March, J. "Footnotes to Organizational Change." *Administrative Science Quarterly* 26 (December 1981).

McLaughlin, M. "Lessons from Past Implementation Research." *Educational Evaluation and Policy Analysis* 9:2 (1987), 171-178.

Meyer, J., and Rowan, B. "The Structure of Educational Organizations." In *Environments and Organizations*, edited by M. Mayer. San Francisco: Jossey-Bass, 1978.

Miles, M., and Huberman, M. *Innovation Up Close: How School Improvement Works*. New York: Plenum Press, 1984.

Moore, W. E. *Social Change*. Englewood Cliffs, New Jersey: Prentice-Hall, 1963.

Nisbet, R. *History of the Idea of Progress*. New York: Basic Books, 1980.

_____. *Social Change and History*. London: Oxford University Press, 1969.

Reimer, J. "The Synagogue as a Context for Jewish Education." Report to the Commission on Jewish Education in North America, 1990.

_____. "What We Know About Jewish Family Education." In *What We Know About Jewish Education*, edited by S. Kelman. Los Angeles: Torah Aura, 1992.

_____. *When Synagogues Educate*. Philadelphia: Jewish Publication Society, 1993.

Schoem, D. "What We Know About the Jewish Supplementary School." In *What We Know About Jewish Education*, edited by S. Kelman. Los Angeles: Torah Aura, 1992.

Schoenfeld, S. "Folk Judaism, Elite Judaism and the Role of Bar Mitzvah in the Development of the Synagogue and Jewish School in America." *Contemporary Jewry* 9:1 (1988), 67-85.

Sergiovanni, T. "The Leadership Needed for Quality Schooling." In *Schooling for Tomorrow*, edited by T. Sergiovanni and J. Moore. Boston: Allyn and Bacon, Inc., 1989.

Sklare, M., ed. *American Jews: A Reader*. New York: Behrman House, 1983.

Spindler, G., and Spindler, L. "Roger Harker and Schonhausen." In *Doing the Ethnography of Schooling*, edited by G. Spindler. New York: Holt, Rinehart and Winston, 1982.

Stake R., and Easley, J. *Case Studies in Science Education*, vol.1. Urbana, IL: Center for Instructional Research and Curriculum Evaluation, 1978.

Stiggins, R.; Conklin, N.; and Bridgeford, N. "Classroom Assessment: A Key to Effective Instruction." *Educational Measurement: Issues and Practice* 5:2 (1986), 5-17.

Suydam, M., and Osborne, A. "The Status of Pre-College Science, Mathematics and Social Science Education, 1955-1975." In *Mathematics Education*, vol. 2. Columbus, OH: Ohio State University, Center for Science and Mathematics Education, 1977.

Tyack, D. *The One Best System*. Cambridge, MA: Harvard University Press, 1974.

Watzlawick, P.; Weakland, J.; and Fisch, R. *Change: Principles of Problem Formation and Problem Resolution*. New York: Norton, 1974.

Weiss, I. Report of the 1977 National Survey of Science, Mathematics, and Social Studies Education. Washington, DC: National Science Foundation, 1978.

Wiggins, G. "Teaching to the Authentic Test." *Educational Leadership* (April 1989).

REFLECTIONS ON THE SOCIAL SCIENCE OF AMERICAN JEWS AND ITS IMPLICATIONS FOR JEWISH EDUCATION

Riv-Ellen Prell

ocial scientists who turn their probing eyes and questions on American Jewish life have come to play an increasingly important role as planners and even visionaries for the Jewish community since the 1970s. They are anxious to help set the agenda to create a vital Jewish community for the twenty-first century. Their demographic profiles, attitude surveys, and community studies convey a much larger story about what will create or undermine Jewish continuity. I want to survey briefly some of this research in order to understand what it can teach us about Jewish education and to explore why the education of Jewish children is at the center of their agenda.

It is ironic that where education fits into the general research agenda of the social scientific study of American Jewry is anything but obvious. Even when researchers explicitly include education in a survey or point to it as a direct cause that explains Jewish commitment, Jewish education is never discussed in its own terms. With a few notable exceptions, social scientists have left the study of Jewish education to educators and have not considered how a focus on education might affect their own research problems. The information that many of these studies yield is, nevertheless, potentially very useful to the long-range planning efforts of visionary educators.

How Important Is Jewish Education?

The social scientists who have focused their attention on Jewish education have come to two oddly contradictory conclusions: Jewish education is a disaster, and it insures a sense of identity. The story is more complicated than that, but for the sake of an overview, it is worth drawing attention directly to this peculiar contradiction. The most recent National Jewish Population Study certainly indicates a strong association between Jewish education and Jewish ritual observances. A person who has had a religious education is far more likely to observe and participate in Jewish ritual and religious life than a person who has had no religious education. At the same time there is some clear evidence that children in Jewish supplementary schools dislike the education they are getting. They appear to learn little and the models used for learning are long outmoded. (Schoem 1989)

This apparent contradiction feels intuitively true to most adult Jews in America today. One learns from casual conversations with any cross section of American Jews born between 1940 and 1960 that they probably went to religious school and disliked it. Jewish education, particularly in the synagogue, loomed large in the Jewish lives of Americans after World War II because it served as the primary instrument to train Jews religiously and socialize them.

In the decades immediately preceding and following World War II, Jewish families essentially ceded the role of religious education to congregational and communal schools. Marshall Sklare's study of a postwar Chicago suburb (Sklare 1967) revealed that most families believed that a healthy Jewish identity was essential for their children, but parents needed schools and synagogues to provide that identity. Sklare later noted that parents turned to Jewish education to insure group survival. The traditional subjects of Jewish education were not designed to "create identity" for postwar America. Jewish families wanted their children to remain Jewish, but not to be taught traditional texts and laws. (Sklare 1971, pp. 160-161) They sought a new type of education.

Sidney Goldstein and Calvin Goldscheider's pioneering population study of three generations of Jews in Providence, Rhode Island, suggests an interesting link among secular education, affluence, and Jewish education. (Goldstein and Goldscheider 1992) The more highly educated, more recent urban residents interviewed had more Jewish education than suburbanites, and 54% of those between the ages of fifteen and twenty-four had seven or more years. This population reflected what the researchers learned in general about college-educated Jews—that they were very likely to identify with the Jewish community. Contrary to pervasive assumptions of the time, the researchers discovered that higher education was a predictor of attachment to the Jewish community. They concluded that Jewish education kept Jews with high secular educational attainment linked to the Jewish community.

Well-educated Jews are often those who epitomize the very educational and social class goals associated with the majority of Jewish immigrants and their children. Parents used educational facilities of the Jewish community precisely as they used the public schools of their cities and suburbs—to train their children for success and to socialize them effectively as Jews.

One cannot overstate the fact that Jewish education, successful or not, is a critical component of American Jewish life and has been so for the decades that were characterized by a remarkably homogeneous Jewish population with a high degree of endogamy and stable households. However important education was for creating Jewish identity in the past, the need for this function seems to have increased directly as a result of the explosion of intermarriage after 1960. The profile of American Jews produced by the National Jewish Population Study of 1990 suggests a far more pressing need for educational institutions to provide socialization precisely because children are less likely to be raised in homes where both parents are Jewish or married to other Jews. In the more "fluid" Jewish population of the next century, schools will be called on to provide a far greater number of components of a Jewish identity. (See Goldstein and Goldscheider 1992.)

Precisely because Jewish education serves the function of making Jews Jewish, educators might become an easy target of blame for failing to make Jews better Jews. Perhaps that is why more recent studies have emphasized the failures of Jewish education to educate well. An even more pressing problem is the simple fact that the social scientists who want very much to help set the agenda for Jewish life in the twenty-first century have not undertaken serious studies of education. Other than a survey question here, a single ethnography there, and a few studies in the 1970s, the realm of Jewish education remains largely untouched by social scientists. The synagogue, the Federation, prayer, ritual attitudes, social mobility, housing, voluntary associations, and philanthropy have all been more systematically scrutinized than one of the most significant modes of Jewish socialization in the United States.

I am interested in briefly reviewing recent social scientific studies of American Jewish life in order to learn what each approach has to tell us about how to evaluate and restructure Jewish education. I will lay out four different social scientific problems or frameworks in order to make clear what they have learned about American Jewish life and what the implications of this work are for educating children. The first and least developed framework is **How do Jews create meaning?** which reveals what isn't working in Jewish education. The second is **What contributes to Jewish social cohesion?** which suggests what seems to make Jews want to continue to educate their children. The third framework is **What promotes Jewish behavior?** which emphasizes what the outcome of decades of American Jewish education has produced. The fourth is **What do Jews believe?** which presents the content of Jewish life as it is currently lived.

How Do Jews Create Meaning?

This question is most closely associated with social scientists who undertake ethnographic research and engage in the observation of participants. The general assumption is that if an outsider hangs around long enough, he or she will be treated increasingly like a member of the community or the school and over time will learn what its members are doing. A close-up look is not good for generalizing, as more quantitative measures are, but it does allow for careful listening. The study made by Marshall Sklare, mentioned above, did just that. Sklare and his assistants learned a great deal about suburban Jewish life by interviewing and talking to the Jews of the community.

Since the 1970s several ethnographic works have examined synagogues and religious communities (Furman 1987; Heilman 1983; Mayer 1979; Prell 1989) Each of these studies has attended closely to how particular groups of Jews create a meaningful religious experience within the context of community. These works probe what it means to be a Jew in a particular time and place. Questions like these have the potential to provide educators with clues for how to build on the powerful sentiments that motivate a Jewish parent or child to want a continuing connection to Judaism.

It is worth comparing the approach of these ethnographic works to the one qualitative study of Jewish education by David Schoem that used ethnographic methods. His conclusions, while undoubtedly accurate, seem entirely to miss the point of ethnographic work. Schoem reported the obvious. He found that barely identified Jews were urging their children on to Jewish education that they themselves hated and that they anticipated their children would hate as well. He found teachers with minimal personal commitments teaching a Judaism they did not practice or personally support. He discovered the inevitables of social life, contradictions, ideologies unsupported by social reality, power struggles, and even despair. Clearly these things are there for the finding, but little is learned by repeating them.

The great potential for ethnographic work, at least as it is practiced by anthropologists, is to find what is below the surface, to explore what is not obvious from superficial observation in a cultural setting. Schoem, however, set the stage for his approach in the first page of his book. He contrasted the Deuteronomic admonition to teach your children with a statement made by a school parent:

> I guess if there weren't so many pressures and directions—
> what with work and bills and taxes and weeds—we might
> sit down with books and read about Judaism. But hell,
> we'd rather watch the Super Bowl.

As I read each chapter on Jewish education, I waited for the moment the writer would pursue the place from which the desire to read books about Judaism developed and ask what nourished and what destroyed it. I wondered why the father who regarded the Super Bowl to be more important than Judaism bothered to send his child to that school and why the teachers taught in and the children attended that school. In short, I wanted Schoem to explore the whole world of that school, how it constituted a world of meaning and how it did not. Then there is the larger question of why study a school that "fails" and not also study one that "succeeds."

My point is not specifically to criticize Schoem's work but rather to hold out the hope for an ethnographic study as a meaningful research alternative. If ethnography will help us to look at the development of values, the construction of meaning, and the sources of persistent identity as cultural matters for Jews in the United States, then it is an approach that may well contribute to providing an alternative vision of American Jewish life.

What Contributes to Jewish Social Cohesion?

Ethnographers take a very close look at community behavior in order to understand what identity and religion mean in the Jewish case. Sociologists interested in social cohesion ask what FACTORS make Jews feel connected to other Jews, and they define those behaviors in terms of what Jews do. These social scientists have learned that even when Jews observe very few of the traditional commandments, many of them still live in Jewish neighborhoods, have mostly Jewish friends, and feel most comfortable with other

Jews. The sociologists and political scientists engaged in this work are interested in how modernization has shaped Jewish life as we know it. (Goldstein and Goldscheider 1992, p. xi)

Their task is to explain the social relations that create Jewish cohesion and hence enable a Jewish identity to persist. Their most radical claim is that the content of Jewishness is far less relevant or important than the structure of Jewish life. They are interested in group strength and cohesion, without appeal to any cultural or moral content. (Cohen 1988, p. 6) In *The Transformation of the Jews*, Goldscheider and Zuckerman develop their view of Jewishness as an "emergent ethnicity." They use this term to suggest that the persistence of Jewish identity is unrelated to "primordial" sentiments that attach people to a series of standard practices and meanings consistently over time. Rather, faced with modern life and its challenges to immigrants and their children in the early twentieth century, Jewish continuity, they argue, is the product of communal interaction. (Goldscheider and Zuckerman 1984) They demonstrate that Jews within particular societies have shared a small number of occupations as well as social and cultural organizations, political movements, and kin bonds and that these have been the source of "ethnic cohesion." This ethnic solidarity is reinforced by bonds of friendship and endogamous marriage. The density of overlapping networks in which Jews encounter one another produces Jewish continuity. (Ibid. 1984, p. 9) Thus Goldscheider and Zuckerman claim:

> For most Jews most of the time, the constraints of economic position and opportunity, place of residence, educational skills, political limitations and rights, and tugs of family and friends have outweighed personal convictions. At a different level of analysis, the same factors structure the Jewish communities. Hence, many Jews who prefer not to be Jews may be bound tightly by occupational, residential, and other structural ties to the community. Conversely, many who want to be Jews may not do so in the absence of those ties. Where Jews share similar residences, schools, occupations, organizations, and friends their community has the highest level of cohesion whether the individual Jews value or desire this interaction, whether they think each other apostates or reactionaries. (Ibid. 1984, p. 241))

According to the reseachers' challenging explanation for the "real" ties that bind American Jews, cultural content reflects rather than causes Jewish continuity. Although they never discuss Jewish education because they are not very concerned with the transmission of Jewish identity through cultural institutions, one can speculate on what role they might assign to that process. The supplementary school might well provide an ideological overlay to emergent Jewish ethnicity. Because Jews, like most Americans, rarely celebrate their occupation or social class identities, they are bound instead by a sense of common origins. The ideology may be relatively superficial. Herbert Gans, another sociologist, calls it "symbolic ethnicity." (Gans 1979) It is individualized and heartfelt, but it is a veneer over the more fundamental if less articulated ties of modern life—occupation, social class, degree of higher education, etc., all of which are widely shared by Jews.

The contribution these social scientists can make to our understanding of how to educate Jews is to encourage our suspicions of any truths or values that some claim unite all Jews and must be transmitted in the education of young American Jews. In fact, the experiences that these sociologists might well suggest are shared by young students may have little to do with Jewish matters and everything to do with a shared American culture based on social class privilege and expectations for attaining a certain degree of affluence and education. Their definition of Jewish cohesion helps to explain why American Jews are so deeply committed to their identity as Jews but appear to be unable to define the content of that identity in terms of values, practices, or shared cultural resources.

What role does or should education play in the reproduction of cohesion for Jews? Does Jewish education reinforce the basic middle class values that figure into the forms of cohesion at work in American Jewish life?

Jewish education may both benefit and be at risk if it is recruited as an ideology to reproduce a cohesive middle class Jewish community. Education linked to Bar and Bat Mitzvah is an important arena for achievement and performance, highly valued elements for a group whose mobility has been directly tied to individual achievement and higher education. Religious education also provides a setting in which Jews meet other Jews and parents are anxious to reinforce the normality of Jewish existence. Finally, Jewish continuity does depend on teaching what it means to be Jewish, something that is difficult to discover in the secular spheres of modern life. Therefore, families are dependent on Jewish education to help them define for their children the meaning of this identity whose content is so minimized in contemporary American life.

The very forces that draw a significant percentage of American Jews to educate their children may, however, complicate the educational process. If Jewish life in the supplementary school basically reproduces the secular world as Jewish teenagers know it, then it is at risk because it cannot compete with that larger secular world. Schoem's ethnography of a synagogue school emphasizes the fact that students and their families are aware that the stakes in Jewish education are very low because they do not lead to either college or jobs. (Schoem 1989) The school does not disrupt the secular school calendar and does not attempt to compete with the many activities that claim teenagers' interests. Religious school "fits in" on many dimensions. Although the content of what is taught-Hebrew, the festival cycle, history—is different from that taught by the dominant culture, the latter is reinforced in every other way.

If students express discontent with the values and expectations of middle-class American life, then Judaism is liable to rejection because it appears inseparable from that world. Deborah Dash Moore's work *At Home in America* (1981) makes this very point for second-generation New York Jews. I have argued elsewhere that much of the expressed discontent between Jewish women and men can be attributed to the link between Jewishness and economic success. (Prell 1992) Paradoxically, American Jews have fashioned a Judaism for themselves that is exceptionally compatible with the demands of a solidly middle-class, achievement-oriented culture. But generational rebellion against the class-based aspirations of parents may also result in their rejection of Judaism.

The very ties that draw students and their families to Jewish education may become the basis of students' disparaging and rejecting it. Not only is the education "irrelevant," it is too much like daily life, while at the same time it describes a world so different from that life. The frank indifference to cultural matters that scholars who study social cohesion possess may help to sharpen questions about what precisely is being taught in supplementary school and why. Should Jewish education challenge the dominant culture of the United States and in what ways?

What Promotes Jewish Behavior?

The social scientists who study Jewish behavior conduct surveys that help them learn what types of Jews do or do not participate in a variety of Jewish activities, rituals, and organizations. They, too, are concerned with what creates Jewish continuity, but they emphasize more specifically the behaviors and choices made by individual Jews rather than the structural features created by modernization. The task of the interpreters of these surveys is to isolate the "independent variables" that are most likely to support Jews' commitments to their children's Jewishness.

The Jewish population studies are one of the most significant developments in the social science of American Jewish life of the past three decades and are the product of this approach. (Cohen et al 1984, Goldstein and Goldscheider 1992) This research, conducted in conjunction with Jewish communities throughout the United States, attempts to gather information about American Jews—their education and occupations, their religious commitments, their residences, and their friends. The studies define relevant Jewish behaviors and suggests axes along which to measure differences in those behaviors. Ritual behaviors, contributions to Jewish charities, choice of friends, and membership in organizations have been used as significant markers of Jewish affiliation. The sociologists who interpret these data rely heavily on the measurement of "behaviors" to understand what produces and maintains a measurable Jewish identity.

Steven Cohen, one of the most important figures involved in this research, analyzed the data from the New York study in light of his larger concern with the issue of Jewish continuity. Cohen argues that sociologists who analyze these data have formed two camps: the transformationalists and the assimilationists. (Cohen 1988, p. 10) The transformationalists understand American Jewish life to be changing but vigorous, whereas the assimilationists claim that Jewish life has been in decline for most of the century. Cohen argues for a middle path. He suggests that there is evidence of some vitality in Jewish life as well as a definite decline in overall behavioral measures.

The direct implications of this research for Jewish education is its close attention to behavior. Cohen, for example, explicitly examines the relationship between Jewish education and the "Jewish continuity" behaviors he and other sociologists have attempted to measure. He argues that Jewish education is in fact, contrary to the flawed studies of the 1970s, likely to affect behavior.[1] He asserts that supplementary Jewish education can be causally linked to adult Jewish commitments. Behaviors that he measures as significant expressions of Jewish life, such as candlelighting, maintaining dietary laws, affixing a mezuzah, and attending a seder, are all positively correlated to sustained participation in supplementary Jewish education. (Cohen 1988, pp. 82-95) Cohen also claims that Jewish education is not strongly correlated to other measures of Jewish continuity such as philanthropy or communal organization membership. (Ibid. p. 89) Cohen's findings support those reported by Sidney Goldstein and Calvin Goldscheider's Providence, Rhode Island, study, the first Jewish population study conducted in the United States. They write, "Whether or not an individual receives a Jewish education may be a key factor in influencing the degree of his identification with the Jewish community in adult life." (Goldstein and Goldscheider 1992, p. 224)

Jewish education, most likely reinforced by the family, emphasizes a particular set of Jewish activities. It appears to train Jews to participate in the cycle of festivals and Sabbath and gives them the skills to appropriate the events that they choose to observe. Since the overall direction of Cohen's data affirms that Jews become, for the most part, less religiously observant with each generation since immigration, he certainly does not argue that education is responsible for maintaining a high degree of religiosity. But it appears to allow Jews to maintain a Jewish identity rooted in part in religious behaviors and symbols.

The various community studies, in addition to the 1990 National Jewish Population Study, are unambiguous about the significance of day school education in particular. Children who attend day school are less likely to intermarry (Phillips 1991, table 19) and to maintain a Jewish identity than children with supplementary or no education. Children who attend supplementary school are less likely to maintain as high a degree of Jewish identity as those who attend day school but are more likely to do so than children who have no Jewish education. Correlation between education and religious commitment in adult life cannot be asserted apart from the Jewishness of families of origin. On the other hand, a survey instrument cannot detect if the family of origin became more religiously committed as a result of their children's attending religious school. These studies can only demonstrate that Jewish education is linked to adult behavior.

Population studies yield data that in many ways are quite hopeful for Jewish education. But the studies pose an even more challenging question about intention and outcome. Did the supplementary curricula from the 1930s to the 1960s seek to create a form of Jewish identity in the United States that was primarily oriented around a small number of ritual activities and a very general definition of Jewish identification? If education is even partly responsible for the outcome that sociologists describe, can we isolate and understand what aspects of suburban synagogue education were central to that outcome? Have curricular changes of the last decade directed Jewish learning differently? Cohen and his colleagues are fairly explicit about the fact that all their data reveal is what people do, not what they think, feel, or understand about their Judaism. In short, the researchers have measured what is measurable and little more. When Jewish social scientists turn into social planners, they are in a position to advocate for the use of community dollars for education. If education is measured by years and hours, then it is inevitable that the social scientists will encourage the development of day schools, perhaps to the disadvantage of supplementary schools. How should Jewish educators enter this debate? Part of their position might well rest on underlining how these surveys define outcome and what the definitions of Jewishness asserted by the data are.

The behavioral/survey approach provides a powerful and consistent picture of American Jewish life. Study after study reveals, as Cohen notes, a set of behaviors and attitudes amenable to different interpretations. Those who were studied in major Jewish population centers persist in identifying themselves as Jews through membership in the Jewish community, identification with Israel, participation in philanthropy, and associating with Jews. Their ritual life is minimal. Indeed, Jews are singularly characterized in the United States by their strong social and political identification and weak religious life. (Cohen 1988, p. 8) These issues are indisputable. However, the quality of Jewish life associated with them and their effect upon generational continuity is a matter of interpretation. Jewish educators must simultaneously contend with these basic realities and decide how supplementary education will affect and shape them.

What Do Jews Believe?

Both the behavioral and structural interpretations of Jewish life are characterized by their attention to what people do rather than what Jewish leaders believe that they ought to do. Both perspectives attempt to understand in differing ways how Jewish life is lived. Neither makes an argument for a coherent system that guides these lives. Two social scientists have attempted to define what might be called a "folk model" of American Jewish life. Charles Liebman and Jonathan Woocher, during two different decades, each laid out an ideology or belief system that they (sometimes critically) described as the widely held beliefs of

149

American Jews. Both described an unofficial worldview that Liebman characterized as "ambivalence" (Liebman 1973) and Woocher as "civil Judaism" (Woocher 1986), which they detect in the activities of American Jews who are committed to Judaism. They contend that their version of that worldview bears very little resemblance to any classical normative picture of Jewish life, but they think it worthy to reveal the existence of their model.

Charles Liebman's work *The Ambivalent American Jew* pioneered this approach by differentiating between what he called folk and elite models. (Liebman 1973) Jonathan Woocher's study of Jewish civil religion took a somewhat more complex form. Borrowing from Robert Bellah's work on an American civil religion, Woocher explores the development of a new set of religious principles that emerged in tandem with a centralized Jewish philanthropic establishment that dominates the secular domains of Jewish life. Woocher lists the principles of this civil religion and then supports them with the results of survey research conducted with Federation lay leaders. His civil religion does not pretend to describe all Jews, but it does describe very active Jews whose lives may vary extensively from normative Judaism. Woocher's principles are as follows:

(1) The unity of the Jewish people

(2) Mutual responsibility

(3) Jewish survival in a threatening world

(4) The centrality of the State of Israel

(5) The enduring value of Jewish tradition

(6) *Tzedakah*: philanthropy and justice

(7) Americanness as a virtue (Woocher 1986, pp. 67-68)

These principles give shape to the life that Jews live, which, as all social scientists have noted, attempts to balance uniqueness and cultural integration. More precisely Woocher demonstrates that these principles speak to specific claims that Jews are "one," that they are endangered, that they are responsible for one another, and that they share a destiny.

In 1973, Charles Liebman listed an almost identical catalog of core values for Jews. He wrote:

> Jewish identity in America, among its other aspects, includes a sense of social intimacy with other Jews; a sense of identification with or attachment to the State of Israel as a political entity; a sense that anti-Semitism, however remote, always

constitutes a threat; a sense that Jewish well-being is interrelated with Enlightenment, rationalism, social justice, political liberalism, and the separation of church and state; and a sense that Jews share a common history. (Liebman 1973, p. 181)

Liebman and Woocher differ on the attention each pays to liberal politics and in their levels of pessimism about American Jewish continuity. In his work Liebman was convinced that Jews had to abandon an integrationist perspective in order to survive in the United States. These differences aside, Liebman and Woocher find very similar principles operating in what each sees as an American Jewish worldview.

Although both Woocher and Liebman describe Jews as profoundly motivated by a series of convictions and anxieties, the two do not examine these ideas developmentally. For example, their methodologies do not include life histories through which they might discover why and how such concerns and fear developed. They do not look at the contribution of Jewish education to these outlooks, not even its contribution to the role of *tzedakah* in the lives of the Federation's leaders. Both Liebman and Woocher begin their work with the condition of Jewish life in America and the fundamental struggle between integration and uniqueness, and they then translate those issues into adult behaviors.

For this work to be fundamentally important to Jewish education, these ideologies must be applied to developmental perspectives that allow us to understand how Jews are made Jewish in American culture. At the same time they make it clear, like the other social scientists, that Jewish educators inherit and compete with a series of values and beliefs that they must address in their efforts to educate Jewish children. If another set of values is what is to be taught, then how to acknowledge the competition between models or worldviews is a serious challenge to educators.

Final Thoughts

The social scientific study of American Jews has provided Jewish educators with a powerful picture of the ideologies, behaviors, and sources of cohesiveness that characterize Jewish life. This research has been affected by the various problems that appear to confront Jewish continuity and survival. Survey research has revealed the importance of Jewish education for reproducing American Judaism as we know it—short on activity and high on commitment—but enabling the commitment that exists. The structuralists have shown that the foundation of Jewish continuity derives from the density of Jewish social spheres. This analysis reveals to us that Jewish education's success is its vulnerability. Education can help thicken the density of Jewish networks, but it can also reproduce them. Insofar as Jewish education resembles American middle-class life it can be discarded along with the latter when young adults seriously reconsider their family's values. The folk Judaism school has also ignored Jewish education, but it could scrutinize that education for the values that constitute the adult civil Judaism that Woocher describes. Both questions about belief and meaning can help shape an education that speaks to the real quest for an integrated identity that members of American society seek in increasing numbers.

Both the profile of American Jews and the issues that challenge our future point increasingly to Jewish education as a critical setting for the transmission of Judaism, a role that is entirely consistent with the development of American Jewish life in the twentieth century. Social scientists are certainly aware that a number of Judaisms have developed in our century. Denominations as well as folk and elite formulations of Jewish life, normative Judaism, and civil religion underline the fact that Jewish educators will need to decide which Judaisms to teach about and how to integrate Judaism into the lives of Jews who, at the end of the twentieth century, yearn for a meaningful religious experience that will not disrupt their secular lives but will not abandon them to the secular world, either.

Notes

[1] Cohen particularly discounts the research of Bock and Himmelfarb done in the 1970s that claimed supplementary school had no effect on continuing Jewish identity unless it exceeded a certain number of hours. They disagreed, however, on the precise number. Cohen persuasively argues that their findings were skewed by their failure to analyze their data by gender. Girls received far less education than boys, thus skewing the overall sample. (Cohen 1988)

REFERENCES

Cohen, Steven M. *American Assimilation or Jewish Revival?* Bloomington: Indiana University Press, 1988.

Cohen, Steven M.; Woocher, Jonathan; and Phillips, Bruce. *Perspectives in Jewish Population Research.* Boulder, CO: Westview Press, 1984.

Furman, Frida Kerner. *Beyond Yiddishkeit: the Struggle for Jewish Identity in a Reform Synagogue.* Buffalo: State University of New York Press, 1987.

Gans, Herbert. "Symbolic Ethnicity: The Future of Ethnic Groups and Cultures in America." *Ethnic and Racial Studies* 2 (January 1979), 1-20.

Goldscheider, Calvin, and Zuckerman, Alan S. *The Transformation of the Jews.* Chicago: University of Chicago Press, 1984.

Goldstein, Sidney, and Goldscheider, Calvin. "Profile of American Jewry: Insights from the 1990 National Jewish Population Survey." In *American Jewish Yearbook*, edited by David Singer. Philadelphia: Jewish Publication Society, 1992, 77-126.

Gordon, Milton. *Jews in Suburbia.* Boston: Beacon Press, 1959.

Heilman, Samuel C. *The People of the Book: Drama, Fellowship, and Religion.* Chicago: University of Chicago Press, 1983.

Jewish Americans: Three Generations in a Jewish Community. Englewood Cliffs, NJ: Prentice-Hall, 1968.

Liebman, Charles. *The Ambivalent American Jew: Politics, Religion, and Family in American Jewish Life.* Philadelphia: Jewish Publication Society, 1973.

Mayer, Egon. *From Suburb to Shtetl: The Jews of Boro Park.* Philadelphia: Temple University Press, 1979.

Moore, Deborah Dash. *At Home in America: Second Generation New York Jews.* New York: Columbia University Press, 1981.

Phillips, Bruce. Tables from the National Jewish Population Study. Association for Jewish Studies Annual Meeting, 1991.

Prell, Riv-Ellen. *Prayer and Community: The Havurah in American Judaism.* Detroit: Wayne State University Press, 1989.

————. "Why Jewish Princesses Don't Sweat: Desire and Consumption in Postwar American Judaism.". In *People of the Body: Jews and Judaism from an Embodied Perspective*, edited by Howard Eilberg-Schwarts. Buffalo, NY: State University of New York Press, 1992, 329-360.

Schoem, David. *Ethnic Survival in America: An Ethnography of a Jewish Afternoon School.* Atlanta: Scholars Press, 1989.

Sklare, Marshall. *America's Jews.* New York: Random House, 1971.

Sklare, Marshall, and Greenblum, Joseph. *Jewish Identity on the Suburban Frontier: A Study of Group Survival in the Open Society*, 2d ed. Chicago: University of Chicago Press, 1967.

Woocher, Jonathan. *Sacred Survival: The Civil Religion of American Jews.* Bloomington, IN: Indiana University Press, 1986.

3

THE PROCESS
OF TRANSFORMATION

An Organizational Perspective on Changing Congregational Education

What the Literature Reveals

Susan Shevitz

magine three congregations five years after each began intensive work to transform its educational program. Each had hoped not merely to expand and enrich what it was already doing but also to make the congregation a center of "cradle to grave" learning. Each had aspired to active congregant participation in defining its educational mission and agenda. When these congregations started the process of reconfiguring their approaches to Jewish education, each was excited by what it hoped to achieve.

After five years each congregation has indeed changed, although not necessarily in the ways it had imagined. One of them looks surprisingly the same as it did before. Some classes were dropped and some programs were added, but the problems that motivated the congregation to try to change are still endemic. After a flurry of activity and experimentation, things somehow reverted to "business as usual." The congregation's school is its primary educational arm. Jewish education is mainly for the children. Some members assert that conditions are now worse than they were five years ago. Since congregants' expectations had grown, members now feel disenchanted with the professional staff and skeptical about the impact of Jewish education. Or, as one board member was heard saying, "The more things change, the more they stay the same."

Although the web of educational offerings in the second congregation is not as seamless as some congregants had hoped it would be, there have been changes. The school more regularly involves families than it did before. Through many "beyond the classroom" activities, students participate in communal life. New educational programs that are coordinated with the school curriculum provide formal and informal educational opportunities to teens and adults. "We're doing more of the same," concedes an active congregant, "only now we're doing it more thoughtfully." While the different educational activities are related to one another, Jewish learning is still not pervasive. For many congregants Jewish education is something that is done for others but not for them.

The third congregation is very different today than it was five years ago. The graded school is no longer the hub of its educational offerings. Instead, families and individuals work together with the staff to develop an annual Jewish education plan. Classes on different subjects are open to people of all ages. Individuals with similar interests are matched and study together. The library/resource center has kits and programs for individuals and small groups. And the set of congregational offerings is adjusted annually to incorporate members' emerging interests and capacities.

The new system is not without problems. It is hard for the staff to keep tabs on all the participants. Much time is spent experimenting with record keeping. Members of the staff are continually being challenged to learn new content and approaches to keep up with congregants' changing interests and worry that they don't always have the depth of knowledge they'd like to possess. Without a lock-step program, groups of students in a class are often on different learning levels. The easiest classes to organize are those for beginners. Other classes encounter problems because of heterogeneous student background, knowledge, and expectation. Use of space is an especially sensitive issue. Not all the rooms are adaptable to the different needs and ages. Overcrowding often occurs during the most popular times for on-site study. With so much happening away from the congregation, some worry that participants' identification with the congregation will erode. Families that prefer a more typical religious school for the youth and ancillary programs for their other members have left the congregation, although some new people, drawn by the excitement of the new venture, have joined. And conflict has arisen over the years as people pushed for the new vision. "Still," claims an involved congregant, "these problems come from a new reality. People do get frustrated; not everything is as good as we would like. But we are clearly committed to educating Jews, not only kids, and this is becoming our congregation's raison d'être. We don't know what the effects over time will be—we hope they will be more positive than our old system—but we can't yet be sure. We can't even be sure that they'll endure another five years... beyond the initial experimentation phase!"

These imaginary but paradigmatic congregations illustrate what personal experience and social history show. Change is never simple. What actually happens often bears little resemblance to the anticipated change. Institutions can be impervious to our best efforts to change them. As congregations embark on the process of planned change, it is fitting to ask what they can do to increase the odds that their efforts will yield significant and sustained improvement. This is a difficult question because while descriptions of new programs in a synagogue do exist, there is practically no literature that deals with the organizational context and the process of change in the congregational setting. How a new approach is incorporated into an institution is not described, as if having a good idea is enough to insure its use.

This paper will address the question of planned educational change in the congregation by (1) describing characteristics of congregational education that emerge from relevant literature; (2) using relevant organizational theory to describe salient aspects of congregational life; and (3) suggesting tentative guidelines for initiating planned educational change in the congregation.

This paper assumes that defining new policies will not necessarily yield the desired changes. Instead, it suggests that significant educational change results from a strategic approach in which flexible strategies emerge through an iterative process. (Pettigrew, Ferlie, and McKee 1992) The type of change, placed on a continuum of evolutionary, additive, and transformative change, will be either additive or transformative. Evolutionary change is a "steady state: new norms, beliefs and values are introduced at about the same rate that others fade away. Over time, the culture acquires new content, but the shift is not radical." (Rossman, Corbett, and Firestone 1988, p. 14) Additive change suddenly modifies "the norms, beliefs, or values in a particular domain of the institutional culture. The new norm or belief then spreads to modify an entire set of beliefs." (Ibid. p. 14) For example, including parents in Jewish educational settings changes notions of who is to be educated, the purpose of Jewish education, and the definition of effective education. Admitting women into rabbinical schools is another example of additive change. The new beliefs reverberate through and change the culture. Additive change can be very powerful.

Transformative change occurs when an individual or group deliberately sets out to change an institution. This usually occurs when an institution that has been besieged over a long period of time realizes it needs to be redefined in order to endure. A dissident inside group or some outsiders lead a process of major transformation so that a new organization is born from the remnants of the old. (Ibid.)

Whether they engage in additive or transformative change, participating congregations in the ECE will need enough stability and security to engage in a process of introspection and improvement. Understanding the organizational context and process of change will be as important to the outcome of their effort as the content of the proposed changes. Hence a careful analysis of these issues is timely.

The way we think about congregations and the models of organizing that we apply to them influence our prescriptions, expectations, and assessments of the process of change. The following will discuss characteristics of congregations and their schools that emerge from the literature about their educational programs. We will argue that the relevant literature reveals several widespread but questionable beliefs about the organizational context of Jewish education and congregational life held by people interested in Jewish education. By recognizing assumptions that are shared in many reports of change in Jewish settings, we will uncover some of the dominant perspectives and behavioral regularities that must be considered as we plan initiatives within our congregations.

DESCRIPTIONS OF JEWISH EDUCATIONAL INSTITUTIONS

Descriptions of many religious school projects, usually written for other practitioners, and published evaluations of particular schools (e.g., Cohen 1992, Stern 1993) are generally concerned with the content of a change (i.e., the new program, curriculum, or policy). While they often ignore the contexts and processes of change, we can extrapolate from them some of the assumptions commonly held by people about educational change in the congregational setting.

Education As Compartmentalized

Like the self-centered dreams of Joseph in Genesis, most studies wishfully place the school, class, or project at the hub of the system's universe and reveal little of what else is going on. While this may be due to the need to focus attention on a particular phenomenon, one wonders about other processes and events at the site or in the community. Is instituting a new curriculum as central to involved stakeholders' decision-making premises as a regional recession or a fight over a rabbi's contract? Probably not. Yet key events and characteristics of the context are often omitted from view.

Only recently has attention been paid to the relationship between the school and its sponsoring congregation. According to Reimer the terms of this relationship may be a critical influence on the school's effectiveness, perhaps more influential than the school's own policies and programs. (Reimer 1991) In his recent study of two "good enough" congregational schools, he demonstrates how these two schools have the status of the favored or mission-bearing child. (Reimer 1992) Reimer posits four possible relationships: boarder, stepchild, child less focused-upon, and mission-bearing child. When the school assumes the mission-bearing status, demonstrated through generous financial support, integration into temple life, and special attention from rabbinic and lay leadership, its excellence is made possible.

The Limited Perspectives of Education Partisans and Others within the Congregations

Hand in hand with compartmentalization is the question of perspective. Education partisans within the congregations often disregard the other needs of the institution, while others fail to consider the needs of the educational programs. Different groups, it seems, have different views of what is important to the congregation. For example, in one synagogue the sisterhood insisted on installing lace curtains in the kiddush room that for twelve hours each week served as a classroom for eleven- and twelve-year-olds. Because the curtains were soon stained, much unpleasantness occurred as a consequence. The ensuing arguments made it clear that neither faction had considered the other's perspective.

The following is a more significant example. Professional and lay education partisans from several congregations who were several years into a process of promoting family education participated in an "envisioning" exercise. They were asked to consider what their institutions would be like were their initiatives to be successful. It took this group of rather sophisticated people quite a while to recognize that if they were to succeed, many other branches of the congregation would be affected. Other professionals would have additional responsibilities, more money and space would be required, space would be used differently, other congregational programs (e.g., youth group, sisterhood, men's club, nursery school, various clubs) might be found to be redundant or unnecessary, the school curriculum would need revision, and so on. By not involving the other groups that would be affected by their program, they would be sowing the seeds of conflict and perhaps defeat! The point is that informed education partisans were reluctant to view the larger context in which Jewish education takes place. This tendency seems to be so pervasive and taken for granted that it has become a behavioral regularity that expresses the deeply held, often unconscious views about the nature of congregational education as isolated from the rest of congregational life.

Dominance of the Professionals' Perspectives

Few descriptions or analyses of an educational change from perspectives other than those of the professionals exist. We don't learn of other stakeholders' reactions or how their viewpoints influence a process. From the written descriptions of programmatic reform (Dorph 1989, for example) and from the exhortations of others (Reisman 1992), it is unclear that stakeholders have a compelling voice in important decisions despite rhetoric that talks of a diverse community and constituent needs. This may be related to several problematic assumptions: that stakeholders follow leaders, that the professional's viewpoint is the legitimate or correct one, or that there is little difference between the stakeholders' perspectives.

Assumption of a Linear Process

Discussions of educational change assume that it is (or should be) a straightforward, linear process. Improvement can be mandated, taught, and then caught by the proper personnel. This rational bias has been repeatedly documented in the literature of school reform and organizational change and is illustrated in many reports about Jewish education.

Examples abound. Teachers, considered deficient in some content or methodological area, are sent to in-service courses. Students don't attend Shabbat services; as a result, a policy that students must attend is passed. There's nasty behavior among cliques in a grade; therefore, teachers are told to establish a sense of community within the classroom. While none of these interventions is by itself wrong, it is misleading to assume that each alone can change the reality.

Or consider the assumption originally built into a plan to encourage families to save money, to be matched by communal dollars, for children's trips to Israel when they become adolescents. It was assumed that the principals of schools that promoted the plan would tell the teachers to teach more about Israel, the teachers would comply, and the children would learn about the Jewish state in preparation for their trip. This did not happen. (Shevitz 1989) The error lies in assuming that a linear, hierarchical process corresponds to the messy, nonlinear processes at work in schools.

Two core beliefs, which function as theories-in-use, are implicit in the way educational issues are discussed: (1) bureaucratic and hierarchical means of control function when change is initiated; and (2) change processes are linear and sequential. These beliefs may then frame the way in which problems are considered and how people work on them. When problems persist, new structures (e.g., curriculum evaluation committees, teacher supervisors, etc.) are suggested or people are blamed. Teachers—or parents—as saboteurs is a common theme when problems persist. Professional and lay leaders become frustrated when a process does not proceed straightforwardly and they blame themselves or others. (Shevitz 1987) They depict the problems themselves as crises in order to galvanize support although the problems may be complex, chronic conditions with no simple and quick solutions. (Shevitz 1988) The dilemma, of course, is that how we frame problems is related to how we try to solve them.

Teams within Congregations

Recently there has been talk of "congregational teams" that sometimes include lay and professional leaders. Not surprisingly, although teams are formed, they do not necessarily have the capacity to work effectively together. Congregations have been professional hierarchies, with the most status, salary, visibility, and authority residing in rabbinic positions. Note the order in which staff members (indeed, even which staff members) are listed on stationery and bulletin boards, invited to events, expected to attend important congregational meetings, bequeathed parking spaces and secretaries, and so on, to get a sense of how entrenched a hierarchy can be.

Different professionals are also trained differently, usually in programs that isolate them from one another. Their vocabulary for professional concepts varies. Each maintains his or her domain, with the senior rabbi—the "first among equals" (Goldberg 1992)—functioning as the leader. Program areas are relatively independent of one another, so that youth committee policies may contradict the school's and the cantor's, Bar/Bat Mitzvah lessons may interrupt Hebrew classes, and family education programs may compete with sisterhood events. Including lay people further complicates issues of ownership and authority. Developing a team that functions effectively requires reexamining and perhaps adjusting long-established rules, roles, and relationships—a difficult process.

For example, of the congregations in which professional teams had been meeting for two or more years, rabbis, principals, and family educators had very different perceptions about their congregation's goals for family education and the problems that were being encountered. (Shevitz and Kaye 1991) Teams flounder because they are uncomfortable exposing dilemmas and dealing with issues pertaining to process. When at a national training program teams were asked about obstacles they have experienced, they overwhelmingly identified communication as the main problem. "We relate the way we always have and this doesn't work when we're trying to do something new," confided one lay leader. The perceived authority of rabbis prevents open discussion, causing many team members to assume a deferential role and then feel unappreciated for what they could have contributed to deliberations. The rabbis feel burdened by multiple demands and expectations. Principals are unsure of their expertise and feel pushed by rabbis and lay leaders to take on more work. Lay people are uncertain how to relate in a planning capacity to congregational professionals. These positions and the attendant dissatisfactions they generate are not uncommon. They correspond to typical upper, middle, and lower positions in organizations, because people's outlooks are predicted by their position in an organization. (Oshry 1986)

ALTERNATE VIEWS OF CONGREGATIONAL LIFE

The characteristics described in the previous section suggest ways people generally think about—and, therefore, act on—processes of change in Jewish educational settings. By using organizational theory to view salient characteristics of congregational education, we will suggest an alternate way to understand the complex realities of the congregation and its school.

Congregations As Pluralist Environments

Perhaps because we think of congregations as families or membership organizations, it is easy to assume that they are monolithic, with members having similar, if not identical, belief systems and values. There is, however, more diversity in congregations and communities today than ever before. One needs only to look at the 1991 National Jewish Population Study to note the wide range of personal belief patterns, family configurations, and views on Jewish life. While the variation might not be as wide within a single congregation as in a random national sample, it is still significant. A single view of what is important in Jewish life cannot be assumed.

Subgroups hold different perspectives on what is important. For example, a congregation might have one subgroup that is devoted to social action and advances its cause whenever possible; another subgroup might want to promote activities for families with young children; and another might be primarily concerned with social networks. The subgroups have different ideas about what is (or should be) central to the congregation and what should be of secondary importance, and they will look for opportunities to promote their agendas. Reimer (1992) documented how one such subgroup in a rather cohesive congregation challenged the congregation's main ideas about Jewish schooling.

The more symbolically charged an issue is, the greater the likelihood that many stakeholders will want to have a say in the decision process. The fact that they bring different priorities to bear complicates the planning process. (Shevitz 1987) Just as in public education, where a wide range of stakeholders—from neighborhood merchants and retired citizens to parents of current students and advocates for special interests—become involved in public education (Peshkin 1982), so, too, in congregational life many of the stakeholders may not be immediately obvious. They include people with previous and potential attachment to the congregation—from the old-timers who remember how things used to be to families who perceive themselves to be marginal. As discussions about the purpose and nature of Jewish education proceed, the opinions of diverse subgroups will become increasingly relevant to the decision-making process.

The Voluntary Nature of Congregations

This characteristic may seem obvious. Yet it can easily be overlooked during the effort to change a congregation's direction.

People choose to belong to the congregation. They vote with their feet, getting involved with issues that they care about and avoiding others. This sense of caring about some things but not others is related to the congregation's pluralism. People's "agendas" are not bad. They are the issues that those people care about, that bind them to the congregation. The challenge to a change process is to affirm the interests of subgroups while simultaneously expanding them so that many of the groups share at least some aspects of a compelling vision for the institution.

Congregations As Nonrational Organizations

As illustrated throughout this paper, congregations are not usually characterized by coordinated, harmonious, systemic action. Rather, action is sporadic. There is limited coordination among subunits and relatively independent action on the part of leadership. Rather than judging these traits to be problematic, we can turn to organizational theories that aptly describe and explain such nonrational characteristics.

Weick coined the phrase "loosely coupled systems" to describe organizations whose subunits affect one another "(1) suddenly (rather than continuously); (2) occasionally (rather than constantly), (3) negligibly (rather than significantly); (4) indirectly (rather than directly); and (5) eventually (rather than immediately)." (Weick 1983, p. 380) Reacting to numerous studies that demonstrate the lack of coordination and control in educational systems, Weick and others suggested that because "attempts to control and coordinate activities in institutionalized organizations lead to conflicts and loss of legitimacy, elements of structure are decoupled from activities and from each other." (Meyer and Rowan 1992, p. 39) Thus one branch of an organization can proceed one way, while others move in different directions. For example, in the congregational setting an instructor might be teaching modern Hebrew despite the school's stated policy of teaching liturgical Hebrew; the junior congregation might be incorporating very little Hebrew into its service even while the rabbi expects fluent recitation of prayers (although children are not welcome in adult services). Such discrepancies are not necessarily due to individual sloppiness or obstinacy but rather to the organization's complex reality in which processes and policy are loosely coupled as a way to preserve the organization's ability to function. While from a rationalist perspective qualities associated with loose coupling may seem wasteful, they actually enable the system to respond to conflicting, simultaneous needs and preferences—the conditions we expect in pluralist and voluntary organizations. This allows the different subgroups within the congregation to move forward.

Cohen and March use the term "organized anarchy" to refer to a subset of organizations characterized by three traits: (1) problematic goals that seem inconsistent and ill-defined; (2) unclear technology that operates on the "basis of simple trial and error procedures, the residue of learning from the accidents of past experiences, imitations, and inventions born of necessity; and (3) fluid participation so that participants vary among themselves in the amount of time and effort given to the organization as do, over time." (Cohen and March 1983, p. 3)

These characteristics capture basic qualities of congregational life. Operating in voluntary and pluralist contexts, different individuals and subgroups have different goals for the congregation. These vary over time and are highly influenced by environmental and contextual factors. Consider, for example, family education. Sensitive to new trends and eager to find solutions to a litany of problems, congregations rushed into family education as if each was discovering in some systematic way the programmatic response to its own specific issues. Once we peel away the layer of sloganeering to probe what is meant by family education, a range of preferences, often vague and sometimes incompatible, emerges. Getting more families to attend services, reaching out to intermarried couples, teaching ritual skills, empowering parents to be their children's teachers, gaining support for the school's programs, making the congregation marketable to young families, etc., become the working objectives. Subgroups and stakeholders hold different views that change over time.

The second characteristic, unclear technology (technology is how things are accomplished), is why we can't codify how a prayer service—or committee—works. When the technology is unclear and highly influenced by contextual factors, intervention is challenging. It is hard to grasp how things are done or to pinpoint problems.

The third trait, fluid participation, is prominent in voluntary settings. Players in congregations have competing commitments. The professional staff members hold multiple responsibilities that are attended to as needed. Laity's involvement is voluntary and is affected by internal and external factors, such as dissatisfaction with a new synagogue policy and the demands of their families or jobs.

These characteristics prompted March to compare leading an organized anarchy to playing soccer "on a round, sloped, multi-goal soccer field (March 1982, p. 36) "Many different people (but not everyone) can join the game (or leave it) at different times. Some people can throw balls into the game or remove them. Individuals, while they are in the game, try to kick whatever ball comes near them in the direction of goals they like and away from goals they wish to avoid."

IMPLICATIONS FOR RECONFIGURING EDUCATION IN THE SYNAGOGUE CONTEXT

Much of organizational theory derives from rationally based models in which means and ends, as well as cause and effect, are assumed to be related directly, efficiency is maximized, and decision making follows a form of logic. As Zey demonstrates in her critique of rational models:

> There is a litany of reasons organizations are not totally rational in pursuit of the dominant coalition's goals. Individual and organizational rationality are not the same. People who make up organizations do not always act rationally in the interest of the dominant coalition or collective good. If they do choose to act in the interest of the dominant coalition or collective good, they seldom have a consistent ordering of goals; they do not always pursue systematically the goals they do hold; there are inconsistencies of individual preferences and beliefs; they have incomplete information; they seldom conduct an exhaustive search of alternatives and they do not always know the relationship between organizational means and ends. (Zey 1992, p. 25)

The analysis offered in this paper is that congregational life is characterized by loose coupling, a pluralistic environment, nonrational decision-making patterns, hierarchical leadership relations, and systems illiteracy. These traits, basic to how congregations actually operate, must be taken into account when plans for adaptation and change are being formulated. Otherwise these traits will derail the best detailed plans. This section suggests several underlying principles for processes of change that recognize and use these characteristics. They focus on three critical concerns: (1) understanding the context of nonrational organizations; (2) strengthening the congregation's culture; and (3) considering how the leadership team does its work.

UNDERSTAND THE ORGANIZATIONAL CONTEXT

Think about Congregational Change and Become Aware of Nonrational Characteristics

A first step in the process of change is for the leaders spearheading the effort to confront how they think about congregational change. To a large extent this will determine how they approach the process and content of change—what they will consider relevant and what they will ignore. It is likely, as Zey argues, that thinking is structured by the rationalist assumptions that permeate our culture's beliefs about organizational life. Without an alternate model, congregational leaders might rely on processes that fit their situations poorly and lead to frustration. The following are some examples:

- "Why do we keep returning to the same issue at each meeting?" a rabbi wonders, neither recognizing a garbage can (see p. 168) nor understanding the symbolic importance of the question being discussed. A committee chair, frustrated by the tangential issues that keep coming up, reigns in the discussion, only to see the same issues erupt again and assume a life of their own. The resulting tendency is to clamp down and overtly or covertly enforce rules of relevance. Meetings are tightly structured to avoid open discussion or disagreement; actions are taken regardless of decisions made. People feel misled as they perceive the openness of the process disappearing; leaders feel betrayed as they sense dissatisfaction and opposition.

- "This process is taking too long; after all, how hard should it be to change...?" complains a tired lay leader. Because people assume that change is linear and sequential, they underestimate the amount of time required to accomplish it. Educational change is never a straightforward process. Instead, there are starts and stops, backslides, detours, and sometimes movement in an unanticipated direction, especially when people capitalize on "windows of unplanned opportunity." (Kanter 1985) All this takes more time than expected or allotted, yielding frustration and unhappiness—and sometimes an effort to short-circuit the process. Five years is the minimum amount of time it takes to institute significant change. Only when the flurry of activities and excitement associated with the change subsides can it be known whether the innovation has staying power.

- "That teacher's still doing the same old thing despite the fact that we introduced a new curriculum!" notes an annoyed principal. Because a policy has been mandated, people want to believe its intent will be fulfilled. Innovation cannot depend on bureaucratic roles and rules. (Timar and Kirp 1988)

A consequence of these problems most often is blame, sometimes of self ("If only I had controlled the process better, the discussions wouldn't have fallen apart!") and sometimes of others ("The rabbi let us down!" or "Those lay people really don't care enough about Jewish life!"). [Shevitz 1987] Each of these positions leads to disillusionment.

How the congregation actually works needs to be understood so that energies are appropriately spent during the planning process. The challenge is twofold: understanding how change actually occurs in the messy world of an organized anarchy and knowing how to work in an organized anarchy to achieve results. Thus a preliminary task for congregational leaders is to figure out how they will handle these two complementary needs. Involving people adept in these skills is a good starting point; so is having a group willing to work together, consider their underlying assumptions, and use outside resources appropriately.

Recognize and Use the Unique Way of Making Decisions in Organized Anarchies

The garbage can model describes the decision-making process in nonrational settings. (Cohen, March, and Olsen 1972) With scant information, erratic participation, and multiple and inconsistent goals, decision making is a process rather than a one-time event. It has four relatively independent streams: (1) problems and concerns of people inside or outside the organization; (2) solutions [people's products or ideas]; (3) participants whose involvement waxes and wanes; and (4) choice opportunities or "occasions when the organization is expected to produce a behavior that is called a decision." (Ibid. pp. 26-27) The garbage can catches and contains both problems and solutions that surface.

Several aspects of the decision-making process have implications for how a congregation could proceed to reconfigure its educational offerings. (Cohen and March 1983, pp. 206-207)

(1) Since participants can give only partial and erratic attention to any decision, most issues have low salience for most of the

people most of the time. That explains why people who are prominent through one set of issues seem to fade as others become important. But when a decision carries high symbolic importance to the group or individual esteem—as we might expect if congregational education is actually reconfigured—it will attract attention from a wider range of stakeholders. People who have cared about the school and/or congregation, as well as those who are currently involved, can be expected to be concerned and episodically involved in the discussions. To return to March's analogy of a soccer field, these people will try to kick their balls toward the goals they think are appropriate.

(2)   The system has high inertia. Because the subunits in a loosely coupled system act relatively autonomously and have their own partisans and participants, it is difficult to start things that require coordinated effort by the whole. Once started, however, they are hard to stop if stopping them also requires coordinated effort.

(3)   Any decision process can become a garbage can for almost any problem. Deliberations about the congregation's educational activities are likely to attract a wide range of issues and, therefore, they are likely to be an institutional garbage can. Having other garbage cans available to absorb some attention and concern will be helpful. Having too many garbage cans, however, will make it impossible for the congregation to focus enough attention on education.

(4)   Because of uneven participation in an organized anarchy, the processes of choice are easily subject to overload. When this happens, decision outcomes are separated from the decision process. The question of how much choice the congregation can handle before overload sets in will have much to do with the eventual outcome.

(5)   The organization has a weak information base. Information about past decisions and events is scant and unsystematic. This gives leaders ample room to maneuver and suggests the wise use of precedent and principle.

The contrast is stark between this decision-making model and the standard description in which alternative courses are investigated and the one that is likely to do the most good (and/or least harm) is selected. It focuses attention on the sporadic influence of people and groups, their inconsistencies, interests, and concerns. It recognizes the limited energy available for system-wide, sustained analysis and action, and it posits that limited coordination and loose coupling will always be part of the institutional picture. Plans need to take these realities into account.

Use the Congregation's Pluralism to Incorporate Ideas and Build Commitment

It is easy to get something done when a group of like-minded individuals is convened. Discussions can be short, disagreements can avoided, and goals can be quickly identified. Even when individuals with divergent views meet, there can be a tendency toward premature settling on the solution that is assumed to be acceptable to respected leaders. (Janis 1979)

If a congregation is to look at itself critically and creatively, it ought not rely on a relatively homogeneous group that supports the projected changes. It needs to develop a process that involves its multiple stakeholders and subgroups. This includes the obvious (e.g., sisterhood members who attend weekly classes, youth group participants, parents of nursery children, teachers in the school, etc.) and the invisible (e.g., uninvolved members, seniors, people without children, people who have dropped out because they felt unwelcome or unserved). If the goals are to develop an educational approach that reflects the community's aspirations and needs (rather than one subgroup's prescription for what it wants to see happen to others in the community) and, at the same time, to build commitment to the approach, then the meaningful involvement of many different subgroups is critically important.

Used appropriately, stakeholders and subgroups can actually improve the plans. And the fact that they have helped define the plans increases the probability that the plans will actually be enacted more or less as intended.

Including the diverse groups entails several challenges. People who may not usually be part of a decision-making process need to be recruited and helped to feel at ease and important. Doing this can be difficult since there are networks among the involved people for whom the congregation functions as a club. Newcomers need information and acknowledgment. They need to feel comfortable. The usual participants need to be helped to hear what these new-comers have to say. Norms for open discussion and good listening must be established.

Participants also need to be encouraged to stay in the process. Given the limited decision-making energy in an organized anarchy and its erratic participation patterns, people who spend time have considerable influence over decision outcomes because they become information sources in an information-poor world and are, therefore, taken seriously. Since they participate regularly, they are likely to be present when important issues are discussed. Routes back into a process after people miss key events are important, as are ways of keeping the multiple stakeholders informed about developments. Clear records of events and deliberations and frequent telephone contact are ways to keep people involved. Learning to encourage those people who feel their ideas are different—or, to use Cohen and March's phrase, " to facilitate the opposition's participation"—is also essential. The idea isn't to "sell" one view of what Jewish education should be but to help the stakeholders define what it will be, based on an articulated and examined vision.

Account for Loose Coupling in Organized Anarchies

While it may be comforting to imagine a congregation in which all elements are coordinated, that is not a viable model. As has been already discussed, loose coupling gives an organization the flexibility to proceed. It is an adaptive response to the pluralist environment, unclear technology, and multiple goals. Some consideration should be given to developing plans that capitalize on traits while bringing all domains within the system into more regular, systematic contact with one another.

Another aspect of loose coupling is the relationship between problems and solutions. In the garbage can model, the solutions offered are more often some group's or individual's idea of what ought to be. They are linked to problems for instrumental reasons. In that way, Cohen and March argue, solutions can be seen a proceeding problems. People tend to promote the same solutions repeatedly. While this is often thought of as "their agendas," it can be seen as solutions looking for problems to attach themselves to, thereby promoting the possibility that the solutions will be adopted.

Severing the comfortable but naive relationship between "the problem" and "the solution" will help a congregation use ideas that have been floating around more freely. It will also reduce the tendency to simplify problems and claim that one solution will solve them—all within a relatively short time frame. This will change the understanding of the planning process itself. Change will not be seen as an episode or intervention but as a process of continual improvement.

171

DEVELOP A STRONG CONGREGATIONAL CULTURE

A challenge to any organized anarchy is how to maintain a strong, identifiable culture that transcends its many subgroups while allowing them to thrive. Because the subgroups have different ideas about what is important, there must be a clear notion of what values are shared by the multiple subgroups without trivializing their very real differences. This helps stakeholders together define what they want to achieve. A congregation in which the different subunits are so powerful and self-identified so as to preclude an overall sense of "our" congregation will probably be unable to mobilize for system-wide change. An important aspect of the process of change, then, involves strengthening the culture of the congregation.

Build Commitment to the Congregation

Schein's work on organizational culture indicates how the basic beliefs and assumptions that a group holds about the nature of reality, human nature, and the relationship of the organization to the environment shape its culture and determine what adaptations and developments will prove viable over time. The beliefs are expressed through the organization's values (reasons for doing things a particular way) and artifacts (the organization's visible and audible expressions) that further reinforce its fundamental beliefs. For example, a congregation that thinks of itself as "classy and serving an elite population" might have a slick, professionally made set of brochures to give to prospective members, whereas a congregation that prides itself on being "grass roots" and "participatory" will have brochures that look quite different. In each case the artifact is proclaiming the institution's values.

Culture is the glue that binds people to an institution. It gives meaning to their actions and provides rationales for their plans. It provides a predictability that helps people know how to behave. Thus the same person who acts one way at a Federation executive committee meeting will act quite differently at a congregation meeting. Culture most often operates unconsciously; it is both "the way things are done around here" and the assumptions that underlie why they're done that way.

Members have come to understand and expect the congregation to be a certain way. The process of change, especially an attempt at transformational change, challenges the culture. Leaders must help people stay connected and committed by focusing attention on the congregation's beliefs and values—those things that bind people to the congregation and one another. Stories about "our way" of doing things, attentiveness to the artifacts, and interpreting what is happening in terms of "our identity" will reduce the turmoil that can accompany change.

Recognize the Limitations of Any Intended Change

Persuasive research shows that if an intended reform is at odds with a group's basic assumptions, it is unlikely to take hold. (Sarason 1971; Schein 1992; Rossman, Corbett, and Firestone 1988) To use an example from the previous section: If the new educational plan for the "grass roots" congregation relies on hiring a cadre of professional staff, it is unlikely to be accepted by the congregation. This is not merely because congregants are not used to having several professional staff members. More significantly, the staffing patterns reflect their beliefs that member-based activities allow people to express and explore their own Jewish identities in ways that would not be possible if they had to rely on professionals. Such a reform, if it is not rejected outright, will be diluted in implementation until it more easily fits the organization's belief system. Understanding the culture and the level at which proposed changes challenge the culture is essential to the success of any process of change.

Envision the Whole: Cultivate Systems Literacy

Given people's compartmentalized views of congregational life, it is important to help them consider the whole congregation. Since perspectives are shaped by positions within organizations, and since it is difficult for people to see the same situation from the perspectives of others, this challenges any process of change. Not attended to, systems illiteracy is likely to yield stereotypical and rigid thinking that prevents collaborative deliberation, planning, and action and results in the tops, middles, and bottoms typically believing certain things about their own reality and that of other people. (McGonagill 1992; Oshry 1986)

> [Tops], as shapers, experience a world of complexity and responsibility in which there is too much to do, too little time, and thorny problems to solve. They face an ever-changing environment and conflicting inputs.... They have a strong sense of being visible, accountable and at risk. They take failure personally. This leads them to hold onto responsibility and control as a strategy for survival. (McGonagill 1992, p. 10)

Because of these pressures, "tops" feel misunderstood. Immersed in detail and demand, they are often unable to step back and provide the vision that is needed by the whole system. "Bottoms" generally feel vulnerable and powerless, as if they have little control over what the system will do to them. They see problems that the tops and middles haven't solved and are suspicious of new efforts at reform and improvement. They believe they need to protect themselves against "them." Because of their vulnerable position, they develop defensive patterns of action and thought. "Middles" are caught between the conflicting expectations of the tops and bottoms and the dynamics of their own world: "In trying to please [the tops and bottoms] they satisfy neither. By allowing themselves to be pulled into the middle, they lose autonomy and thereby sacrifice the independent perspective that might have enabled them to bring tops and bottoms together." (McGonagill 1992, p. 13) Applying these categories to synagogue leadership is not hard. It is interesting to note that one person can belong to two categories; for example, a family educator may be a bottom when working with the rabbi and principal but a top when working with staff and volunteers.

Systems literacy can be taught. (Ibid.) The starting point is helping people understand systems thinking: "... there is no outside; you and the cause of your problems are part of a single system." (Senge 1990, p. 67) The ability to shift perspectives, check assumptions with others, and understand the ramifications of a proposal on other subunits within the congregation become essential ingredients for developing viable plans for congregations. How this is done will vary in different settings. In some, an outsider might help participants learn to question perceptions and assumptions; in others, people involved in the process may have (or learn) the tools to do so. In either case, the group would be helped to incorporate procedures that enable participants to probe the meaning and intent of others.

Although McGonagill's suggestions are aimed at labor negotiations in public education, several of them can be applied usefully to congregations:

- Use strategic planning as a way to develop a shared definition of the problems and a commitment to ways of dealing with them. This will forge a nucleus of key people who have the opportunity to work closely together and overcome systemic stereotypes.

- Create vehicles to enhance system understanding.

Well-conceived forums, task forces, and experiential activities are powerful tools.

- Provide training in systems literacy. In supportive settings help people see the typical mind-set of their position and confront its pitfalls; help them reframe the situation and consider new actions and possibilities.

- Provide training in the skills of collaborative dialogue. Help participants learn ways to express their ideas so that other people can hear them and develop their own ability to listen to others.

- Focus on the receiver of services: The internal dynamics and tensions of a process of change can easily distract people from the goals of the process. Focusing on the experiences of the people being educated could "provide an integrating framework around which to mobilize the different parts of the system." (McGonagill 1992, pp. 29-30)

These suggestions will create conditions of mutual trust and collaboration by seeing and interpreting ambiguous events from others' perspectives, giving appropriate benefit of the doubt, and responding in ways that take into account others' realities and interests. Such habits of perception and behavior are a critical resource.

See the Planning Process As a Ritual with Group Maintenance Functions

With all the attention that is paid to the difficulty of processes of change, it is easy to forget that it is also an elaborate ritual that serves many purposes for the group. It defines "us" and "them," reaffirms commitment to "our way," lets people gain attention, links the congregation's future to its past, and provides vehicles for shared celebration and, sometimes, mourning. (Bolman and Deal 1991) Participation can be pleasurable: it identifies and certifies who and what is important, worthy of celebration and incorporation. (Sproull, Weiner, and Wolf 1978)

Ceremonies that confer legitimacy and status can be developed. (Deal and Kennedy 1982) From the simplest expression of participation—logos, tee shirts, newsletters, etc.—to elaborate symbols of the direction being taken—community conversations, questionnaires, planning documents—attentiveness to the symbolic aspects of the process of change buoys people's beliefs that something good

175

will result. This encourages their ongoing involvement since the process is both important and fun!

Develop Transition Rituals

As new directions are considered, the need for ritual grows more intense. The congregation as an entity and its individual members are being asked to accept change. We are aware from psychological, sociological, and organizational studies of the profound difficulty of change for individuals and groups. Loosening people from their conceptual moorings, change creates ambiguity and tension. Even when change is expected and desired, people struggle with the powerful feelings that it evokes. In organizations such feelings are often expressed in the form of a sudden deification of past procedures—even when those very procedures were the catalyst of people's insistence on change.

Creating transition rituals can help the institution and individuals cope with the prospect of change. Rituals can acknowledge the "death of the old way" while reaffirming its legacy and value. People need to mourn that loss and be helped to connect what has been meaningful in the past to the institution's future. (Peshkin 1982) Deal, for example, describes the cathartic effect of the Ma Bell coffin made by employees after the divestiture.(Deal 1986) Manthei portrays the painting of the walls of a consolidated school by parents as group recognition by them that despite the tensions of the past months, they must provide a constructive educational environment for their children. Helping people enact their losses, commitments, and aspirations through a scripted ritual can enable them to move more readily through the process of change.

CONSIDER HOW THE GROUP'S SPEARHEADING THE CHANGE PROCESS WORKS

Most congregations have little experience using teams for significant work. If the process of reconfiguring education is to involve the range of stakeholders in a meaningful way, both lay and professional leaders will have to play critical roles in that process. With little experience in ongoing planning, they will need to attend to ways in which they can work together effectively.

Define the New Group Process

Working in a pluralist environment is a new challenge to professional and lay leaders. Each has a voice. Many have a legitimate say in the organization's future. This presents challenges to the individuals and the system. How can the members of the working group (or leadership team) define responsibility, authority, power, and control in a way that makes use of their expertise, while acknowledging different roles and perspectives? On what basis will the opinions of different subgroups be evaluated? How will decisions be made? Will they be subject to review and adaptation? These questions did not have to be openly explored when people assumed a set of rules about professional and lay roles that were based on hierarchical institutions.

Who makes the decisions and how? Whose views are advisory? How will the range of positions be interpreted and transformed into a plan? Clarity on these issues provides flexible boundaries to a nonrational process while fostering widespread involvement and ownership.

Cultivate Symbolic Leadership

Leadership in a pluralist setting requires special orientations and skills on the part of professionals. Friedman, writing from a family systems perspective, shows how both consensus and charisma-driven rabbis flounder in the congregational setting. He develops a model of self-differentiation and nonreactivity. Sergiovanni, Deal, and others show that the leader who merely facilitates the process, in the style of a civil servant, may find it impossible to steer a course of action. The danger that too many unorchestrated voices may make noise but yield no sustained theme is real. On the other hand, the leader who uses charm and persuasion to sell a vision of how Jewish education ought to be loses the ongoing commitment of others to the process.

Recent literature on professional leadership in pluralist settings develops the notion of symbolic or cultural leadership. (Sergiovanni 1989; Deal 1986; Schein 1992; Peters and Waterman) The underlying premise is that the organization is a culture to which participants bring their need for meaning-making and coherence. The role of the leader is dynamic and integrative. By giving meaning to events, aspirations, and processes, the leader helps participants maintain commitment to the enterprise, understand its values, and engage in its activities. In a pluralist setting in particular, to which individuals and groups come with different assumptions, the symbolic leader develops a context in which all can function. Defining a vision that reflects the aspirations and needs of many of the stakeholders is an important element of success. While different writers emphasize different activities, they agree that the leader's primary task is to develop allegiance to the organization's dynamic culture. Storytelling, creating rituals and ceremonies, using symbols, connecting with people, and interpreting reality are more important for this kind of leadership than technocratic expertise is. Schein asserts that the primary function of the leader is to understand an organization's culture and to help it adjust to new challenges.

Insure That the Process Symbolizes the New Approaches

How the reconceptualization process is conducted seems as important as the content of its discussions. If people talk of an inclusive approach to Jewish education but conduct the planning with just a few *machers*, that tells onlookers that not much will be changing. If the professionals say they will empower lay people but instead hoard information and retain decision-making authority, it will not be possible to build a team committed to the imagined changes. If lay leaders disregard the professionals' perspectives, they perpetuate an us-them attitude that reinforces defensive behavior. Like a school's hidden curriculum, the way the business of change is conducted will deeply affect the possibility of change. Consequently several questions should be asked during the time that a process is being designed and initiated:

- Are diverse stakeholders being included?
- Is weight being given to disparate opinions?
- Is the process collaborative?
- Are formal, hierarchical relationships being maintained?
- Is it clear how decisions will be reached and by whom?
- Are there ways to help the group learn together?
- Is attention being focused on what is shared and valued by congregants?
- Is a stance of experimentation and exploration being maintained?
- Does the process foster people's identification with the vision of the institution as it might become?
- Does the process take into account people's need for continuity as well as change?
- Has the group developed norms of open, civil, and respectful deliberation?
- Has the group defined clear, respectful ways in which to handle problems?

ENABLING CHARACTERISTICS OF RECEPTIVE SETTINGS

Several traits have been associated with successful processes of change in other nonprofit sectors. Given congregations' organizational characteristics, the following seem relevant to the likelihood of a successful process of change.

Stability and Harmony of Key Personnel

The presence of knowledgeable lay and professional personnel who are respected by the congregation and its subgroups is needed to lead a community through a process of change. The latter have several roles. A local champion   disseminates new approaches throughout a system. The figurehead or leader of change is a person who embodies the values of and is perceived by others as the one who makes things happen. (Pettigrew, Ferlie, and McKee 1992) For example, in the case of supplementary school consolidations, there needed to be clusters of interest; a solitary lay or professional leader was unable to catalyze change. (Shevitz 1987) Since the reconfiguration process will look at the whole congregation, it is reasonable to assume that the senior rabbi must support the endeavor even if others will play a more vital role in the day-to-day proceedings. The need for symbolic leadership cannot be underestimated. Consider the example of a congregation whose associate rabbi was working hard to develop an alternative *minyan* that included a potluck lunch. The caterer tried to claim the luncheon space for *B'nai Mitzvah* on several *Shabbatot*. Despite the entreaties of the *minyan* participants and associate rabbi, upheaval continued until the senior rabbi publically stated that a group that wants to pray and eat together should have priority with regard to the use of space in this congregation. No objections followed and, as a result, the group had permanent space every Shabbat afternoon for as many hours as it wanted. According to the associate rabbi and *minyan* members, it was the clear statement from the senior rabbi that signaled the primary importance of the *minyan*. (Shevitz 1993)

The ongoing involvement of lay people and a rotational system that insures continuity are important, especially since participation in an organized anarchy is erratic or episodic. Training people who will assume leadership in the future is important.

Another aspect of this is the ability of key leaders to work together. Although they may not yet have the skills of ongoing collaboration, they need to have enough trust and confidence to learn how to collaborate in a long-term process. Having a history of harmonious relationships is helpful.

Key leadership should also be committed to an institution for several years. Since change brings upheaval, there must be some stability among professional and lay leaders.

Financial Resources

At the start of the process of change, it is not possible to know how much money will be needed to develop and sustain the new approaches. The congregation must have a general sense that it will be able to find sources of funding as needed or have an idea of how changes will be otherwise instituted.

Time and Energy

Time and energy are precious commodities in an organized anarchy. For the development and maintenance of the kind of preparatory processes envisioned in this paper, there must be some time and energy available within the institution. This suggests that the congregation should not be simultaneously involved in several major, time-consuming processes. If it is, the congregation will not have the ability to sustain the work, thereby resulting in upheaval and frustration. Are respected, fair-minded lay leaders available with the interest and ability to lead the process? According to Cohen and March, people with the time to persist in the process will exert great influence on it. Is there staff to assume the requisite responsibilities in a timely fashion? Can the congregation's attention be captured and held at this point in time for this particular issue?

Aspects of the Congregation's Culture

Most of the recent literature about institutional change asserts that the environment more than the individual makes the crucial difference in whether innovation will be accepted and, once it is accepted, whether it will endure. This is directly related to the organization's culture—how it understands its reality and its underlying belief system. Aspects of an organization's culture that seem relevant (Pettigrew, Ferlie, and McKee 1992; Kanter 1985) are:

- A history of experimentation, risk taking, bias toward action, and "can do" beliefs about itself.
- A willingness to learn.
- A commitment to exploring goals and values.

- Flexible mechanisms for planning and development.
- A strong sense of pride in past achievements.
- Use of its own (internal) human resources.
- An appreciation for the political dynamic of the process of change, especially bargaining, campaigning, lobbying, coalition building, and sharing information, rewards, and recognition.
- An integrative approach.

In the congregational setting the following factors may be central:

- A belief in the importance of Jewish learning not as a tool for building the congregation but to enrich the lives of Jews.
- A commitment to the congregation as a community in which all have an interest.
- A sense of the congregation as a responsive and adaptive community.
- A commitment to experimentation and learning.

Aspects of Receptive Contexts

Derived inductively from their long-term, large-scale study of innovation in mental health settings in Great Britain, Pettigrew, Ferlie, and McKee have developed a heuristic of eight linked factors that support the process of change: (1) environmental pressure; (2) supportive organizational culture; (3) change agenda and its locale; (4) simplicity and clarity of goals and priorities; (5) cooperative interorganization networks; (6) good managerial-clinical relations; (7) key people leading change; (8) the quality and coherence of policy. (Ibid.)

These factors are interrelated; each affects the others. They are dynamic; they can build, shift, change, or recede according to planned and unplanned circumstances. Although they are present in all the sites, they are constructed idiosyncratically so that the overall picture looks different in the different locations.

We do not know which if any of these factors are the most relevant in the congregational setting. Many seem appropriate, but whether these are the critical factors that support the process of change will only be known if comprehensive and systematic study of the Experiment in Congregational Education and other current attempts to transform congregational education is conducted. The literature of institutional change agrees on the following general point: There is a complex, dynamic interplay between clarity and ambiguity, environmental factors and individual leadership, and supportive policy and flexible strategy in successful processes of change. How exactly these are played out in the congregational setting has yet to be determined.

REFERENCES

Bolman, L., and Deal, T. *Reframing Organizations: Artistry, Choice and Leadership.* San Francisco: Jossey-Bass, 1991.

Cohen, B. *Case Studies in Jewish School Management.* Orange, NJ: Behrman House, 1992.

Cohen, M., and March, J. *Leadership and Ambiguity.* New York: McGraw Hill, 1983.

Cohen, M.; March, J.; and Olsen, J. "A Garbage Can Model of Organizational Choice." *Administrative Science Quarterly* 17 (1972).

Deal, T. "Educational Change: Revival Tent, Tinkertoys, Jungle or Carnival?" In *Rethinking School Improvement: Research, Craft and Concept,* edited by A. Lieberman. New York: Teachers College Press, 1986.

Deal, T., and Kennedy, A. *Corporate Culture.* Reading, MA: Addison-Wesley, 1982.

Dorph, S., ed. *Project Ezra: A Handbook for Training Congregants as Rabbinic Aides.* Los Angeles: Pacific Southwest Region of United Synagogues of America and Torah Aura, 1989.

Goldberg, David. "First Among Equals: The Rabbi as Leader of the Professional Staff Team." Unpublished substantive paper. Hornstein Program, Brandeis University, 1992.

Huberman, A. M., and Miles, M. *Innovation Up Close: How School Improvement Works.* New York: Plenum Press, 1984.

Israel, S. "Working Group Draft Proposal: Institutional Readiness." Unpublished paper. Commission on Jewish Continuity of Boston's Combined Jewish Philanthropies, 1993.

Kanter, R. M. *The Change Masters: Corporate Entrepreneurs at Work.* New York: Simon & Shuster, 1985.

Janis, I. "Groupthink." In *Organizational Psychology: A Book of Readings,* 3rd ed., edited by D. Kolb, I. Rubin, and J. McIntyre. Englewood Cliffs, NJ: Prentice-Hall, 1979.

Louis, M. "Organizations as Culture-Bearing Milieux." In *Organizational Symbols,* edited by L. Pondy, G. Morgan, and T. Dandridge. Greenwich, CT: JAI Press, 1983.

Manthei, J. "A Reconsideration of School Consolidation Issues." Unpublished qualifying paper. Harvard Graduate School of Education, 1983.

March, J. "Footnotes to Organizational Change." *Administrative Science Quarterly* 26 (1981).

_____. "Theories of Choice and Making Decisions." *Society* 20:1 (1982).

Martin, J.; Feldman, M.; Hatch, M.; and Sitkin, S. "The Uniqueness Paradox in Organizational Stories." *Administrative Science Quarterly* 28:3 (1983).

McGonagill, G. *Overcoming Barriers to Educational Restructuring: A Call for "Systems Literacy."* Arlington, MA: McGonagill and Associates, 1992.

Meyer, J., and Rowan, S. "Institutionalized Organizations." In *Organizational Environments: Ritual and Rationality,* 2d ed., edited by J. Meyer and W. R. Scott. Newbury Park, CA: Sage, 1992.

Olsen, J. "Choice in an Organized Anarchy." In *Ambiguity and Choice in Organization,* edited by M. Cohen, J. March, and J. Olsen. Bergen, Norway: Universitetsforlaget, 1976.

Oshry, B. *The Possibilities of Organization.* Boston: Power and Systems, Inc., 1986.

Patterson, J.; Purkey, S.; and Parker, J. *Productive School Systems for a Nonrational World.* Alexandria, VA: Association for Supervision and Curriculum Development, 1986.

Peshkin, A. *The Imperfect Union: School Consolidation and Community Conflict.* Chicago: University of Chicago Press, 1982.

Pettigrew, A.; Ferlie, E.; and McKee, L. *Shaping Strategic Change.* London: Sage, 1992.

Project Ezra: A Handbook for Training Congregants as Rabbinic Aides, edited by S. Dorph. Los Angeles: Pacific Southwest Region of United Synagogues of America and Torah Aura, 1989.

Reimer, J. "Between Parents and Principal: A Social Drama in a Synagogue School." *Contemporary Jewry* 13 (1992).

_____. *The Synagogue as a Context for Jewish Education.* Cleveland: North American Commission on Jewish Education, 1991.

Reisman, B. "The Role of Lay People." In *What We Know About Jewish Education,* edited by S. Kelman. Los Angeles: Torah Aura, 1992.

Rossman, G.; Corbett, H. D.; and Firestone, W. *Change and Effectiveness in Schools: A Cultural Perspective.* New York: State University of New York Press, 1988.

Sarason, S. *The Culture of the School and the Problem of Change.* Boston: Allyn and Bacon, Inc., 1971.

Schein, E. *Organizational Culture and Leadership,* 2d ed. San Francisco: Jossey-Bass, 1992.

Scott, W. R. "The Organization of Environments: Network, Cultural and Historical Elements." In *Organizational Environments: Ritual and Rationality,* 2d ed., edited by J. Meyer, and W. R. Scott. Newbury Park, CA: Sage, 1992.

_____. *Organizations: Rational, Natural, and Open Systems.* Englewood, NJ: Prentice-Hall, 1981.

Senge, P. *The Fifth Discipline.* New York: Doubleday, 1990.

Sergiovanni, T. "What Really Counts in Improving Schools?" In *Schooling for Tomorrow: Directing Reforms to Issues That Count,* edited by T. Sergiovanni and J. Moore. Boston: Allyn and Bacon, Inc., 1989.

Shevitz, S. *An Evaluation of the Israel Incentive Savings Programs.* Unpublished paper. JESNA, 1989.

_____. "Changing Jewish Schools." In *What We Know About Jewish Education,* edited by S. Kelman. Los Angeles: Torah Aura, 1992.

_____. "Communal Responses to the Teacher Shortage in the North American Supplementary School." In *Studies in Jewish Education,* vol. 3, edited by J. Aviad. Jerusalem: Magnes Press, 1988.

_____. *Supplementary School Consolidation in the Jewish Community: A Symbolic Approach to Communal Decisions.* Unpublished dissertation. Harvard University, 1987.

_____. Unpublished program evaluation. Avi Chai Foundation, 1993.

_____. *What Have We Learned? An Evaluation of the Projects of the Task Force on Supplemental Education.* Newton, MA: Bureau of Jewish Education of Greater Boston, 1992.

Shevitz, S., and Kaye, J. "Writing for *Sesame Street,* Directing Traffic, or Saving Souls: Jewish Family Educators Describe Their Practice." *Journal of Jewish Communal Service* 67:4 (1991).

Sproull, L.; Weiner, S.; and Wolf, D. *Organizing an Anarchy: Belief, Bureaucracy and Politics in the National Institute of Education.* Chicago: University of Chicago Press, 1978.

Stern, J. *Ten Studies of Jewish Schools.* New York: United Synagogues of America, 1993.

Timar, T., and Kirp, D. *Managing Educational Excellence.* New York: The Falmer Press, 1988.

Tucker-Ladd, P.; Merchant, B.; and Thurston, P. *School Leadership: Encouraging Leaders for Change.* Cambridge, MA: National Center for School Leadership, n.d.

Weber, M. "Basic Sociological Terms." In *Economy and Society,* edited by G. Roth and C. Wittich. Berkeley, CA: University of California Press, 1947.

Weick, K. "Educational Organizations as Loosely Coupled Systems." *Administrative Science Quarterly* 21 (1976).

_____. "Management of Change Among Loosely Coupled Elements." In *Change in Organizations,* edited by P. Goodman and Associates. San Francisco: Jossey-Bass, 1983.

Zeldin, M. "A Framework for Understanding Change in Jewish Education" In *Studies in Jewish Education,* vol. 2, edited by J. Aviad. Jerusalem: Magnes Press, 1984.

_____. "In Yesterday's Shadow: Case Study of the Development of a Jewish Day School." Unpublished paper. Conference of Research in Jewish Education, 1989.

Zey, M. "Criticisms of Rational Choice Models." In *Decision Making: Alternatives to Rational Choice Models,* edited by M. Zey. Newbury Park, CA: Sage, 1992.

REIMAGINING CONGREGATIONAL EDUCATION

A CASE STUDY OF A WORK-IN-PROCESS

Linda Rabinowitch Thal

An Opening Caveat

t is difficult to tell a story while one is at its midpoint. The conclusions drawn today will undoubtedly appear simplistic, perhaps even mistaken, in the light of tomorrow's developments. Even more difficult is the challenge of locating the proper voice with which to recount a story one is witnessing from multiple perspectives. By academic training I am an anthropologist, by profession a Jewish educator, by affiliation a congregant, by birth and personal commitment a member of *Am Yisrael* with a stake in its future, by religious need a Jew in search of deeper connections to the wisdom and meaning inherent in Jewish tradition. The voices attached to these various perspectives all appear in this paper. Often they are mixed—or shift without warning—as they do inside me, as I witness the process of educational change unfold. Consequently the view presented in this paper must be considered a personal one, although I do believe its elements are broadly shared. It has benefited from the suggestions of and feedback from many of those who have participated in the process it attempts to describe.[1]

THE SETTING—AN INTRODUCTION TO
LEO BAECK TEMPLE

Leo Baeck Temple is a Reform synagogue on the Westside of Los Angeles, an affluent community neither fully urban nor quite suburban. Since it was founded in 1948, the congregation has had only two senior rabbis.[2] Its first cantor served the congregation from 1954 until his retirement in 1988. Congregants became accustomed to this stability of clergy, and to a large degree they identified the temple and its culture with the values, interests, and styles of these three men.

The congregation's membership, as well as its leadership, remained remarkably stable, especially compared to that of other synagogues in the Los Angeles area. In large measure this could be attributed to the congregants' respect for and personal loyalty to their rabbis and cantor. It could also have been the result of the temple's decision to limit its membership. Although waiting lists have existed only a few times in the temple's history, the ideology of limited membership contributed to the congregation's sense of itself as being unique.[3]

The defining ethos of Leo Baeck Temple was social justice. The congregation embraced the Reform movement's conception of prophetic Judaism and was proud of its reputation as a "social action temple." What Leo Baeck Temple was and what being Jewish meant were clear. An unspoken corollary of the congregation's strong identification with social action was a sense that too strong an endorsement of or too much attentiveness to particularistic Jewish practices and beliefs would distract congregants from devotion to the universalism of the prophetic message.

The synagogue developed a style of both worship and program that was characterized by dignity, self-reflectiveness, a sense of esthetics, and decorum. The Leo Baeck Temple Way meant a certain elegance of style. In the domain of aesthetics, standards were diligently maintained. In matters of Jewish belief or practice, the value of individual autonomy was paramount. Adult education was highly intellectual. It often focused on the issues of social justice current in the secular culture. Questions about God or prayer tended to be explored in the context of comparative theology. As was generally true in the 1960s and 1970s, discussions about personal religious experience or meaning were rare. Jewish practice and skills were taught infrequently. Children's education operated in a separate sphere. The detached set of classroom buildings was emblematic. One went out (the doors) and down (several sets of stairs) from the temple to the school.

At approximately the same time that the cantor and the founding rabbi retired, the congregation established an early childhood center that offered both preschool and toddler programs. The decision to expand the congregation's program in this direction was the direct result of the leadership's realization that the congregation's membership was aging. Even though the number of temple members had remained stable, the population of religious school-aged children was declining dramatically.[4]

Thus two significant changes were introduced into the

congregational system simultaneously: a new group of young families and new (women) clergy.[5] The latter accelerated the emergence of women into lay leadership roles, placed greater emphasis on the connection between study and personal experience, and introduced new forms of spiritual expression.

The nature of the new families was different as well. Many were attracted to the temple less by its reputation for social activism or intellectual solidity than by its early childhood center, which had won an award for its architecture and accolades for its developmentally sound educational program. These families were joining the temple at an earlier point in their family's life cycle than previous generations of new members had. They also made different demands on the temple. They wanted programs that served their needs directly, particularly programs that were child- and family-centered. Although most of the adults had relatively little Jewish knowledge or experience, they were receptive to Jewish practice and celebration if they strengthened their families and connected them to community. Similar value changes were taking place in both the secular and Jewish communal culture at that time. Separating out the influences of each factor is less important for this analysis than noting that the process of educational change was introduced during a transitional period in the congregation's history. The opening of the Early Childhood Center and changes in the clerical leadership were as responsible as anything else for the fact of change. Educational planning helped to give the change shape, direction, and intentionality.

Initiating a Process of Educational Change

In response to the changes the congregation was beginning to experience, it was proposed that my part-time position as principal of the Sunday morning religious school be made full-time. Supervision of the heretofore separate afternoon Hebrew school would be added to my responsibilities.[6] This proposal provided me with the opportunity to think about education at Leo Baeck Temple systemically, and I concluded that both the types of educational programs we were offering and the role of education itself in the life of the congregation required reexamination. It seemed impossible to teach about prayer if a praying community did not exist, futile to teach a Hebrew heritage vocabulary of ethical concepts in the classroom if no one in the synagogue was using these words in reference to the acts of *gemilut chasadim* they performed, shortsighted to proclaim Jewish study a lifelong pursuit if only preadolescents and retirees were engaging in study with regularity. I concluded that I was not interested in an expanded position if educational programs continued to be defined as discrete spheres of activity with religious school, Hebrew school, adult education, early childhood education all separated from one another and from other aspects of temple life. Unless we viewed education from a holistic, congregational perspective, it felt that my work would be limited to the introduction of small-scale, incremental changes that would leave the real educational – and Jewish – issues unaddressed.

Consequently I recommended that my new job include the development of this kind of perspective. Suggesting that the reenvisioning of education at Leo Baeck Temple would require "a process that would have broad congregational support, involvement, and investment in whatever direction(s) we might choose to go," I proposed the creation of a special task force on congregational education that would do the following:

- Explore the issues of our vision and goals for education on all levels of congregational life.

- Brainstorm many and experiment with the implementation of a select number of educational programs.

- Examine the goals and structure of our children's educational program in the context of this new, larger congregational perspective.

- Develop a set of proposals based on its year of study, discussion, and experimentation.

- Take responsibility for introducing the congregation to and involving congregants in the new programs.

Neither the congregation nor I knew exactly what we were undertaking. Had we known the enormous investment of time the process would require, the amount of energy each change would demand, the impact that every educational decision would have on other aspects of congregational life, or the fact that our work would result in the need to find new sources of funding, we might have hesitated to begin.

In fact, when I first proposed this agenda, "educational improvement" and "long-range planning for education" were the only concepts that were effective in explaining my goal to the participants and the congregational leadership. The notion of developing a new educational vision made little sense to them. Moreover, had it been possible in those early stages to spell out the vision that was to emerge, that vision would probably have been perceived to be unrealistic, if not altogether threatening.

The realization that this process was about fundamental change[7] emerged slowly. As the ramifications of the ideas we were discussing became apparent, participants began to realize that we were not just dealing with the educational system. While our mandate may have been to reenvision education at Leo Baeck Temple, participants began to remark, "If we really do this, *everything* could change!"

CHANGE AS A PROCESS

The process of change that has emerged at Leo Baeck thus far appears to be less linear and our organizational model less "rational" than what is outlined in much of the planning literature we originally consulted.[8] We invented as we proceeded. I believe that we functioned in this way because it was an effective means of introducing change in a congregation that was accustomed to stability. Understanding and working within the culture of a congregation is critical, even if the ultimate goal is to change that culture.

Chronology and Structure of the Planning Groups

Until now, our process has occurred in three phases. Over time, these phases have become overlapping rounds of planning and implementation that have lost their discreteness. The first phase lasted ten months. It dealt with vision, mission, and philosophy. Phase two dealt with the further development and application of these abstract principles to two specific aspects of our educational program. At the end of six months, the philosophy and goals for family education and Hebrew education had been developed and the initial steps for programmatic change had been proposed. By phase three, each planning group was working on several levels: implementing the first round of change, developing plans for more profound change, and working toward an understanding of how their work fits into the larger vision.

Phase One

Although Leo Baeck's established programs of children's and adult education were strong, they existed in a vacuum. During a period of low volunteerism in the temple as a whole, the Religious School Committee dissolved itself, saying that "things are great – call if you ever need us." The Adult Education Committee sponsored excellent programs but did not work from an overview of the congregation's educational needs or mission. At one point it briefly considered renaming itself the Adult Programming Committee because that name better described how it saw its role. There was no setting nor shared language in the congregation for serious discourse about Jewish education—its importance, goals, or complex nature. Therefore, the first challenge was to help the new Educational Task Force reach a level of reflectiveness and sophistication about Jewish education that would enable its members to enter into such a conversation.

The Educational Task Force met twelve times over ten months. Early meetings combined discussion of a series of articles that task force members read as "homework" with exercises designed to help them explore and articulate their own Jewish values and goals. For example, in preparation for one meeting every member was asked to present a metaphor about Jewish education. We used these metaphors to elucidate the issues we would need to address in future deliberations.

One member suggested that Jewish education was "like pearl formation: There has to be an irritant," she said, "to stimulate development." Two members argued about whether Jewish education was more like a jigsaw puzzle that can be assembled starting with any piece or more like a house whose foundation must be laid first. Such conflicting metaphors stimulated the group to debate whether there is a basic core of Jewish information, skills, and competencies that everyone needs to have. The member who compared Jewish education to "trying to grab a handful of sand" provoked us into looking at the way defeatist attitudes limit our vision.

The metaphor that has been reinvoked most frequently throughout our planning process is the one that compares Jewish education to a health food restaurant.

> It serves meals that are tasty, attractive, nourishing, and good for you. People come because it has wonderful food and they can get something special here that they don't ordinarily eat at home or at other restaurants. There is a philosophy or set of values that underlies what is served. Sometimes people come because of that. Sometimes they just come in for something different. Then they are exposed to the values espoused by the restaurant and may start to think differently about how they eat. The restaurant becomes so successful that it opens a take-out counter so that people can take home the food

they've sampled and enjoy it in their own home and share it with friends. Finally the restaurant opens a health food market so that people can learn to make this kind of food for themselves, experiment with the ingredients, use their own creativity, and put the ingredients together in new ways that suit their own tastes.[9]

The health food restaurant metaphor has helped us discuss the extent to which Jewish education should be consumer-driven and the extent to which it should be vision-driven. It has been particularly important in helping us remember that this is not an either-or choice, and it has helped us clarify the dynamic and complex relationship between the vision that motivates educational leaders and the interests, felt needs, and receptivity of the congregants they serve.

At another early meeting we broke up into groups to answer the question: If we had the most solid and successful program of congregational education imaginable, how would things appear five years from now on a Sunday morning at Leo Baeck Temple? At the Ploni family's Shabbat table? In a car pool going home from Hebrew school? On Super Sunday? While the task force was not yet able to imagine wildly, its members found this exercise liberating. They saw that they could search for new possibilities.

Eventually common themes began to emerge in our discussions. Over several months we wrote our Mission Statement, an elaboration or commentary on the Mission Statement that we call our Rashi,[10] and a set of eighteen We Believe Statements (containing other ideas, both philosophical and methodological, that we had come to believe about Jewish education). Over several months, drafts of these documents were introduced and discussed with nine stakeholder groups.[11] Revised versions, along with a proposal for the next phase of the planning process, were adopted by the Board of Trustees. (See Appendix for these documents.)

Phase Two

The proposal for this next phase of planning mandated the establishment of a standing committee called the Coordinating Committee for Education. It replaced the original Educational Task Force. The chair of the Coordinating Committee for Education became a member of the Board of Trustees. The core of the new CCE was composed of *vatikim*, "old-timers," from the original task force. The committee was expanded to include members of the other temple committees whose programs had educational components, as well as additional members at large.

191

Both the structure and content of phase two were influenced by the need to address a particular educational issue: the time required for the study of Hebrew. Had we not needed to turn our attention to Hebrew school issues at this point, the process might have taken shape quite differently.

For several years there had been mounting pressure from parents to reduce the educational program for children who were studying Hebrew from three days a week to two. This change had already been made by virtually every other Reform congregation in our city. With the senior rabbi's support I had maintained that a decision about the days and hours of Hebrew school could only be made in the context of larger educational issues. After ten months of discussing vision, mission, and goals (and after a further year's delay due to my sabbatical), it became clear that this issue had to be addressed.

In order to keep the discussion about the Hebrew school schedule related to educational goals, we decided that the CCE would be divided into two working task forces: one on Hebrew education and one on family education.[12] We believed that if the CCE understood itself to be a unified body with an educational agenda, the Hebrew Education Task Force's recommendations would more likely be educationally sound as well as politically acceptable.

The strategy worked well. By meeting together as a group twice before breaking up into separate task forces, the Coordinating Committee for Education did, in fact, come to perceive itself as responsible for looking at specific areas of education from a holistic or congregational perspective. The two task forces understood that their mission was to implement the foundational documents that had been created by the original planning group. Their subsequent joint meetings combined study sessions that reinforced this perspective with opportunities to consult with one another on work-in-progress.

During the six months of phase two, each task force met five to six times; the entire CCE met four times. The Hebrew Education Task Force made changes in the structure of the Hebrew school, reducing the number of days of study for the Alef class but increasing the number of hours of study per week for all other students. It also mandated the introduction of Hebrew into the curriculum of the primary grades of the religious school and the hiring of a Hebrew specialist who would facilitate the incorporation of Hebrew into the religious school program. It recommended the development of a program of Hebrew cultural literacy that would be based in the school but would extend to the adult community. Finally the Hebrew Education Task Force committed itself to exploring and promoting the role of Hebrew for the entire congregation.

The Family Education Task Force mandated a number of new projects: a weekly family education newsletter, an opening-day-of-school program and a series of follow-up meetings in homes designed to get the family education message across, a family *Shabbaton*—"Shabbat retreat"—a project to get Jewish books into families' homes, the expansion of our home sukah-building project, the creation of family study *chavurot*—"fellowship groups"—a new pre-Bar and-Bat Mitzvah program that included twelve parent-child sessions, a new consecration ritual, and the development of congregation-wide *Gemilut Chasadim* Days (opportunities for congregants of all ages to participate in community service projects linked to the study of texts about *gemilut chasadim*—the "doing of good deeds").

Phase Three

Phase three has combined the implementation of the two task forces' program and policy decisions with processes of formative evaluation and continued planning. The Hebrew Education Task Force invited consultants from the Bureau of Jewish Education to work with it and the faculty on a process of goal-free evaluation. That evaluation has led to a decision to reorganize the Hebrew curriculum around syntactic structures instead of vocabulary. The Hebrew Education Task Force has also begun to develop programs and projects that address its primary goal: the development of a synagogue culture that supports and affirms the importance of Hebrew and Hebrew education.

The Family Education Task Force has continued to develop its vision of a comprehensive plan for congregational education.[13] It has applied for two grants that will enable it to implement its program.

The work of this third phase has brought us face-to-face with a new set of questions: How do we assure that what we are doing is not just adding programs to a congregation that is already rather well programmed? How do we knit things together? How do we develop each project so that it is rich and multifaceted, so that it has a deep and lasting effect on individuals and on the culture of the congregation? How do we make sure that the cumulative effect of our programs does, in fact, move us toward our emerging vision of an integrated learning community?

The CCE realized that before it continued to generate more programs, a new round of system-wide envisioning and planning was needed to address the above questions. A third task force, which includes four past presidents of the congregation, has been assigned the task of tending to the larger vision. Their tripart mandate includes:

1. Promoting awareness of, support for, and participation in all levels of education at Leo Baeck Temple. Articulating the message that Leo Baeck Temple is (becoming) a "learning community."

2. Conceptualizing and strategizing the planning process as it moves forward. Determining which steps come next.[14] Thinking about how to integrate the pieces. Being the keepers of "the big picture." Asking the underlying goal/philosophy questions.

3. Finding resources for implementation. Looking at the personnel, space, and monetary needs created by the changes in our program.

The third task force, composed as it is of experienced temple leaders (including the chairs of the Family and Hebrew Education Task Forces), has moved ahead with policy and programmatic decisions more quickly than the preceding groups did. For example, it tends to imagine on a grander scale, proposing a set of educational goals to be achieved by the congregation's fiftieth anniversary (in 1998). Although education was not previously an area of primary concern for most members of this task force, their collective learning curve has been rapid. Most would have had little patience for the slow, deliberative, nonlinear style of the previous task forces' early work. Now that the direction in which we want to move is becoming clearer, these well-seasoned congregational leaders who "know how to make things happen" have an important role to play.

Admittedly there is a somewhat cumbersome nature to the structures that have emerged. There was far more elegance to the design of the CCE as it was originally proposed to the Board of Trustees. However, the congregation's need to resolve "the Hebrew question" called for something else. The organizational culture of the congregation was also a factor in shaping the process. Because the temple had little prior history of serious educational deliberation by congregants, it was most effective to focus the work of the task forces on discrete areas of educational interest or concern. By concentrating on the specific issues of Hebrew and family education, it was possible to develop a large group of knowledgeable and reflective educational advocates and planners.

The Nature of the Process

Like the planning structures themselves, the process unfolds in ways that are often unanticipated. We often plan two or three meetings ahead but just as frequently revise our plan as we approach each meeting. We encounter points of turning, moments when it clearly seems time to move on to the next task, but we cannot always predict precisely when these moments will occur. Particularly for the early stages of each task force, we have devised exercises and strategies to help move the group forward and give structure to its discussion. Frequently, however, the group's energy cannot be contained by the structure, and the conversation takes on an excited and somewhat jumbled quality. Time for unstructured exploration needs to be allowed before the group can refocus.

The CCE chairperson has described this process as "a ritual dance—a lot of back and forth before everyone can agree on how the work will be done." The result is often close to what she and I have anticipated, but the plan sometimes has to reemerge from someone in the group before there is consensus about proceeding. There are frequently a few members who protest and ask, "Do we know enough? Are we really ready to go on?" The rest of the group usually convinces them to try. Eventually we reach a critical moment at which time the work plan emerges.

Although the process doesn't have linear neatness, we've isolated a number of elements that have been important in moving us forward: constructing the planning group, establishing the leadership team, focusing and investing the group, engaging in a process of self-education through reading assignments and inviting guest experts, distributing narrative meeting minutes, and procuring the support and participation of the full temple staff, especially the senior rabbi.

1.   Constructing the Planning Group

Our goal was to include as broad a representation of the congregational membership as possible. It was important that the many voices and perspectives that exist in our temple be heard. We also wanted to insure our ability to reach back into the congregation through the committee's members to engage and enlist the support of the congregation's many constituencies. We included members at different stages of the life cycle and different stages of temple membership (ranging from founding members to members affiliated less than a year) on each task force. There were supporters and critics, educational consumers and congregants on the periphery, women and men, religious school faculty members and older students, people who hold leadership roles and former activists whom the senior rabbi hoped to reinvolve in congregational life. The members represented many Jewish perspectives and many professions. Representatives of key temple committees (Adult Education, Early Childhood, Youth, Social Action, Finance, and Membership) were included.

2.   *Setting Up the Leadership Team*

The single most important step in establishing the planning group was selecting the chair of the original Educational Task Force and its successor, the CCE. The chair needed to be someone of long-standing stature in the congregation; someone with good leadership skills, particularly in areas that would complement mine; someone who grasped the mission and was excited by it; someone who would be an advocate and ally for Jewish education but whose Jewish background and communal experience were strong enough to provide her with an independent perspective. We used similar criteria in selecting the chairs of the three task forces within the CCE.

Achieving the proper balance between lay and professional leadership was critical. This can be a complex, even delicate matter. In many ways the goal of this process is the empowering of lay people to take responsibility for and give direction to their own Jewish lives. At the same time rabbis and educators have Jewish expertise and passions that can both inspire and guide the process. Moreover, they are the professionals who will be responsible for implementing the new vision and the new programs. It is a challenge for the professionals to provide guidance without being overly directive, to maintain momentum without pushing too forcefully in their own preferred direction.[15] How the lay-professional roles evolve in each congregation will be influenced by personal leadership styles and skills, but they also must fit (or be consciously designed to change) the organizational culture of the congregation.

3.   *Focusing and Investing the Planning Group*

The initial process of group formation is critical. It was essential to give each group a clear sense of its mission and to assure participants that their service would be stimulating, their time well spent. The rabbi's presence and his charge to each group at its first meeting sent a powerful message about the importance of their work. The introductory activities, which extended over several meetings, were designed to provide information about the current educational program and clarify the group's mission. The activities also foreshadowed the complex and challenging issues with which we would be dealing. We introduced planning language and concepts, engaged in envisioning exercises, and assigned reading and other homework.

4. Engaging in a Process of Self-Education through Reading

Reading assignments have played an important role in all phases of the process. They have provided both general orientation and specific information for participants who had previously done little systematic thinking about Jewish education. Committee members have consistently come to meetings well prepared and stimulated by their reading. They have spoken with excitement about this process of self-education. They value the insights they have had about their own Jewish commitments as much as their new appreciation of the complexities of Jewish education.

More than anything else, the reading assignments gave participants a shared language and a common set of conceptual frameworks. A paper by Jonathan Woocher[16] provided the CCE with a set of concepts for exploring what it means to be a learning community. That paper crystallized the CCE's understanding that education was the vehicle through which we could create the kind of community in which the education that we really want to be doing will "make sense."

The reading assignments required and helped to elicit a serious commitment from task force members. During the six months of phase two, the whole CCE read three papers and each task force read four or five additional articles. It was important for the selected readings to be directly relevant to the specific issues a task force was confronting at the time and appropriate for the level of sophistication its members had developed until that point.

5. Inviting Guest Experts

Inviting guest experts has been another key element in the CCE's self-education process. At the first meeting of the Hebrew Education Task Force, Dr. William Cutter, professor of Modern Hebrew Literature at HUC, spoke about the role Hebrew has played throughout history in the life of the Jewish community, the role language plays in cultural transmission, and the particular ways in which Hebrew plays this role within Jewish culture. Had the members of the task force not been provided with this kind of background, it would have been very difficult to move them away from their immediate preoccupation with the narrow problem of how many days per week the Hebrew school should meet.

Dr. Cutter provided some of the concrete information about Hebrew and language acquisition that the group members needed in order to wrestle with their dilemma, but his visit also had symbolic importance. The presence of a scholar and the intellectually challenging nature of his presentation underscored the importance of the Hebrew Education Task Force's deliberations and the significance of the issues the task force would be addressing. By the end of that first meeting, the group was already talking about extending the use of Hebrew in the congregation. One of the most ardent proponents of a two-day-a-week (rather than a three-day-a week) program remarked, "You know, I'd never realized that studying Hebrew is about more than Bar and Bat Mitzvah. I just didn't get it. We have to let parents know that Hebrew connects you to the Jewish people across history and geography!"

When Dr. Isa Aron, professor of Education at HUC, presented the first draft of her article that appears in this volume to the combined task forces of the CCE, it had a similar impact. Both task forces could hear in that paper echoes of the issues they had been discussing. Dr. Aron's paper excited them because it restated some of the things they had been saying to one another, because it helped crystallize some of their still inchoate thoughts, and especially because it invited them to think more boldly. It gave them permission to depart from existing paradigms.

All guests have been carefully selected and briefed on the work of the task forces. In each case, the experience of interacting with someone from outside our own system has had the dramatic effect of moving the group to a new level of sophistication and insight.[17]

6. Distributing Narrative Minutes

Another important tool in our process has been the use of narrative minutes. Six to eight pages of single-spaced minutes are sent to task force members after each meeting. The notes bring anyone who missed the meeting up-to-date; they also remind those who attended of what was said.

Because the early discussions of each task force are often conversational and meandering, the meetings result in few definitive conclusions, making it easy to forget all but the key points. Narrative notes allow ideas to stay alive and be recalled months later when we are ready for them or to ripen slowly as they come into clearer focus with each subsequent session.

The minutes also keep our rabbis informed and orient the guest experts. Guests arrive fully aware of the issues about which the task force has been deliberating and with an understanding of the group's level of sophistication. Narrative minutes also assure members that they have been heard and that their ideas have been recorded, even if they have not been fully accepted.

I often use the minutes to do some of the teaching or commenting that I have refrained from doing during the meeting itself. When I insert my own comments, I bracket them to make it clear that they are postmeeting additions. In this way I have been able to provide additional information, raise questions, or clarify issues. Occasionally I include excerpts from articles that address issues raised during the meeting. We have also invited task force members to contribute their own postmeeting reflections or proposals, and several have done so.[18]

7. Procuring the Support and Involvement of the Rabbi and Full Staff

As the educator, I have been the primary staff person for the CCE, but clearly no effort of this kind can be successful unless the entire professional staff is aware of what is happening, is supportive, and is working as a team. The rabbi's involvement is essential. Congregational life is such that there are some things only senior rabbis can do. Capturing the attention or igniting the imagination of the congregation is at least partly dependent upon the rabbi's strong and frequent endorsement of the new vision and the new programs. The senior rabbi needs to be willing to risk some uncertainty (and occasionally some messiness) and must be prepared to step in at times to push across certain barriers — political, economic, and personal.

Ultimately, however, success depends upon the involvement of the entire professional staff. For example, the assistant rabbi, who staffs the Adult Education Committee, selected congregants who had served on the Family Education Task Force as chairs of the Scholar-in-Residence Weekend Committee and the Adult Retreat Committee. She saw that as a way of insuring that the educational concepts and perspectives that the CCE had been developing would also take root in the Adult Education Committee. The executive director frequently makes a point of talking about our changing view of education when he meets with potential new members. His sensitivity to and support of the space, budget, and support staff needs of our changing educational program are critical. When the Family Education Task Force suggested that consecration be recognized as a rite of passage for the parents of children beginning their religious education, as well as for the children themselves, it was the cantor who helped fashion the new ritual.

Inclusion of the religious school faculty proved to be a particularly sensitive matter. Teachers who had been at Leo Baeck for a number of years suddenly found themselves being asked to implement ideas and programs that had been generated by strange new groups called task forces. Although members of the faculty sat on these task forces, the change was disconcerting for some, especially because in their early stages, it was difficult to explain what these groups were and what could be expected of them.

The Up Side and the Down Side of Process

Although the full vision toward which we are working may not be clear yet, the process itself has been transformational. Among its by-products are the expanding circles of congregants who can enter into increasingly sophisticated discussions of the kind of Jewish lives they want to create for themselves and their families, the renewed energy for programmatic experimentation and risk-taking, the emergence of new congregational leaders, and the lively intergenerational exchange that takes place between newer and older temple members. Engagement in this process is exciting, at times exhilarating, for both staff and lay people. Ideas and insights often come with stunning rapidity. As one CCE member noted, "No matter how tired I am before a meeting, I am always energized by the evening's combination of unstructured dialogue and structured goal setting."

There are also, however, periods of confusion and uncertainty.[19] Progress is uneven. At times we seem to be stalled in our tracks; there are moments when it seems like everything we have been working toward is about to fall apart. Every decision made, confirmed, and even acted upon at one meeting may need to be rediscussed and reconfirmed several months later. When attendance at an experimental program is low, we are reminded how much groundwork still needs to be laid before the rest of the congregation's thinking catches up to that of the CCE. Only persistence and *emunah* sustain us through these moments of retrenchment. We have learned to regard them as episodes from which we can learn about the areas of genuine tension that exist in the synagogue and those that are inherent in the process of change itself.[20]

Anatomy of a Hot Spot

It is not surprising that our most difficult moments to date have occurred as a result of the Hebrew school issue. This "hot spot" predated the planning effort and was, although somewhat indirectly, intimately linked to its initiation. Certainly it would be preferable to begin a planning process free of such back-burner issues, but that may not always be possible. While we did anticipate many of the difficulties the Hebrew Education Task Force encountered, we were unable to navigate a smooth course around them.

By the time the Hebrew Education Task Force got underway, there was intense pressure from parents to reduce the number of days per week that students preparing for Bar and Bat Mitzvah attended Hebrew school. The issue had been raised several times, both by the Board of Trustees and by the membership committee. Several members of the task force were themselves advocates of such a change. The task force, nevertheless, accepted the challenge of trying to make decisions about the Hebrew program based on educational goals as well as parent satisfaction and membership retention. The conflict between what the task force members came to believe about the importance of Hebrew education and the obligation they felt to be responsive to the legitimate needs of congregants proved to be wrenching. There were several tense, even anguished meetings.

The Hebrew Education Task Force struggled with the different meanings that the term "time" has in this issue. Is it clock time: i.e., hours and days and numbers of trips to the temple? Seen from this perspective, time is a scarce resource. Families feel pressed for time, and each additional hour taken away from a child's homework or after-school activity time or added to a parent's commute time is perceived as adding stress to the family's life. But time has more symbolic meanings as well. Statements about time can be statements about degree of commitment. Time can be treated like a yardstick that measures a family's priorities, with the number of hours of a child's week devoted to Hebrew study compared to the number of hours spent in other extracurricular activities.[21] It is no easy matter to separate these various meanings.

Pressed by time, the task force made an initial decision that precipitated significant upset. There was bad feeling about both the decision and the decision-making process. In hindsight, we can identify four factors that contributed to the creation of this brief crisis. They represent areas of unresolved ambiguity both in the political culture of the synagogue and in the change process itself.

1. The issues with which the Hebrew Task Force was struggling were incredibly complex. Members had been exposed to an enormous amount of new information – about the history and structure of the Hebrew language, about various rationales for teaching Hebrew, about the multiplicity of goals possible for Hebrew instruction in supplementary schools, about the existing Hebrew programs in our community, about the structure and curriculum of our own program. They had also discussed the nature of children's schedules, the stresses on working parents, traffic and carpooling problems. Members were on information overload. Their questions sometimes indicated that they were having difficulty processing so much new information. At times task force members could not see the logical inconsistences in the solutions they were proposing. It remains unresolved in my own mind how much complexity can be handled by a group that starts out with little educational expertise. Such a group is dependent on the educator's or on guest experts' interpretations of educational information. Given the limited amount of time they can spend on research and self-education, lay people may find themselves having to accept or reject interpretations that they are not fully able to evaluate independently.

2. While the task of the CCE was defined as educational planning, the Hebrew Education Task Force was playing on a political as well as educational field. Issues of parent satisfaction and even membership retention were discussed, but how the political factors were to be weighed against the educational issues was not adequately addressed. Consequently some task force members contended that "certain voices weren't being heard," while others believed that illegitimate (noneducational) points of view were being given too much weight.[22]

3. The relationship between lay authority and professional authority was also not confronted directly. When lay people are asked to devote a great deal of time and thought to issues, can their role be merely advisory? To what extent are educators or rabbis willing to empower lay people to make decisions that they will not want to implement? Ambiguity was built in from the

beginning because while these key questions were considered, they were left unresolved.

4. Finally the Hebrew Education Task Force was working against a deadline. As the end of the year approached, parents of third-grade students were waiting to be informed about the structure of the Hebrew program that their children would begin in the fall. At its final scheduled meeting for the year, the task force found itself trying to make a complex set of decisions under enormous time pressure. The hour was late, but everyone was too exhausted and tense to suggest that an additional meeting be held. Repair of both the decisions the task force made that night and its equanimity took several weeks and the senior rabbi's facilitation.

These factors were not, of course, working in isolation. It was their combined force and the messy way in which they were intertwined that brought us to crisis. Had we not been working against a deadline, it is possible that we could have negotiated our way through the first three elements of systemic "irrationality." With or without the pressure of time, however, it is important to recognize the potential inherent in these factors to act as land mines. Nevertheless, the overriding lesson is that with enough good will, openness, and genuine dedication to Jewish learning on everyone's part, even moments of crisis can be worked through to a positive end.

It is probable that the task force was able to weather this difficult period because the group had participated together in a process of study that committed it to the importance of Hebrew. That commitment became the common ground upon which all members stood. After six weeks (and three very difficult meetings), the Hebrew Education Task Force got itself "back on track." The group spent time analyzing what had gone amiss in its process as well as reconsidering and revising its original decision. In the year since its crisis, the task force has worked harmoniously and productively.

The task force perceives the revised set of decisions it reached to be a workable compromise. While it made some concessions to families' needs to make fewer trips to the temple, it added both time and resources to the program in order to enhance the quality of Hebrew education. The task force also committed itself to work toward the development of a synagogue culture that supports and affirms Hebrew and Hebrew education.

Change Begins to Break Out of the Structures and Becomes System-wide

There are certain kinds of trees that, once they are established, drop shoots of their own and after a fashion give birth to unanticipated offspring. A good change process probably works like that, too, and we are beginning to experience something comparable at Leo Baeck. Here are a few examples:

- Congregants have begun to propose and take responsibility for implementing programs they want to see happen. Historically programming at Leo Baeck Temple has been largely staff generated. In the past when program ideas did come from congregants, the primary responsibility for their implementation has been assumed by the staff. But now, particularly in the areas of family programming, parents are developing their own vision of what could or ought to be. In those cases in which the staff responds, "Yes, that's a terrific idea, but the staff [or current committees] can't take on one more program," congregants are beginning to respond, "Well, what if *we* can make it happen?" A programmatic approach to High Holy Day child care and a congregation-wide program of *Gemilut Chasadim* Days have been developed with the staff's providing guidance and resources but with congregants' bearing more responsibility for designing as well as implementing these programs than in the past. These changes represent more than new or enhanced programming. They may prefigure a fundamental shift in the role that congregants take in shaping their own Jewish lives and their synagogue community.

- Members of the CCE have begun to introduce both the concepts and the visions they have been discussing in the task forces to other committees on which they sit. The Families with Children Committee incorporated *divrei Torah*—literally, "words of Torah"—into their meetings because its chair had been present when the idea was developed in the Congregational Education Task Force. "Starting with a *d'var Torah* has changed the whole tone of our meetings," she reported back. It was at an earlier meeting of the same committee that a member of the Family Education Task Force, exasperated at committee members' hesitation to move ahead on a particular project, cited the article she'd been reading in the task force and said, "Come on! We just have to suspend our disbelief and act as if we already are the community we want to become!"[23]

- Hearing that discussions about the need to create community in the temple were also taking place in the educational task forces, the membership committee proposed a monthly Sunday morning bagel bar. They set up tables with coffee and Jewish periodicals over which parents could meet and schmooze after bringing their children to religious school. Coordination between the Membership Committee and the Family Education Task Force has furthered both groups' agendas.

- The CCE's ongoing articulation of the need to develop a vision has begun to affect other areas of temple life. As the idea of developing a vision penetrates the thinking of the Board of Trustees and various temple committees, there is some confusion about how the emergence of a truly shared vision can be fostered in a congregation that seems so much more diverse than it once was. A strategy for creating a coordinated vision has not yet been clarified, but the very fact that the question is being asked is likely to contribute to the creation of greater synergy among the groups that are doing the asking.

THE CONTENT OF CHANGE
Does the Emperor Have Any Clothes Yet?

Sometimes I wonder where this is all leading or whether it is leading anywhere at all. Is change really taking place or does the process merely feel exciting? Are the changes cosmetic and superficial, or will they be deep and profound? Will lives be changed and the synagogue transformed? Is a unifying vision emerging, one that will help us articulate who and what we want to become, one that can guide its own further unfolding? Or will we be one of the congregations about which Shevitz would write "more of the same but thoughtfully" or "business as usual"?

About the process of personal transformation, Adin Steinsaltz makes the following observation:

At every rung in [the] ascent... [one] perceives mainly the remoteness. Only in looking back can one obtain some idea of the distance already covered, of the degree of progress.[24]

Looking back at the process of institutional transformation from our current vantage point, this is what we see. Leo Baeck Temple is no longer the synagogue it once was, although it is not yet fully clear what it is becoming. Nevertheless, some of us do have what we like to call an "emerging vision" of our future. It is not yet widely shared, and its articulation is sometimes vague.[25] Moreover, even those of us who see the vision most clearly are not certain about the extent to which it is achievable.

Since, as Steinsaltz notes, remoteness from the goal makes it difficult to trust that one is really on the path, pausing to reflect on the distance traveled is a helpful exercise. The issues, questions, solutions, and new understandings that have emerged along the way serve as signposts of our progress. Below I briefly discuss three of the areas in which educational discourse in our temple has deepened significantly.

Expanding the Meaning of Being Jewish at Leo Baeck Temple

When the Mission Statement and the We Believe Statements were complete, I found myself vacillating between two opposite reactions. "Have we accomplished anything at all?" I wondered. "This sounds like the motherhood and apple-pie version of Jewish education." When I reread the statements, I was incredulous that these documents had been written at Leo Baeck Temple. Suggesting that Jewish study is not merely an intellectual pursuit but something that should have an impact on one's life was a new concept for this community. Stating that Jewish study ought to be a lifelong activity for everyone and not just a personally satisfying leisure-time pursuit for our "adult-edniks" was unusually prescriptive for Leo Baeck Temple. Asserting that the values of peoplehood and ritual practice must be stressed equally with ethical action could have been regarded as "not Reform." Arguing that the home—and not just the synagogue—was the locus of Jewish living was likely to be perceived as "meddling." As benign as these statements sounded to my Jewish educator ears, cloaked as they were in language that was purposefully gentle, I knew that their content represented dramatic change. So did the Educational Task Force. Each of these statements had been the subject of lively, often heated, debate. There had been disagreement and compromise about both the statements' substance and their exact wording.[26]

In spite of the task force's long evenings of debate, discussions with congregational stakeholder groups about the Mission Statement and other documents produced little opposition. The conversations were animated but abstract. No one, including the members of the Educational Task Force, was really clear about what these statements would mean once they were operationalized.

Noteworthy, however, was the fact that almost every stakeholder group expressed concern that the statements did not address the issue of "how we fit into the American or non-Jewish world."

"I don't feel as if I 'live Jewishly'; that's not universal enough for me; I live as a human being."

"We need to be committed to world issues, not just Jewish issues."

"To identify with Israel sometimes [makes me] feel out of step with the rest of the community. We need to find the ways in which we fit in as well as understand our own marginality."

"How do we relate to, include, and affirm our non-Jewish relations (especially grandparents)?"

The Educational Task Force briefly considered adding a We Believe Statement that would address such concerns but after much debate concluded that the proposed statement sounded too apologetic.[27] The majority believed that the Mission Statement's reference to "the world" was adequately universalistic and saw "no need to defend or dilute the strong Jewish messages we are trying to send."

While few changes were made in the original documents as a result of discussions with stakeholder groups, those sessions accomplished several important things. They extended the new conversation about Jewish education to wider circles within the congregation. They solidified the task force's commitment to the "strong Jewish message" the task force had chosen to send. And they foreshadowed themes to which the CCE has returned as it has continued its work. The Education Task Force's final report to the Board of Trustees contains the following conclusions based on discussions with stakeholder groups:

1. *Participation* continues to be a nettlesome issue. Adult learners were frustrated that adult education programs are not better attended and that a relatively small percentage of the adults in the congregation engage in serious Jewish study.

   Parents of school-aged children exhibited an ambivalence about family education. They clearly understand the importance of adult learning and parent participation. Nevertheless, many are reluctant to commit time to them.

If Jewish education is truly to be viewed as "a lifelong pursuit" that "requires commitment of time and resources for individuals and families as well as for the temple," we will need to educate toward this goal.

With the exception of adults already engaged in regular Jewish study, the congregation still tends to view Jewish education as an activity for children.

2. *The experience of community* (or lack thereof) is a key concern. Every group expressed a strong desire to provide opportunities for people to feel included, welcomed, and connected. Some see an organic connection between the experience of gathering together for ongoing Jewish study and the natural formation of community, while others see Jewish educational programs from a utilitarian perspective – as a means of providing social connections for temple members. The interplay between Jewish study and social connectedness needs to be thought about in a way that acknowledges its complexity.

The tension between serving the special needs of the diverse groups that make up our congregation and bringing the whole congregation together in communal activity needs to be resolved.

3. *Jewish ambivalence/minimalism* continues to characterize discussions about Jewish education. On the one hand, there is a very healthy looking outward to the world, acceptance of diversity, and welcoming of a multiplicity of perspectives. On the other hand, there is excessive concern about being "too Jewish," too insular, too limited. One of our educational goals must be to help individuals balance their universalistic and particularistic concerns.

In the two and a half years since the original Education Task Force made its report to the Board, the culture of the congregation has begun to change and there is less concern or tension around some of these issues. The role of parents as active partners in their children's education has been widely accepted, and many parents have begun to look at opportunities for adult Jewish study as addressing their own needs as much if not more than their children's. As more adults of all ages engage in Jewish study, especially text-based study, the congregation is beginning to define Jewish learning as normative Jewish behavior, not merely the activity of a small, interest-based subgroup of the congregation. As the Hebrew Education Task Force continues to support the introduction of a particularistic Hebrew vocabulary for universal as well as particularistic concepts, the perceived tension between these two perspectives has dissipated. For those who remain uncertain, the senior rabbi acts as the articulator of the message. "If we want to build community here by becoming *ba'alei rachmanut* and if we then want to extend that *rachmones* into the world around us, first we must be grounded more deeply, more firmly in our tradition. [The educational task forces have] launched us on a search for deeper Jewish life by challenging us to know more and do more, and the agenda... is profoundly right."[28]

Was Hebrew Education Too Narrow a Focus for an Effort That Aspires to Fundamental Change?

The changes made by the Hebrew Education Task Force and its endorsement of the importance of Hebrew may seem like rather limited manifestations of the CCE's vision, but the task force's work has begun to have a significant impact on the congregation. Both the task force members and the staff talk about the importance of Hebrew whenever the opportunity arises. The task force's specific decisions are described as part of a larger effort to reexamine the role of Hebrew in the congregation. Because the importance of Hebrew has been officially endorsed, it is possible to use more Hebrew vocabulary in messages sent home to parents and to include a weekly lesson for parents in *L'Mishpacha* (our family education newsletter) on the school's *Milat Hashavuah*—"Word of the Week." A column on Hebrew has begun to appear in the temple bulletin each month. Often it deals with Hebrew cultural literacy and the heritage vocabulary that is being taught that month in the school. Sometimes it contains an explanation of how the three-letter root system of Hebrew allows for a kind of intellectual playfulness and religious contemplation. Once it included a poem about falling in love with Hebrew. Enrollment in the adult Hebrew Marathon program has increased, as has the attendance in our two-year Adult B'nei Mitzvah Class. It is clear that there are more Hebrew readers at Shabbat services, and the rabbi has recently been writing the Hebrew words he uses in his *d'var Torah* at the beginning of Board meetings on the chalkboard in Hebrew letters as well as their transliteration, although many Board members don't yet read Hebrew. The "Hebrew message" is becoming ubiquitous. As one congregant remarked, "You have to be asleep not to know that something new is afoot at Leo Baeck."

Was Hebrew education too narrow a focus? In our case, necessity was the proverbial mother of invention. Working from the premise that language lies at the core of a culture and is one of its most potent elements, the Hebrew Education Task Force has come to believe that steady, persistent emphasis on Hebrew can have a dramatic impact on the congregation and on congregants. Since language conveys the key concepts and values of a culture, possession of a Hebrew heritage vocabulary gives Jews a set of Jewish categories with which to experience and think about the world. Knowing Hebrew can serve as a key to a sense of one's authenticity as a Jew and a perception of oneself as an insider – a member of *Am Yisrael*. The task force believes that Hebrew has the power to transform Jewish life on both the individual and the institutional level. The very fact that Hebrew and Hebrew education is such a locus for conflict is probably indicative of its transformational power. Hebrew lies at the heart of the universalistic-particularistic tension that is undergoing readjustment at Leo Baeck Temple.

Family Education Becomes Congregational Education

From the charge to the Family Education Task Force:

We currently have a strong family education program in the religious school and a number of other family education experiences such as the Family Retreat, our Simchat Torah program, etc. In order to create a coherent program, however, we need to examine the premises on which family education programs are based and to articulate (and sometimes choose among) the various goals that family programs are designed to meet. Should the primary goal of family education programs be to provide knowledge, skills, and motivation for families to intensify their Jewish home life or should the main goal be to provide a positive Jewish experience for families in the context of a synagogue community? Should family education be school-based or completely separate from the school structure? What is a family? Is it possible to create truly intergenerational experiences that include older and younger singles and couples without children, as well as families that are defined by a parent-child relationship? What is the relationship between family education and other congregational programming and holiday celebrations?

Although some parents had expressed resistance to the increase in parent-child programming in the religious school, there were no pressing issues or time-bound decisions confronting the Family Education Task Force. Moreover, in order to compensate for the Hebrew Education Task Force's narrow focus, this group was encouraged to be expansive in its thinking and to define family education as broadly as possible.[29] It was important to remind members regularly to maintain a congregational perspective and not merely imagine programs targeted for families with school-aged children. Indeed, an all-inclusive definition of family emerged early in the process, and the task force defined its target population as "the whole Leo Baeck Temple family." By doing so the task force – like the Hebrew Education Task Force – signaled its understanding of the fact that transformation must occur on two levels: the individual (or individual family) and the community, which nurtures and supports individuals and families.

Early meetings of the Family Education Task Force focused on the need to build community and on the tension between participation based on "enticement" and participation based on "expectations."[30] The themes adumbrated in the original task force's report to the Board of Trustees (participation, community, minimalism/ambivalence) reemerged without any effort by members to raise them directly. For this task force in particular, reading assignments played an important role by introducing educational concepts and Jewish content into discussions that might otherwise have focused on the rather abstract goal of "creating community." An article by Jonathan Woocher[31] gave the task force language for understanding the dialectical relationship between education and community.

When the task force began to generate specific proposals, they fell into two categories. Therefore, one subcommittee devoted itself to creating family education programs (a family *Shabbaton*, a home-starter library project, a Shabbat tape, family study *chavurot*, *Gemilut Chasadim* Days). Another concentrated on projects that would "communicate the family education message" (i.e., education about education, such as a first-day-of-school program, a series of parents meetings in members' homes, a family newsletter, parent forums). The two agendas were, of course, intimately interconnected and reflect, but do not exactly parallel, the enticement-expectations debate. As the Family Education Task Force moved into phase three, it began to conceptualize its goal in a fashion that one member dubbed "spiraling *na'aseh v'nishma*."[32] The label was an acknowledgement of the dialectic between doing and understanding – program and message. The Family Education Task Force has begun to explore the role that consciousness and self-reflection play in Jewish growth both for families (or individuals) and for a congregation. Woocher's insight that we must "suspend our disbelief" and "act as if we were the community we wish to become" is the *na'aseh*. *V'nishma* is the vision, the articulated understanding of what we wish to become as individuals (and families) and as a community. *V'nishma* is thus both the understanding we gain by doing and the inspiration that can further motivate the leaps of faith that *na'aseh* so often requires.

The process of applying for grants helped the Family Education Task Force consolidate its ideas into a comprehensive program of congregational education – a program based on its understanding of the interconnection between doing and understanding and of the power of Jewish study to both affect individuals' lives and create the foundation of a supportive Jewish community.

Toward a Holistic Educational Vision

A central challenge of phase three has been the weaving together of the work of the CCE with the work of other committees and constituencies within the congregation. This task is most easily accomplished by finding areas in which the work of one group connects to that of another.

- The Maot Chitim[33] Committee is composed of older adults. Unless we work with them to be sure that the religious school schedule is taken into account when they plan the distribution of Pesach food baskets, we will miss an opportunity for family education in the area of *gemilut chasidim*.

- The home sukah-building committee of the Family Education Task Force wants to extend sukah building to more congregants who do not have school-aged children. It, therefore, needs to make an alliance with the Environmental Task Force, which wants to use the Sukot festival to sponsor adult study on Judaism and the environment.

- The Hebrew Education Task Force plans to ask the congregational choir to participate in a program on the role of Hebrew in Jewish life. Preparation for such a program could create an educational opportunity for choir members, as well as enable them to make an educational contribution to the congregation.

- The new Task Force on Congregational Education has recommended that every temple committee meeting begin with a *d'var Torah* led by congregants. The task force plans to develop a manual explaining how to prepare a *d'var Torah*, create a *d'var Torah* resource center in the temple library, hold an orientation session at the beginning of each year to introduce committee chairs to the idea, and sponsor workshops to help congregants use study resources.

Much of the work of phase three might be summarized as the CCE's effort to implement We Believe Statement 18: We believe that there should be an element of Jewish study in all temple work.

Interfacing with other committees has not been easy. When other temple committees recognize the commonality of their work with that of the CCE, the difficulties of collaboration are primarily logistical and administrative. At times, however, the CCE's proposals have been perceived as impositions by other committees. The introduction of new ideas or the establishment of a collaborative relationship requires an attitude of respect for the other committee's agenda and a sensitivity to the fact that the perspectives (and especially the jargon) that have developed in the CCE are not yet shared.

The issue of collaboration is only the beginning of a process of more integrated synagogue-wide planning. The Board of Trustees and the Membership Committee, as well as the CCE, are feeling the need to reimagine the temple's future. How central a role the CCE will play in this reimagining is yet to be seen.

Stitching Together the Garment

And of the emperor's new clothes? The pieces of the vision are still being stitched together, but the participants themselves let us know that their lives have already been affected:[34]

"I am particularly aware of the difference it has made to me personally. I am more deeply convinced of the importance of Judaism in my family's daily life. Shabbat has come to our family. Holidays, too. I see this in other families as well."

"This process has helped me reevaluate the attitudes I held when my two daughters were growing up. I regret that this process didn't happen then. I see how much more I could have done to build their Jewish identity. I want to share my new understanding and excitement with other temple members."

"Before I got involved in this process, I didn't even know I had a spiritual side. I was brought up in Israel, and my family was secular. I've learned a lot about education, but I've learned more about myself."

"My husband, who was confirmed at Leo Baeck Temple but had no Bar Mitzvah, is now a student in the Adult B'nei Mitzvah Class. His involvement can be traced directly to the changing and inviting environment that's being created at our temple. The two of us have learned that Jewish learning is a lifelong process, that adults can "pick up the pieces" they missed as children, and that families can and must grow together."

There are moments when it is possible to imagine that Leo Baeck might someday be a radically different place. The transformative vision that has begun to emerge, however, is hardly radical. In Steinsaltz's words it can be understood as "return to prototype."[35]

For a long time, I was puzzled by the frequency with which CCE meetings strayed from the subject of education and focused on the desire for community. At first I concluded that in this increasingly impersonal and fragmented city, people are hungry for a refuge of familiarity, a more intense set of social networks. Until this emotional hunger is satisfied, it seems that congregants cannot think about education (a postmodern version of *Im ayn kemach ayn Torah*, "If there is no sustenance there is no Torah"). Upon further reflection, however, I have begun to believe that what we are really hearing is the expression of a deep longing to be part of a community of meaning, a religious yearning to be a *kehillah kedoshah*—"holy community."

Can a Reform Temple really become a *kahal*, "community"? A *kehillah kedoshah*? It won't be easy. The centrifugal forces of postmodern life are powerful. Most of us experience our lives as so fragmented that it may be difficult for us to imagine wholeness of person, let alone wholeness of community. Belonging to community – particularly a community that strives toward holiness – requires a kind of surrender that challenges the autonomy, rationality, and universalism that Reform Judaism once glorified. How do we begin to build such a *kehillah*?

We are told that the world stands, and consequently any authentic Jewish community must stand, on the pillars of Torah, *avodah*—"worship"—and *gemilut chasidim*. These pillars are also portals, gateways for reentry into Jewish life. We must be prepared to greet congregants at each of these gateways because each individual and family may choose a different point of entry. We must also be sure that the community into which we usher those people who cross any of these thresholds is so vibrant and contains such a richly woven tapestry of Jewish possibilities that they will be drawn from their particular antechamber of welcome into the inner sanctuary of vital Jewish living. This vibrancy depends upon using our stories, our symbols, our language, our rituals, and our texts. It is the interconnectedness of the pathways that lead from one portal to another, that provides the possibility of personal integration and allows individuals and families to experience Jewish life as a whole garment.

That is why no program can be purely Jewish study. At the least it must have threads of spiritual connection. At the least it must indicate how study informs the way we live our life in the world of action. That is why the work of groups like the choir, the Environmental Task Force, the Maot Chitim Committee, and the educational planners needs to be integrated in a manner that goes far beyond coordination or occasional joint efforts. The vision we offer must be one of organic integration for the individual and for the *kahal*.

CODA

When I proposed that David (not his real name) be invited to sit on the CCE, I was recalling a conversation I had had with him at a *shivah minyan* for his brother. "I wish there were other families who were interested in celebrating Shabbat," he told me. "It's hard to get started. It would be easier if there were other families to share it with." I was also remembering a parents' meeting at which David had spoken passionately about his experience growing up at Leo Baeck Temple. "We felt proud to be Jews," he said, "especially proud to be members of Leo Baeck Temple. And we knew what that meant. We knew that being a Jew meant being committed to social justice. It was a clear and powerful message." At the same time David confessed, "We didn't learn much about Jewish practice or about our tradition. I don't know the Torah stories my children are learning in religious school. I feel as if I missed a lot." At the first Family Education Task Force meeting I was surprised and a bit dismayed by David's assertion that the congregation was already asking too much of parents. Instead of insisting that parents join their children at occasional religious school programs, David felt that the congregation ought to be serving the real needs of families.

My question is: How can temple be of service to families with crazy Westside lives? The temple community needs to draw families in and offer help in running their complex lives, perhaps by providing services that also require participation (like cooperative child care). The temple needs to give first. Then people will be ready to give back.

In our family, shopping is a "together" activity. It's something we need to get done, but we make it into family time. We're likely to go to a place where this activity of family shopping can feel like an event, where we get what we need emotionally as well as practically. The temple has an enormous parking lot. Maybe we should hold a farmer's market in our parking lot on Sundays so that families can get their shopping done after religious school. That would also provide an opportunity for families to get to know one another and make us feel like a community.

This suggestion did not strike me as a propitious way to begin our discussion of family education. I wondered where David's desire for a deeper connection to Judaism had gone.

David's fantasy of a Leo Baeck Temple farmer's market resurfaced from time to time. More popular was his suggestion that we establish a mini-café on Sunday mornings so that parents could hang out and read the Sunday papers while their children were in class. However, the task force's efforts moved in other directions.[36]

When I decided to launch a project to encourage members to build sukot at their homes, David was one of the parents I called. "I want every child in our school to know that Sukot is a home holiday," I told him, "and I need a sukah for your daughter's class to visit. I'll be holding a workshop on sukah building and on the celebration of Sukot at my house for every family that agrees to build a sukah and host other temple members." David and his family decided to participate.

At the end of Sukot, David called. His family had loved having a sukah, and he offered to put together inexpensive prefab sukah frame kits that could be provided to other families in the congregation. Although he now sits on the Board of Trustees and the Finance Committee, as well as on the Family Education Task Force, in some temple circles David's primary identity is "The Sukah Man."

The Family Education Task Force hasn't mentioned David's farmer's market fantasy in a long time, but periodically I think about it. I imagine grocery sacks (the ecologically sound canvas ones, of course) with the *brachot* for different kinds of food printed on them. Perhaps there would be signs reading *Pri Ha'adamah,* "Fruit of the Earth," above the vegetable stands and *Pri Ha'etz,* "Fruit of the Tree," above the stands where fruit is sold. I imagine committees that check weights and measures and establish some sort of reapings, gleanings, and *peah*[37] policy that would provide food for homeless shelters. My fantasy includes David's café, with copies of the *Jerusalem Report, The Jewish Journal,* and other Jewish periodicals, as well as the *Sunday Times.* Herschel the Puppet, who tells stories in our religious school along with his ventriloquist friend Ilene, would be there to hang out with the children. Parents would be welcome to listen to the stories they missed when they were kids. Our new library cart with Jewish books, audiotapes, and videos could be wheeled out to the parking lot café.

Why do I find myself musing over such an unlikely possibility? Initially I understood David to be saying that if the temple would serve members' immediate needs, he and others might then be willing to pay attention to its Jewish agenda. But perhaps David was really asking us to address his deeper, existential issues in a way that validated their spiritual essence. Perhaps at the core of his vision lay these profound questions: What would it mean to market as a Jew? How would I feel not to have to separate my role as a consumer from my identity as a Jew? How do I reconcile my desire to be an attentive, nurturing Jewish father and my participation in a world whose demands pull me away from my family?

The synagogue must become a community that addresses these questions not only by engaging members in abstract or philosophical speculation but by weaving opportunities for encounters with Torah, *avodah*, and *gemilut chasadim* into the fabric of daily living. That is the first step to transforming it into a *kehillah kedoshah*, a community of sacred meaning. If the synagogue could become a place in which an ever-increasing number of our human needs are filled—using the idioms, rituals, and values that are specifically Jewish—we would indeed become the kind of community for which our congregants seem to yearn. As long as the synagogue addresses only the Jewish parts of our lives, the notion that our Jewish identity is but one among many coequal roles is reinforced. If, on the other hand, we can make the synagogue into a community that helps us find sanctity in all parts of our lives, we will have established the kind of place that allows us to live with a sense of wholeness.

And the role of *talmud Torah,* "Torah study"? Jewish education is both the object of change and its agent. In our era, Jewish study may be the portal through which Jews most easily reenter the tradition. We need both *Torah lishmah,* "Jewish study for its own sake," and Torah for the sake of revitalizing Jewish practice, Jewish prayer, and Jewish participation in *tikun olam.* In our era *Talmud Torah keneged kulam* may truly mean "The study of Torah is equal to them all because it leads to them all."[38]

APPENDIX

LEO BAECK TEMPLE EDUCATIONAL TASK FORCE
January 27, 1992

The following is a succinct statement of the educational mission of Leo Baeck Temple. In order to make it useful as a planning tool, we have kept it concise and focused. In order to capture some of the richness of thought and meaning that informs the statement, a sentence-by-sentence commentary (referred to as Rashi) has been attached.

Sound planning must not only be based on clarity about our institution's mission but must also be informed by a set of understandings and shared assumptions about the educational enterprise. Accompanying the Mission Statement are a series of statements that lay out what we believe about Jewish education.

Using These Materials

The materials can be used for several purposes:

1. To guide groups and committees as they plan their educational programs.

2. To make an overall evaluation of the temple's educational programs.

3. To set individual goals for adults who want to broaden and deepen their Jewish learning.

Mission Statement

At Leo Baeck Temple we view Jewish education as a lifelong pursuit, leading people to live their personal and communal lives in consonance with Jewish values.

Our educational programs provide the knowledge and teach the fundamental skills of Jewish living so that individuals can feel comfortable as Jews at home, in the synagogue, and in the community and create their own way of living Jewishly. We strive to develop a temple community that embodies Jewish values and looks outward to the world with a sense of responsibility. We foster in individuals and families a sense of belonging to a series of communities: the temple, the Jewish community, Israel, and the world. Our educational programs are designed to help people find personally meaningful ways to worship, participate in Jewish ritual, and encounter the Sacred in their lives.

Rashi on the Mission Statement

1. At Leo Baeck Temple we view Jewish education as a lifelong pursuit, leading people to live their personal and communal lives in consonance with Jewish values.

    a. Jewish education at Leo Baeck Temple should generate an ongoing learning community.

    b. Jewish education should foster in individuals an eagerness to grow Jewishly throughout their lives and a pattern of setting personal Jewish learning goals.

    c. Adults as well as children should be engaged in ongoing Jewish study.

    d. The educational process itself should teach the value of Jewish study and create the expectation that the active pursuit of Jewish learning continues throughout one's lifetime.

    e. Jewish study is not merely an intellectual pursuit; it is a valuing enterprise that affects the way one lives.

    f. Jewish values are manifest in both the personal and the social domains.

    g. Jewish values address both ethical and ethnoreligious concerns.

2. Our educational programs provide the knowledge and teach the

fundamental skills of Jewish living so that individuals can feel comfortable as Jews at home, in the synagogue, and in the community and can create their own way of living Jewishly.

a. Knowledge, understanding, and the ability to put what one knows into practice empower individuals to make meaningful Jewish choices in their life.

b. Although they may be flexibly defined, there are basic bodies of Jewish information and sets of Jewish competencies and understandings that provide a foundation for Jewish comfort and self-esteem.

c. While personal choice about Jewish belief, values, and practices are both honored and encouraged by Reform Judaism, an individual's decisions must be based on knowledge of Jewish texts and traditions.

3. We strive to develop a temple community that embodies Jewish values and looks outward to the world with a sense of responsibility.

a. Our educational programs should strive to facilitate the formation of community at Leo Baeck Temple, as well as meet the needs of students as individuals.

b. The community we wish to create will be one that is informed by a commitment to Jewish values.

c. Concern with Jewish values directs us to consider ever-increasing circles of social awareness, responsibility, and action.

4. We foster in individuals and families a sense of belonging to a series of communities: the temple, the Jewish community, Israel, and the world.

a. An essential part of an individual's experience of himself/herself as a Jew is the sense of being a member of a larger community or a series of communities.

b. Members should experience the temple as a community and not merely as a place that services their Jewish needs.

c. The individual's sense of Jewish community should extend beyond synagogue affiliation to the larger Jewish community.

d. Israel refers to *Am Yisrael*, the "Jewish People," *Eretz Yisrael* refers to the "Land of Israel," and *Medinat Yisrael* refers to the "State of Israel." Our educational programs should help individuals establish and define their particular relationship to each of these aspects of Jewish peoplehood,

e. Jewish education must also help a person define his/her place/role in the world at large.

f. Membership in any of the communities includes both a feeling of belonging and a sense of responsibility.

5. Our educational programs are designed to help people find personally meaningful ways to worship, participate in Jewish ritual, and encounter the Sacred in their lives.

a. Our programs should not only familiarize students with the structural and conceptual aspects of Jewish worship but should also help students explore the ways in which prayer can be meaningfully brought into their life.

b. Our programs should not only teach traditional forms of ritual practice but should also offer opportunities to experiment with Jewish ritual and explore its role in our life.

c. Our programs should help people identify religious moments in their life and provide individuals with the language that will help them conduct their spiritual explorations.

d. Our programs should recognize and encourage people to explore many different ways of relating to God.

We Believe Statements

1. That Jewish education addresses life's important questions * and can touch the deepest parts of people's lives. Our educational programs should help people understand these questions as religious issues and help them develop the inner strength to confront them.

2. That Jewish education should engage the whole person – the intellectual, the emotional, and the spiritual sides of every student.

3. That a basic knowledge of our tradition enhances one's Jewish experience. Our programming strives to provide this, covering the complete spectrum of Jewish content areas: Torah, history, literature (traditional and contemporary), holidays and celebrations, Hebrew, prayer, practice, ethics, values, and the arts.

---

* For example, What does it mean to be a human being? What is the meaning of life? How do I face death? How do I go on in the face of crisis?

4. That study of Jewish tradition and texts helps one develop a system of values for the contemporary world.

5. That Jewish education should result in the building of strong and positive personal Jewish identities. It should help people see themselves as a link in a chain, connected not only to the past but also responsible for the door into the future.

6. That shared Jewish experiences, practice, and discussion in the home are central to a person's Jewish development. Our educational programs foster the creation and strengthening of Jewish homes and provide opportunities for shared Jewish experiences.

7. That Jewish education requires a serious commitment of time and resources on the part of individuals and families as well as on the part of the temple.

8. That the primary responsibility for funding Jewish education rests with the temple community as a whole.

9. That our educational programs must reach out to people of diverse backgrounds and foster respect for different ways of living and believing.

10. That while there are diverse groups with particular needs within the congregation, our temple educational programming must be broad enough to serve the entire congregation, encompassing crossgenerational programs that appeal to participants of varied ages, family status, and Jewish backgrounds.

11. That learning may require nontraditional structures and may employ a wide variety of forms and modes of study (intellectual, emotional, interactive, artistic, structured, informal, etc.).

12. That Jewish education should be both creative and joyful. It should challenge as well as inform and attract.

13. That Jewish education must take place in an environment in which people feel free and safe to question and explore. Our educational program should affirm a multiplicity of Jewish beliefs, perspectives, and practices.

14. That those who take on the honorable role of Jewish teacher, whether in formal or informal education, whether as classroom teachers or as parents, serve as models of Jewish values and behavior. This requires them to be dedicated to their own Jewish growth.

15. That Reform Jewish education helps people address the concept and practice of *mitzvot* in their life.

16. That the Hebrew language is a basic component of the Jewish experience. We strongly encourage both adults and children to study Hebrew, and we offer programs that provide students with a meaningful foundation in this part of our people's culture and tradition.

17. That *Torah lishmah,* "Jewish study for its own sake," is as important as goal-oriented learning and leads to a different kind of knowing. We encourage both kinds of Jewish study.

18. That an element of Jewish study should be embedded in all temple work.

PROPOSED IDEAS FOR
COORDINATING COMMITTEE FOR EDUCATION
January 26, 1992

Format and Structure

1. Chairs (or appointed representatives) of all committees with educational roles (e.g., Adult Education, Early Childhood Center, Families with Young Children, 20/30/40's, Festivals, Outreach).

2. Seven to nine members at large (initially members who served on the Educational Task Force).

3. The chair of the CCE should be a member of the Board of Trustees or the Board of Trustees should appoint a liaison to sit on the CCE.

4. Staffed by director of education.

5. Should meet monthly in the first year, at least bimonthly thereafter.

Function

To stimulate and encourage various bodies of the temple to implement the educational Mission Statement and conduct themselves in accordance with the We Believe Statements (via their representatives on the CCE).

Tasks

1. The committee's first task is programmatic: developing new educational program ideas and strategies that would further the implementation of the Mission Statement. The committee would also take initial steps to put these programs in place.

2. The second task is establishing liaison with all the other educationally related groups (preferably the chair of each group will sit on the CCE).

    Communication between the CCE and the various educationally related groups should result in:

    a. The review of existing or scheduled programs to see whether they further the goals of the Mission Statement and reflect the philosophy of the We Believe Statements.

    b. The coordination of educational efforts temple-wide in order to:

    - Coordinate calendar, avoid duplication of efforts, and combine resources and constituencies where beneficial.

    - Provide a forum for making an overall assessment of our educational programming.

    - Issue an Annual State of Jewish Education at Leo Baeck Temple Report at the annual meeting.

    - Review and revise the Mission and We Believe Statements every three to five years.

Notes

1   I am particularly indebted to Rabbi Deborah Bronstein who not only read with care, critiqued, and proposed modifications of this paper but who for five years was my partner in educational development. Her insights often helped me determine what steps needed to be taken next; her unwavering optimism and steadfast support helped me negotiate moments of confusion and frustration. In writing I have also been able to call upon several volumes of detailed, frequently verbatim meeting notes and the written reflections that have periodically been solicited from educational task force members.

2   The current senior rabbi served as the congregation's first assistant rabbi in the 1960s and returned to the congregation as associate rabbi in 1972. He became the senior rabbi upon the founding rabbi's retirement in 1986.

3   "In a huge, impersonal, and sometimes dehumanizing city, it's important to have a place where there is an attempt to keep things on a human scale, a place where clergy can get to know congregants and congregants can get to know each other in a more human and intimate way." Rabbi Sanford Ragins, opening remarks at the Conference on Reconfiguring Congregational Education, Malibu, May 1993.

4   A number of factors accounted for this decline: The general school-age population of West Los Angeles had decreased significantly and the cost of housing had risen dramatically, making it difficult for young families to buy homes near the temple. The congregation's limited membership policy functioned to discourage the active recruitment of new members as the temple's founding generation aged.

5   The assistant rabbis and the cantor who have served Leo Baeck Temple since 1986 have been women.

6   The Hebrew school had first been directed by the former cantor and then by the new assistant rabbi.

7   See Larry Cuban's paper in this volume.

8   In the recently published book *Change Forces: Probing the Depths of Educational Reform* by Michael Fullan, New York: Faliner Press, 1993, the chapter titled "The Complexity of the Change Process" helps to explain why this is so.

9   This metaphor originated with my colleague Melanie Berman at a retreat of the Rhea Hirsch School of Education's clinical faculty. I shared it with the Educational Task Force, which found it very suggestive.

10 Calling the document Rashi was the beginning of our attempt to use Jewish language to describe what we are doing. What began as a desire to make use of an educational opportunity (i.e., to teach about the importance of the eleventh-century Torah commentator) quickly evolved into something more. Once we applied the name Rashi to the elaboration of our planning document, the process in which we were engaged could be conceptualized in a Jewish way.

11 Board of Trustees, Families with Young Children, Adult Learners, Parents of School-Aged Children, Adult Education Committee, Membership Committee, The Outreach Committee, Early Childhood Center Advisory Board.

12 There were a number of reasons for our selection of family education as the second area of concentration:

    * In 1991 we had increased the number of class-based parent-child activity days in the religious school program and had invited parents to spend the previous Sunday morning in parallel, preparatory study with one of the rabbis. The individual programs (both the parent-child sessions and the adult study sessions) met with a great deal of praise, but the *idea* of family education did not. A small but vocal number of parents resented "losing" their Sunday mornings. They made it clear that they had enrolled their *children* in religious school, not themselves. It seemed important to explore the resistance and develop strong lay support for family education.

    * Concentrating on family education had the potential to move the CCE's thinking about education beyond the notion of schooling.

    * If "family" were defined broadly enough, we would really be dealing with congregational education. "Family education" was a term that did have some meaning to people; "congregational education" was too vague for this stage in our development.

13 The Leo Baeck definition of "family" includes families of all configurations (including singles) and at all stages of the life cycle. This inclusive definition means that family education is really congregational education. While some programs are especially targeted for families with children at home, most have elements that are inclusive of the entire congregational family.

14 For example, at what point will we no longer need a full task force concentrating on Hebrew education? In what order should we begin to reexamine other areas of our educational program, such as Adult Education, the religious school structure and

curriculum, and the link between the families of the Early Childhood Center and the congregation?

[15] See "*Tzimtzum*: A Mystic Model for Contemporary Leadership" by Eugene Borowitz in *What We Know About Jewish Education,* edited by Stuart Kelman, Los Angeles, Torah Aura, 1992.

[16] Jonathan Woocher's "Jewish Education: Crisis and Vision" (for full citation see note 31).

[17] Other guest experts have included Vicky Kelman (family education), Aviva Kadosh (Hebrew), Ron Reynolds (evaluation), and Sara Lee (the ECE project). One of the most powerful presentations was made by a panel of four congregants who spoke about their personal relationships to Hebrew.

[18] Sometimes my notes summarize the key discussions that have taken place at a meeting; sometimes they are almost verbatim transcripts of the meeting; sometimes they cluster comments made at different points in a discussion in order to bring the dialogue—or sometimes the dialectic—of the meeting into sharper focus.

[19] Shevitz's suggestion in this volume that this kind of planning resembles "organized anarchy" evoked in me the same kind of relief I experienced when, as a mother of a six-week-old infant, I discovered the term "periodic irritable crying" in Dr. Spock. Naming the chaos and knowing that someone else has survived to tell the story is of great consolation!

[20] Here, too, a metaphor that comes from the experience of parenting can provide perspective. Child development specialists claim that major developmental leaps are often preceded by a period of behavioral disintegration and even regression.

[21] Joseph Reimer's paper (in this volume) deals with a different set of symbolic meanings that may be attached to the debate about Hebrew. Loyalty to classical Reform Judaism and sensitivities about intermarriage do not seem to have been major factors in the Hebrew school issue at Leo Baeck Temple, although they are not entirely separable from the issues of commitment and priority. Debates within the congregation about how much Hebrew is used in services often do make reference to understandings of what Reform Judaism values, the efficacy of prayer in the vernacular, and the alienation and sense of exclusion experienced by congregants who do not know Hebrew. What is important to note is that Hebrew education does have the potential to be a magnet for a large number of unresolved tensions within a synagogue community. This should not be particularly surprising since language plays such a complex (and largely unconscious) set of roles in shaping individuals, cultures, and communities.

[22] The jumbling of educational and political issues is reminiscent of the term "garbage can planning" introduced in Shevitz's paper (in this volume). Solutions and problems are only loosely connected to one another when the multiple agendas on which the group is working are not clearly acknowledged.

[23] Her reference was to Jonathan Woocher's "Jewish Education: Crisis and Vision" (for full citation see note 31)

[24] Adin Steinsaltz, "On Repentance," *The Thirteen Petal Rose,* New York: Basic Books, 1980.

[25] The process of developing a shared vision based on dialogue among individuals who are simultaneously developing and clarifying their personal vision is analyzed in *The Fifth Discipline* by Peter Senge, New York: Doubleday, 1990. Although we were introduced to this "learning organization" literature only recently, it has been helpful in conceptualizing the process in which we have been engaged. Michael

Fullan (ibid.) argues that "vision emerges from more than it precedes, action.... Ready, fire, aim is the more fruitful sequence.... Productive change is very much a process of mobilization and positive contagion."

26 The use of the words *mitzvot* and *God* were most controversial. *Mitzvot* made the cut; *God* became "The Sacred," although the word *God* did make it into the Rashi.

27 The proposed statement read: "We believe that our status as a minority in America is the source of creative tension. Our educational programs should encourage individuals to develop strong Jewish commitments without becoming insular and strong Jewish identities without denigrating the traditions or interests of other groups."

28 Rabbi Sanford Ragins, sermon at the installation of temple officers given on June 3, 1994.

29 The fact that there is no clear agreement on the definition or goals of family education in the field made it possible to encourage the task force to think expansively.

30 "Enticement" and "expectations" became part of our task force lingo. The tension was between the belief that if congregants understood why Jewish study was so important they would accept or internalize the expectation that they participate and the somewhat opposing position that the congregants' participation had to be wooed by offering programs that were irresistibly enticing.

31 Woocher, "Jewish Education: Crisis and Vision" in *Imagining the Jewish Future*, edited by David Teutsch. Albany, New York: State University Press, 1992.

32 *Na'aseh v'nishma*, "We will do and we will hear/understand," was the Israelites' response to receiving the Torah on Mt. Sinai. The rabbis comment on the order of the verbs, noting that the Jewish people committed themselves to doing the commandments even before they fully heard or understood them.

33 *Maot Chitim*, "wheat money," is a form of *tzedakah* that, since the talmudic era, Jewish communities collected annually before Pesach in order to provide matzah, Pesach wine, and other Pesach essentials for the poor. At Leo Baeck Temple, congregants pack and deliver over 200 bags of Passover food goods for immigrant and elderly Jews each year.

34 At the end of each year, all task force members are asked to reflect in writing on their year of service.

35 Steinsaltz, see note 24.

36 Ultimately, David's concept resurfaced in the Membership Committee's Sunday Bagel Bar.

37 The corners of the field, which are to be left for the poor. (Leviticus 19:9)

38 From *Gates of Prayer*, the Reform siddur.

A PILGRIM'S PROGRESS

EDUCATIONAL REFORM AND INSTITUTIONAL TRANSFORMATION AT CONGREGATION BETH AM

Richard A. Block

ome years ago my remarks to parents on the first day of religious school included an anecdote I had heard from the mother of students in our school. Asked by another parent, "When your kids say, 'I don't want to go to Sunday school today,' what do you do?" She replied, "I say, 'Get into the car!'" The story elicited knowing laughter from parents accustomed to struggling with recalcitrant children who would rather be sleeping in, watching television, playing with friends, or doing almost anything other than receive the Jewish instruction to which they had been consigned.

In sharing that story, I did not intend to concede that every child dislikes "formal" Jewish education, although some surely do, nor did I want to imply that we do not care whether our students like our program, since we care very much. Rather, I used the anecdote to acknowledge the understandable reluctance of many children to devote their precious and limited free time to an activity they had not chosen, one whose perceived value was often unclear to them. By doing so, I hoped to strengthen the resolve of ambivalent, weary, or conflict-averse parents to insist that their children attend religious school notwithstanding the latter's occasional or recurring resistance.

Eight years into my tenure as Beth Am's senior rabbi, I believe more strongly than ever in the importance of parental support and reinforcement for student-learners. However, looking back with the insights I have gained as a result of our efforts of recent years, I see that my well-intended advice, too bold for some families to carry out, was, nonetheless, too timid and may have missed the mark. Even when it was coupled with an emphasis on making the home a center of active, joyful Jewish observance and on participation in family-oriented congregational programs, it called for and offered too little.

I now realize that I was engaged in little more than "marketing." I was asking our parents to support the educational status quo and become better "consumers" of our existing educational "product." This product (for which we had no reason to apologize) had been designed by professionals who felt they understood their customers' needs and best interests implicitly, on the basis of knowledge and experience, but it had little explicit input from the customers themselves. Rather than attempt to confirm that we and they shared a common vision of Jewish education, offer a more ambitious vision, or invite them to become active partners in creating and realizing such a vision, we were taking their agreement for granted. (The same turned out to be true with regard to our teachers, who were assigned textbooks and asked to create fun and effective lesson plans but were rarely given the opportunity or the challenge to participate in shaping the larger educational process.) The parents were there, after all. They had enrolled their children in "our" program, hadn't they? What greater confirmation could there be that we were on the right path and that we were all on the same wavelength? And, in fact, from what I could tell, people were largely content with the program. Therefore, it seemed that what was called for was a pep talk, not a challenge.

However, I understood none of this at the time. Rather, our congregation's efforts at educational reform and institutional transformation did not begin for several more years. I did not bring a coherent vision of Jewish learning in a congregational setting to Beth Am when I became its senior rabbi in 1987, nor was I asked to provide one. In the process that led to my selection, the Board had adopted four goals for the first few years of the new senior rabbi's tenure: (1) to elevate the intellectual character of the congregation's adult-oriented programs and services; (2) to enhance the vitality of our youth groups; (3) to focus on "inreach," i.e., to build a stronger sense of community within the congregation; and (4) to strengthen the congregation's financial stability. I had much to learn and do in assuming the rabbinic leadership of a large, active congregation and in trying to help the congregation achieve the goals articulated by its lay leaders. I set about those tasks in earnest.

When I became senior rabbi, the congregation consisted of about eight hundred households, with approximately four hundred students enrolled in pre-kindergarten through confirmation/tenth grade in a conventional large congregation arrangement that had been in effect for a number of years. Religious school was held in two Sunday morning sessions for pre-kindergarten to eighth grade; the older grades met on Monday evening. Students in Hebrew school attended either Monday and Wednesday or Tuesday and Thursday afternoons. (We have since grown to more than eleven hundred households and about six hundred and fifty students and a richer, more varied structure.)

During my first three years at Beth Am, I was in close and frequent communication with our educator but was not substantively involved in the leadership of our congregation's youth education program. I thought it prudent to observe and evaluate the program for a while before forming a judgment as to what, if anything, needed change or improvement. I visited classrooms to tell stories and interact with the students, participated in class dinners, children's services, and other school programs, helped *B'nai Mitzvah* students with their speeches, and taught the confirmation class with our assistant rabbi and educator.

Prior to my arrival I had received several letters from parents criticizing the eighth- and ninth-grade program and curriculum. We assessed and addressed those criticisms early on, principally by introducing electives (hardly a ground-breaking innovation) and providing an opportunity to socialize over pizza each week before class. Beyond that, although I invited direct communication from my new congregants and received a good deal of it, I received relatively few complaints about Sunday or Hebrew school in the early days of my tenure. Those that came my way tended to involve dissatisfaction with a student's schedule, the congregation's Bar/Bat Mitzvah requirements, or a class or teacher.

I wanted to be helpful and supportive, but I was new at the congregation, had not earned a degree in education, didn't know the teachers or my professional colleagues well, and understood the importance of supporting my staff; as a result, I tried to minimize rabbinic interference. I saw my role principally as that of problem solver and facilitator. I listened carefully and worked to resolve problematic situations to the parents' and students' satisfaction, whenever possible by facilitating direct communication with the teacher involved or our educator.

Some problems were solved, others proved intractable, especially when their origin lay primarily in the family rather than the school, but they did not seem unusual in number or character. At first blush, our school, well regarded in the Bay Area, appeared to be functioning as well as could be expected in light of the challenges and limitations faced by supplementary Jewish education. Things were far from perfect but were "under control." In light of that fact and of the priorities the congregation had placed before me, none of which bore directly on our religious and Hebrew school, I focused my initial efforts elsewhere.

My primary teaching assignment was tenth grade, our confirmation class, an experience that proved to be both thrilling and frustrating. Some evenings after class I would go home saying to myself, "That is why I became a rabbi." On other occasions I would ask "Why did I become a rabbi?" I have come to love teaching confirmation and, for all its challenges, consider it among my favorite tasks.

Like the young people in other affluent suburban congregations, Beth Am's students are a privileged and talented lot. Many of them are bright, some astoundingly so, and are high achievers in our outstanding public and private schools. As I began to know them, however, I was struck by a contradiction: Many of them possessed a very strong, positive sense of their Jewish identity yet seemed to know little about Judaism. This included even those students who had attended our school since early childhood. The former fact told me we were accomplishing an important goal, but the latter fact alarmed me greatly. I wondered how it could be that such gifted students did not know the order of the Jewish holidays or could not identify the basic content of more than half of them. How could students who had spent as many as eleven years in our school not be able to define *Tanach*, name its three main parts, or even differentiate it from the Torah?

I wasn't sure why this was so, but I sympathized with students' difficulty remembering the name, season, and content of holidays that they only learned about but did not practice. Nor was the problem confined to the area of ritual observance. Even with regard to the subject of ethics, something important appeared to be missing. Despite their textual study and regular reminders about *tzedakah*, these wonderful young Jewish people had great difficulty remembering to bring money (not their parents', their own) to contribute each week. Obviously some of the fault, if fault must be found, lay in the home rather than in the synagogue. But having designed and implemented the curriculum at the synagogue, we had to accept an ample share of the responsibility. At best, we seemed to be giving our students a Jewish identity largely devoid of content.

I observed signs of this phenomenon for several years. At times I was comforted by how much knowledge some of the students had attained, the Jewish commitment they demonstrated, and the sense of Jewishness many of them felt, even when they could not articulate its meaning. I also took comfort in the privilege of teaching, challenging, and getting to know such terrific young people (and filling in some of the gaps). In dark moments of self-doubt, however, I experienced a sense of dread and the fear that we were content with raising a generation of proud Jewish illiterates.

The same good news/bad news scenario was true for the other students with whom I had a sustained relationship, our *B'nai Mitzvah*. For two months prior to their service, I met with each of them weekly for a half hour (work I later split with my assistant, when he came on board after my first solo year), getting to know them better, discussing their Torah portions, and guiding them in the preparation of a speech. I was pleased that so many of them had chosen to pursue the challenging course of studies leading to the ceremony, since we demanded a considerable degree of preparation, but I was taken aback by the fact that so few of them understood the meaning of the event in traditional terms.

To their credit and that of their parents, relatively few of the students seemed focused on the material aspects of the occasion, the party and the gifts. For most of them, Bar or Bat Mitzvah was about tradition. It was an important event that had taken place in their family for generations (at least among the males), which they were carrying on for that reason. Some said they were going through the process "because I'm Jewish." Although a majority of the students intended to continue their Jewish education through confirmation, few could cite more than one or two Jewish activities that they intended to perform in the future. Three years later, when these *B'nai Mitzvah* became confirmands, only a handful of them retained their Hebrew skills or possessed the confidence to employ them in the confirmation service.

I do not contend that this gloomy assessment does justice to the educational program that existed at the time. Our teachers worked diligently to accomplish their assigned goals, and a visitor to our classrooms often discovered learning taking place in a very positive atmosphere. To a considerable extent our affective goals were being accomplished. Our cognitive goals, however, at least in terms of retention, were not. As that fact began to sink in, I started hearing certain complaints more consistently: "My daughter says they just do the same things over and over every year"; "When I ask my son what he learns at Sunday school he says, 'Nothing'"; "My child is bored"; "My child wants to learn, but other kids disrupt the class and make it impossible."

Such comments are difficult to assess and even when true can be attributed to a multitude of causes. Consider a child's statement that he or she is learning "nothing." It is conceivable that the cause may be a terrible teacher or curriculum, a student's bad attitude, consistent lack of attendance, emotional problems or a serious learning disability, disruptive fellow pupils, unsupportive parents, a seriously dysfunctional family situation, or other reasons. "Nothing," however, may also mean "nothing useful or of apparent relevance to my life," especially if a child's home is not the site of active Jewish practice. Furthermore, a child may be learning but may be unable to assess his or her progress. Finally some children, of which I was one, use "nothing" to fend off inquisitive parents or deny their parents the satisfaction of knowing they're enjoying themselves and accomplishing something in an activity that their parents insist they do.

Or take the complaint of repetitiveness. Repetition is not inherently bad. It is an accepted pedagogical technique. There is a cycle to the Jewish calendar that we joyfully repeat each year, we hope with a higher level of content and understanding.

I confess that I am not entirely sure whether I began to take such complaints more seriously because they had become more numerous or because I had become convinced, through my independent observation, that they might be justified. Many of our students did not learn or retain much. We did, in fact, do many of the same things in the identical way each year. As I grew more and more concerned about the results of our educational efforts, I tried to be less defensive about complaints. While I recognized that there were and would always be many things beyond the synagogue's control, I wondered if we were fulfilling our institutional responsibility to influence the things we could control.

Despite my growing sense that something fundamental needed to be done, I hesitated. My educator, an experienced, credentialed Jewish professional and a *mensch*, took great pride in the program, which had taken shape under his leadership. He shared my distress at our students' paucity of home observance opportunities but saw little need for change on the synagogue's part. I did not relish the notion of conflict with him and I wasn't yet certain he was wrong. Perhaps this *was* the best we could do. My associate rabbi shared my concerns, but neither of us had a clear idea as to what needed to be or could be done. There was a lay committee that we might have consulted, but, to my knowledge, it had never involved itself with educational policy. Rather, it had traditionally confined itself to such mundane though necessary tasks as organizing the Purim carnival.

My hesitation was also grounded in more personal and somewhat selfish concerns. I was already extremely busy and I shuddered to think of the time and energy that working for serious educational reform would demand. In addition, I was still new in my position. Why, I asked myself, should I venture into areas with which my lay leaders appeared satisfied and risk neglecting the priorities they had set for me and upon which my tenure might depend? If I presented a serious critique of our youth education program, wouldn't I be endangering my credibility and wounding myself unnecessarily? After all, education was an area over which I held ultimate supervisorial authority. If I declared the program inadequate, wasn't I in effect criticizing myself, admitting that I was a failure?

At war with these self-protective concerns and questions were other, more fundamental ones. Had I become a rabbi and assumed the pulpit of a distinguished congregation, one that strives for excellence in so many other areas, only to acquiesce in an educational program that did little more than aspire to mediocrity? Would I look back someday upon a career at Beth Am knowing that I did not attempt to address that situation? How could I face myself or a generation of children whose learning was given into my care, knowing that we could have tried for more but had not? I spent many restless nights and troubled days trying to decide what I should do and when.

As I wrestled with these questions, we began to plan for our annual leadership retreat, attended by members of the Board and other committee chairs. Looking back on the past few years, we concluded that we had largely achieved the goals that had been set at the outset of the rabbinic search process, and I was asked to facilitate a discussion aimed at identifying new goals for the synagogue. After an initial discussion, I broke the group into four sections and had them share their suggestions at the conclusion of an allotted time. In some manner, each group expressed a desire to focus on our youth education program. There was a consensus that we should make the program more engaging so that students would be eager to attend and parents would encounter less resistance from their children.

At this point, I realized that we had reached a critical moment, a genuine window of opportunity. Resolved to take advantage of it, I drew aside key members of the Board's executive committee and made a suggestion whose full implications I did not realize at the time but which turned out to be pivotal. I do not recall my exact words, but they were something like this: "When we talk about making religious and Hebrew school more engaging, is the goal just to get kids off their parents' backs, or do we have something more ambitious in mind? If our goal is the former, we can 'potshky' around and try to make things more fun. There may be some things we can do, but they won't bring about fundamental change or make a lasting difference. If we want to raise these programs to a level of excellence, we need to examine every aspect of them, from the ground up. We should form a special task force and bring together the best and the brightest of our parents, teachers, and students, as well as representatives of every significant constituency within the congregation. We should hire an outside consultant to provide expertise and help guide us through the process. That will take money. Are you willing to provide it?" One of the members asked the logical question, "How much will it cost?" I replied, "My guess is that a consultant might cost as much as $10,000, but the real money will come later if we decide that we need to put more resources into the school." The response was heartening and characteristic of Beth Am, a congregation that is willing to take risks and rise to a challenge. They all agreed, "Let's go for it."

My first call the next morning was to Sara Lee, director of the Rhea Hirsch School of Education at HUC-JIR. Sara argued persuasively that before we could evaluate our program, we had to define our congregation's vision, values, and goals with respect to Jewish education, something that had not occurred to me or the Board. Only then would we have the criteria by which we could judge what we were doing and which would help us determine what we needed to do. Sara's questions were penetrating and her observations were keen. She was intrigued by the challenge but unsure she could commit the time to the project, and she requested a clearer definition of her potential role. Were we looking for someone to facilitate the process, one that was sure to be labor intensive and time consuming if it were done well, or did we seek a person with expertise in Jewish education who could assist us in defining the issues, ask the right questions, and help keep the process on track? I wasn't sure.

Rosyland Bauer, then president of the congregation, suggested that we had a perfect in-house facilitator in Eddie Reynolds, an organizational development consultant by vocation and a committed, active congregational leader by avocation. Eddie readily agreed to organize and lead what became the Beth Am Education Task Force. I put him in touch with Sara to see if they could work out a mutually beneficial arrangement.

As they proceeded with their conversations that led to a wonderful, productive partnership between ourselves and Sara, and as Rosyland, Eddie, and I continued to consult, another issue that I had not considered presented itself. What would my role be in this process? As I thought about it, two things seemed clear: The course upon which we were embarking would need my continuing involvement and input, but whatever plan resulted from it could only win the support of the congregation if it were the congregation's plan and not just the senior rabbi's plan. For that to happen, I knew I needed to be circumspect and remain in the background as much as possible.

Eddie Reynold's chapter (which follows this one) describes the process that ensued, which he led with incredible devotion and skill. That process continues to this day and is not yet complete. I will, instead, attempt to illuminate key factors in its success and significant areas of difficulty that we encountered.

One of the first assignments I undertook after the Board agreed to move forward as I had suggested was to seek our educator's support. This proved difficult because the process was not one that he had proposed, nor did he believe that it was necessary or appropriate. While I understood his reticence and respected his professional judgment, I disagreed. More to the point, this was an initiative that our lay leaders had now made their own, and our cooperation as professionals was demanded whether we agreed with the synagogue's leaders or not.

As I saw it, this undertaking was not grounded in criticism of our congregation's professional staff or our existing program, although both could improve as a result. Rather, I believed then and now that this was the opportunity of a rabbi's and an educator's lifetime in that our congregation was prepared to enhance significantly its commitment to Jewish education and we had vital roles to play in shaping the outcome. Also, our willing participation would be a clear indication of our confidence in ourselves, our program, and our congregation. Although our educator served on the task force, he did not share its enthusiasm and ultimately left the congregation to pursue other goals.

A process like the one we undertook can be unsettling. Even a very secure rabbi or educator is likely to feel at times that an attempt to improve or change the existing program implies a degree of personal or professional inadequacy on his or her part. This thought had crossed my mind earlier and I had to overcome it before I could suggest that we embark on what has proven to be an exciting enterprise. To the extent that a congregation's professionals feel secure in themselves and their positions, the easier it will be to attempt educational reform and institutional transformation. It is extremely difficult to envision the above things happening without at least the rabbi's active support. I would argue, however, that should the congregation's educational aspirations exceed those of its professionals, the latter must yield.

Among our other initial challenges was identifying and recruiting people who were capable of and willing to make a sustained commitment to the task force. Once we succeeded in doing so, logistics proved difficult. We determined that we would need to meet over a period of at least six to twelve months, including several day-long retreats. Agreeing on meeting dates was a nightmare. Early on, Eddie and I decided that the task force could and should meet without me if a date that worked for most of the others was incompatible with my schedule. This demanded a considerable element of trust on my part, but it also provided an opportunity to enhance the lay members' "ownership" of the process and its conclusions. In fact, even though I was unable to participate in several of the most important task force meetings, I rarely disagreed with the conclusions or felt the need to question or supplement them. For me, this constituted a crucial validation of the process and confirmed the wisdom of my self-imposed restrictions.

I cannot emphasize sufficiently the issue of trust. To give educational reform and institutional transformation a chance to succeed, the rabbi and, if applicable, the educator must be able to trust their lay people to be full and equal partners in the education process and must be willing to accept the outcome of a process that they, the professionals, do not control. The professionals must also be able to trust that their input will be sought and valued and that no hidden personnel agenda lies behind the process. In return, the lay people must be able to trust the rabbi and educator to support fully their participation in the conceptualization and actualization of the congregation's emerging educational vision.

We had not anticipated that we would have to search for an educator just as the task force got underway, and we struggled with process issues as we considered the impact of a change in educational leadership. On the one hand, we did not want to proceed too far or too fast without the participation of the professional who would bear the primary responsibility for implementing the conclusions of the task force, nor did we want to forego the benefit of his or her expertise. On the other hand, we were unwilling to delay the process for months, fearing that once the process was derailed, we would find it difficult or impossible to restart it. We concluded that the educator we hired would have to be comfortable with the process we were pursuing and willing to support its major tenets with enthusiasm. Thus resolved, we carried on.

We sought a creative and dynamic educator who would be in tune with our process and committed to our vision, values, and goals. Our new educator, a creative professional with a flair for innovation and experience in a conventional congregational setting, came on board just as we were beginning to shift from vision to implementation, and the transition proved difficult. Arriving shortly before the beginning of a new school year, she had to establish herself in a new congregation and community, take the helm of a large, multidimensional, existing program, and find her place in the dynamic and complicated reformation already well underway.

We have learned that institutional transformation is at best a long-term, complex process that requires leadership, clarity of vision, commitment, good will, tremendous effort, and widespread congregational support. Despite the sometimes overwhelming urge to do everything at once, we discovered that sustained, significant innovation can only take place gradually in stages over time. It involves a considerable amount of improvisation and experimentation, trial and error. But the congregation's present program cannot stop operating in the meanwhile. Recognizing that directing the educational enterprise of a large congregation is a full-time job, we wondered how an educator, especially a new one, could help guide a seemingly unprecedented process of educational reformation at the same time. To put it differently, if the director of education is to play his or her proper role in the synagogue's transformation into a community of learners, who is going to supervise the existing program in the meanwhile? And how and by whom can these two major pieces of the puzzle be coordinated and made to fit together?

This cluster of interrelated questions led directly to the issue of financial resources. Among the conclusions of the task force was that we would need to commit significant additional sums of money to our education program, including its administration. Our goal was to create an education leadership team, supervised by the director of education. This team would manage and coordinate the ongoing program, including the significant innovations being introduced and those to come, while primary responsibility for managing individual aspects of the program would be assigned to different members of the team. This plan, we hoped and expected, would allow our director of education to play the appropriate leadership role in the ongoing (and possibly endless) reformation process. All of this, however, involved recruitment, organization, delegation, quality control, accountability and, of course, money.

We have been able to move in this direction because we are a financially stable congregation and have had the Board's devoted support of the task force process and report, but we have not yet been able to generate resources internally to the extent that has proven necessary. Consequently we have sought private, community, and foundation support to expand our educational team, seed innovative programs, and continue our work, now coordinated by the successor to the task force, the Beth Am Education Council.

While we have gratefully received support from a number of sources, our most significant backing to date has come in the form of a bold and generous three-year grant from the Koret Foundation, which has enabled us to hire a full-time program coordinator. Her primary role is to implement significant aspects of our education plan. Based on our experience, I am convinced that Jewish educational reform will be possible on a meaningful scale only with the substantial support of charitable and family foundations and local Jewish Federations whose leaders understand the centrality and the indispensability of Jewish education and the synagogue to Jewish continuity.

An additional financial issue emerged at Beth Am, one that is related to our beautiful but inadequate facility, which was planned for a congregation half its present size. As the task force went about its work and began to envision new, creative, interactive, and intergenerational programs, it soon saw that we would need additional learning and administrative space, both dedicated and multipurpose. After considerable interaction by the task force with another specially constituted group, the Future Facilities Committee, the education plan emerged as the primary impetus to a major renovation and expansion campaign, presently being planned. In the meanwhile we are doing the best we can within our physical plant's limitations, knowing that we have no choice, at least for the next couple of years. For some congregations space will not be the issue it has been for us, but the relationship between a congregation's facilities, staffing and administration, and prospective educational programs cannot be ignored.

Even with the support we have generated and received, the outcome of the reformation and transformation process is not yet fully assured. Although the task force saw as its goal enhancing the learning of congregants of all ages, the primary impact of its efforts to date has been felt in the area of youth education. And with regard to the latter, major aspects of our vision still await the time, effort, and resources that are needed to bring about their implementation.

Among the most crucial elements of success in creating lasting change is winning widespread support for the process in the congregation as a whole, something to which we have devoted considerable time and effort. The psychology of the congregation's response has been very revealing. When we invited congregants to a series of meetings to learn about the task force's work in progress, we did not know if anyone would come or who would attend. Would only chronic complainers show up? In fact, few of those who did attend came to express their discontent. Rather, their initial response to the efforts of the task force was enthusiastic. However, as they began to envision an educational program that would be considerably more exciting than the present one and as it dawned on them that perhaps they had been settling for too little, considerable frustration emerged. For that reason we tried to "pick low-hanging fruit," to produce signs of early, visible progress that demonstrated the seriousness of our efforts and would build confidence in our prospects for success on a larger scale.

From this project, we learned that those who engage in the process of educational reform and institutional transformation must be careful about the matter of expectations. Inevitably, settled expectations will be unsettled and new, higher expectations will be created. Having embarked on a novel and untried course, we found that we had to constantly mediate between impatience with what is and patience in waiting for what will be. We did not want our congregants to settle for the status quo, but we could not change everything that needed changing overnight. Indeed, the more we learned about the process of reformation and transformation, the more we felt certain that we would never reach a final, static outcome. What we discovered was that we were engaged in a dynamic enterprise that we would need to assess, plan, implement, reform, and innovate continuously in the years to come. As Jewish history has demonstrated, waiting for the Messiah is neither an idle nor a secure occupation.

For me, one of the most wonderful surprises of our continuing efforts has been the creativity they have unleashed among our teachers. Urged to take risks rather than play it safe, to try new things instead of falling into familiar patterns, many of our teachers have risen marvelously and creatively to the occasion. Those for whom risk and change have proven too uncomfortable have gradually gone elsewhere. Among the sweetest fruits of our work are a new partnership between our lay and professional leaders and enhanced collegiality among our professional colleagues. It is too soon to tell whether our monumental effort will be crowned with the success of which we dream. We have experienced numerous setbacks, unpleasant surprises, and no common disappointments, as well as considerable uncertainty and frustration. Undoubtedly there will be more. Nonetheless, each step forward, whether small or giant, and every obstacle overcome renew our sense of sacred mission and confirm the blessing that is ours in working for a vibrant future for the Jewish faith and the Jewish people. Blessed are You, *Adonai* our God, Teacher of Torah to Your people Israel!

PROCESS OF THE BETH AM EDUCATION TASK FORCE

Eddie Reynolds

he following is an outline of the process of the educational task force at Temple Beth Am. At the end are some of the initial products of the task force, including our core values, our vision statement, and some questions that we asked along the way.

The task force adopted up front and modified along the way the following process to accomplish its chartered outcome of creating a long-term, strategic plan for education at Beth Am:

1. An initial retreat of the entire task force on April 20-21, 1991, to establish a guiding vision for the entire planning process.

2. A series of "parlor meetings" with various groups and groupings of Beth Am members in order to seek feedback on the outcome of the first retreat.

3. A second retreat on August 25, 1991, to reach a common understanding of the "parlor meeting" themes and to determine what key areas were to be the strategic foci of the investigation and planning stage.

4. Further communications with the congregants, including the presentation and solicitation of input and volunteers on the opening day of religious school, a letter to the congregation on the task force's work, and High Holy Day speeches by the president and rabbis on education at Beth Am.

5. Formation of four topic-specific task forces, involving some thirty-plus additional individuals, to solicit information nationwide on the best practices and thinking in each of four strategic areas and then to create recommendations for the nineties in each of these areas. (Because the work of these groups was interrupted by the selection process for a new educator, the time period stretched from October 1991-May 1992.)

6. A third retreat on May 17, 1992, to hear the reports of the four subtask forces and to determine final recommendations and proposed next steps.

7. A proposal by the task force in June 1992, to the Board of Directors to create the Beth Am Education Council.

8. A presentation of this report to the Board of Directors in September 1992, with the recommendation that copies go to all congregants and that a meeting for further discussion be held with those who are interested.

9. Establishment of the Beth Am Education Council (BAEC) to coordinate education programming from all sectors of Beth Am (professional and lay efforts), to oversee the implementation of the long-term plan, and to monitor and revise as needed the vision and values.

10. Quarterly meetings of the approximately twenty-person BAEC and annual retreats to revisit the vision.

11. Establishment in April 1993, of the first annual education theme for all Beth Am, a subject toward which all committees and professionals are to gear a portion of their education programming for the upcoming year.

12. Continued communication efforts that include monthly articles in the synagogue newsletter on innovative changes in the education system, a new education page in the newsletter, a president's column dedicated to education once per quarter, values and vision being the topic of sermons on an ongoing basis, etc.

THE VISION RETREAT

The first retreat of the task force produced three important products that guided all subsequent work and that will guide the implementation in the next several years of the following:

1. A set of Limiting Assumptions, things that we in Beth Am may be acting on as if they were true even though they may not be true and that, as a result, may be limiting the possibilities of what education can be at Beth Am.

2. A set of Core Values, those beliefs that are the most important to the Beth Am community with regard to education and that should serve as the ultimate criteria in the decisions and choices that we make concerning education at Beth Am.

3. A Vision consisting of elements that are common to congregants' thinking of what they most want the education system at Beth Am to be.

These three products are detailed in the following sections.

Our Limiting Assumptions concerning Jewish Education

Limiting Assumptions are things that we may be acting on as if they were true and that, as a result, may be limiting our possibilities.

1. Jewish education is only for children.

2. Religious school should consist of two hours per week on Sundays; Hebrew school should be separate.

3. The secular school model is the one to follow (i.e., the classic "teacher as expert and student as one-who-is-to-be-taught" model).

4. If you learn something (e.g., how to observe a holiday), you will like it and, therefore, do it. (Cognitive learning => Doing.)

5. Kids don't and probably won't like their Jewish education experience. Thus parents will feel bad that their kids must attend religious school and parents will have low expectations of Jewish education.

6. Our students need a critical amount of knowledge before they can begin raising and addressing questions about their Judaism.

7. Significant learning and significant questioning cannot occur at the same time (at least for children).

8. Jewish education is low on the list for what seems to be more and more competition for people's time.

9. Achieving in religious school is the same as achieving in secular school. Thus learning things/facts well is our goal for our kids. There should be a method that measures whether or not our kids are achieving—that is, if they are doing well in religious school.

10. If my kid is learning well in religious school, then he or she is learning how to become (and is thus becoming) a good Jew. Therefore, I as a parent can concern myself less in this regard. (Or, maybe I don't need to worry at all.)

11. Kids (as inherent achievers) see no inherent value in the noncognitive part of Jewish education.

12. We place much of our definition of Jewish education on the cognitive realm.

13. Spirituality is (wholly) separate from mainstream Jewish education.

14. Parents cannot to be significantly involved in the Jewish education of their kids because parents lack the needed knowledge.

15. The teachers we need to implement the kind of Jewish education we want are by and large not available.

16. If we reach the kid, we reach (change) the family.

17. If we push Jewish education back into the home, people will not regard the synagogue to be as important as it is regarded now (and thus will not want to pay the synagogue dues).

Our Core Values: Jewish Education at Beth Am

1. We value students.

2. We value people of all ages interacting with the Jewish tradition in a questioning mode.

3. We value reaching out and responding to all levels of interests and commitments and to all constituencies in our Jewish community.

4. We value creating an environment in which people feel free and safe to question.

5. We value community building as a part of the education process.

6. We value the broad definition of Jewish education as an essential building block for establishing personal Jewish identity.

7. We value the development of an individual's love for himself or herself as a Jew and his or her love for the Jewish people.

8. We value the learning of Jewish skills that enable people to participate fully in Jewish life.

9. We value Judaism and the teachings of Torah as resources for answering some of the most important questions in life.

10. We value all forms and modes of Jewish learning.

11. We value the home as the primary source of Jewish continuity.

12. We value creating opportunities in which God can be encountered.

13. We value an understanding of what being a Reform Jew means.

14. We value Jewish pluralism.

15. We value fostering an appreciation of and a commitment to the State of Israel.

16. We value forming a commitment to *tzedakah* and *tikun olam*.

17. We value the Hebrew language as an integral element of Jewish observance and identity.

Common Elements of Our Vision for the 1990s
Jewish Education at Beth Am

1. Learning is an interactive process.

   Questioning is actively encouraged.

   A two-way relationship exists between student and teacher and between student and student.

   Students are engaged in studying Judaic source texts.

   Critical thinking is encouraged.

   Teaching methods, materials, and settings are varied.

2. All congregants are involved in lifelong learning.

   As students.

   In some cases as teachers (i.e., teachers for students, teachers for teachers, experts on special topics, etc.).

3. The home and synagogue are interdependent in the education process.

   Each enhances the other.

   Each is necessary.

   The synagogue is investing lots of resources and energy in the effort to make the Jewish home capable of playing its role.

   People are personally motivated to make this happen.

4. Intergenerational learning is occurring.

   The mixing of ages is being incorporated into many settings and in the curricula.

   Some student groups consist of people of different ages.

   There are teachers of all ages (e.g., young people teach younger children and even adults).

   Leaders of all ages are being cultivated.

5. A variety of nontraditional structures support our education system.

> Team teaching; a mentoring system.
>
> Teachers for short segments of a year.
>
> Specialty teaching; thematic teaching.
>
> Spanning of all committees presently involved in learning by the Beth Am Education Committee.
>
> Alternative time structures for our schools; classes of all ages.

6. We have an articulated, integrated curriculum that addresses a set of competencies. These competencies are derived from a Beth Am model of a fully participating, educated Reform Jew (i.e., the skills, behaviors, values, affective qualities). The curriculum is developmentally appropriate.

7. Education is seen as an obligation of the entire congregation.

> It is viewed as our responsibility, not as a service.
>
> We create equal access for all congregants to all educational services and offerings held at the synagogue.
>
> Congregants are called upon to provide all kinds of resources to support education at Beth Am.
>
> We seek alternative and creative means of funding education.

8. The core values are integrated into and are evident in all that we do.

Our Overall Goal for Education at Beth Am

What we most strive for as the outcome of our education system at Beth Am is a deep love and understanding of Reform Judaism by every individual who participates in that system. This goal will only be accomplished if we focus diligently on the pursuit of our Vision and if we are guided by our Core Values.

THE SUMMER 1991 PARLOR MEETINGS

Background

Once the Limiting Assumptions, Core Values, and Vision were created, the task force felt it imperative to test its sense of reality and aspirations by seeking input and feedback from the temple's constituents. After a letter was sent to all congregants inviting them to come to a parlor meeting, nine two-hour sessions were held along the following groupings:

1. Religious Practices and Music Committees
2. Dues, Budget, and Outreach Committees
3. Religious School and Adult Education Committees
4. Former Presidents of Beth Am
5. Yachad, Sisterhood, and Seniors members
6. Parents of School-aged Children
7. Parents Whose Children Had Graduated from Beth Am Schools
8. Young Families and Outreach Committees
9. High School and College Students
10. Social Action Committee and Board of Directors

Themes That Were Stressed in Summer Focus Groups

From these meetings attended by over one hundred and twenty people, a number of themes emerged. Listed below are the themes and the number of the groups for which each theme was a major topic of discussion:

1. Involve families in the school more. Involve family as a whole. More coeducation. (8)
2. Make religious school fundamentally different from secular school. Come up with a different model. (6) Change the language of how we talk about the "school." (3)
3. Plan for socialization at all ages. (6)
4. Focus on teacher training and on in-service experiences. (6) Use our many Beth Am educators as teachers of teachers, curriculum advisers, and ongoing mentors/coaches. (3)
5. Create more intergenerational learning experiences. (5)
6. Integrate Hebrew with the rest of the students' Jewish education. Do not separate schools. Start Hebrew early. (5)
7. Stress comparative religions. (4)
8. Stress use of congregant teachers. (4)
9. Install a better ongoing evaluation system, including input from the students. (4)

In addition, about fifty distinct suggestions for specific changes were made. These included such ideas as forming *chavurot* of families with students in the early grades, introducing prayer into all education settings, sharing high school education sessions with neighboring congregations, "modularizing" religious school into six- to eight-week segments, and allowing more congregants to teach in the school.

More important, a startling realization was made by most of the people who attended the parlor meetings. When confronted with Limiting Assumption Number Five ("Kids don't and probably won't like their Jewish education experience. Thus parents will feel bad that their kids must attend religious school and parents will have low expectations of Jewish education"), they invariably realized that they had been complacent about and had mediocre expectations of the Jewish education experience for their children.

Most members had not had a rewarding Jewish learning experience when they were children, and their assumption was that the experience of their children at Beth Am would not be much better. What was heard over and again is that people saw religious and Hebrew schools as something to get through—a rite of passage —and that most people did not have the same set of high expecta- tions and demands for the Jewish education system as they did for the public education system. Once parents were confronted with that assumption, an amazing metamorphosis occurred. People attending parlor meetings immediately decided that now was the time to make greater demands, to want more of the Jewish education system than it had delivered heretofore. In meeting after meeting, the emotions and interest of the attendees increased at this turning point, and they began talking with new determination.

THE SECOND RETREAT

Bringing the themes and experiences of the summer parlor meetings with them to the August 25, 1991 retreat, the task force set out to define what areas should be the focus for the next stages of nationwide data gathering and of planning recommendations. Listed below are the four areas decided upon, the key points pertaining to each area made in the summer parlor meetings, and the key questions that the task force charged each area to investigate.

Strategic Focus Number One: Creating a More Effective Structure for the Jewish Education of Our Children

Points from the task force and the parlor meetings: Create more variety. Stress the cultural aspects of Judaism more. Look at non-traditional days and times. Stress the socialization possibilities. Create a "new" model for Jewish education.

Questions Charged by the Task Force to the Structure Task Force

1. Are there other models that deal with time structure, program structure, group structures, and age groupings?
2. How do we meet the diversity of families and situations in our structure and requirements?
3. What are the regularity of meetings alternatives?
4. What do we know about different classroom sizes and their implications for learning?
5. How much variety can we bear? Must there be some sameness and consistency across the board?
6. What constraints do physical space, equipment, etc., bear on the alternative structures that are feasible for us?
7. What support systems or modifications would we need to make for any structure changes?
8. How do we make the religious school different from the secular school, no matter when we meet?
9. What are the range of opportunities that we want to offer people (i.e., art, drama, music, culture, sports, book clubs, dance, etc.)?
10. How can we increase the choices and alternatives for students of all ages?
11. How can we evaluate our structures on an ongoing basis?
12. Is there a common core of experiences that we believe people should have here?
13. Are there educational experiences outside Beth Am that we want to be necessary parts of the education experience (e.g., camp, Israel, trips, service, youth groups, etc.)?

Strategic Focus Number Two: Creating an Articulated, Coordinated Curriculum

Points from the task force and parlor meetings: Curriculum = The total learning experience in a particular context. Building in such ideas as learning Hebrew from the beginning of religious school, studying comparative religions, God in prayer, and pluralism.

Questions Charged by the Task Force to the Curriculum Task Force

1. What are the set of "competencies"?
2. What do we mean by Reform Jewish identity?
3. How do we reconcile having an articulated curriculum in a possibly nontraditional, nonsecular structure?
4. What are the top priority areas of Jewish content that we wish to include?
5. What expectations do we have of parents and students? How do we measure these expectations?
6. How would we form a curriculum over time? Who would be involved? Who would lead the process?
7. When should we introduce Hebrew? Where? How? Can we do this with our faculty or in our structure when the students are younger than they are now?
8. What models of curriculum design should we consider?
9. How do we combat the perceived repetitive syndrome?
10. How much latitude should we give individual teachers?
11. How do we identify curriculum models? What curricula are already available? How and when do we evaluate what is available?
12. What is a reasonable expectation and timetable for implementation?
13. What human, physical, and material resources are implied by these different models?
14. How can we involve congregational experts in implementation?
15. What is the relationship between the cognitive and affective realms?
16. What kinds of learning experiences do we want people to have?
17. How can we insure that our curriculum will help people "encounter God"?
18. What meaning do we attach to the various content areas? Why do we think an area of content is important?

Strategic Focus Number Three: Redefining Who Educates within the Congregation, and Enabling This to Happen

Points from the task force and parlor meetings: Broaden the teacher base. Increase ongoing teacher training, including overtime for the preparation of people to become teachers. Insure that all these teachers in the congregation are people who will be seen as a role model in building and living Reform Jewish identity.

Questions Charged by the Task Force to the Redefining Who Educates Task Force

1. What qualities, characteristics, and commitments must a person have in order to be a role model in the Beth Am context?

2. Can the school have part-time teachers?

3. What levels of commitment are acceptable for those who want to teach?

4. What patterns of deployment can we imagine (team, short-term, mini courses, etc.)?

5. What degree of continuity must students have and at what age level? What are various models for achieving that continuity (i.e., must continuity always be attained through the primary teacher)?

6. How do we identify the possible universe of teachers out there?

7. At this stage how can we measure the potential interest with in the congregation?

8. How do we connect teachers to the Beth Am community if they are not Beth Am members?

9. How as a congregation do we show our esteem and value for those who teach?

10. What do we mean by "teacher"?

11. How do we support the continuing growth of these teachers?

12. How do we handle issues like teacher selection and the supervision of congregant teachers? What issues of evaluation does a congregant's teaching in the school raise?

13. How do we prepare people for their roles as educators?

14. How do we motivate and model for young people in the congregation to help them see that aspiring for education roles is worthy?

15. What are the implications of this potential broadening of the teacher base for the professional staff?

Strategic Focus Number Four: Integrating Family and Home Learning

Points from the task force and parlor meetings: In-home ways to create educational experiences. Bringing families together. Increasing parental [and other adult] involvement in the school.

Questions Charged by the Task Force to the Family Education Task Force

1. What are some of the operational dynamics of the different family clusters that we encompass? What are the financial, ideological, and logistical implications of single-person, two-career, intermarried, single-parent, two-Jews-of-differing-commitments/expectations households?

2. What are the developmental needs of different kinds of families? How would these impact involvement opportunities and expectations that we might structure?

3. What are other congregations doing to bring families together and involve parents in Jewish education?

4. What support systems must we create to help the home fulfill the coeducational role?

5. Are there target-age kids' families that might benefit more than others in this emphasis of family involvement (e.g., early childhood, pre-Bar Mitzvah, etc.)?

6. What is the state of our current family program (e.g., family weekend, Young Families Committee, Mispacha)?

7. What are the ways in which families are currently oriented and socialized into the congregation?

8. What commitments can we realistically ask of parents? Is there a contract involved? How can we entice/motivate parents?

9. What areas of study are conducive to family involvement?

EDITORS

ISA ARON is Professor of Jewish Education at Hebrew Union College-Jewish Institute of Religion Rhea Hirsch School of Education, where she teaches courses in philosophy of education, teaching skills, and research and directs the Experiment in Congregational Education. She holds a Ph.D. in Philosophy of Education from the University of Chicago and has published articles in such journals as the *American Journal of Education, Philosophy of Education, Religious Education, Tikkun*, and the *Journal of Reform Judaism*.

SARA LEE, Director of the Hebrew Union College-Jewish Institute of Religion Rhea Hirsch School of Education in Los Angeles, holds degrees from Radcliffe College, Hebrew Union College-Jewish Institute of Religion, and the University of Southern California. Leadership and organizational phenomena in Jewish educational institutions are her areas of specialty. She serves on the North American Commission on Jewish Identity and Continuity and the Wexner Foundation Graduate Fellowship Committee.

SEYMOUR ROSSEL is Director of the Department of Education of the Union of American Hebrew Congregations and Director of the Reform movement's Commission on Jewish Education. He served as Vice-Chairperson of the Coalition for the Advancement of Jewish Education and on the National Executive Boards of CAJE, the Jewish Education Service of North America, the Jewish Book Council of America, and the National Association of Temple Educators. He is the author of many articles and more than a dozen books for Jewish and public schools, including *A Child's Bible, When a Jew Prays, When a Jew Seeks Wisdom, Israel: Covenant People, Covenant Land, Journey through Jewish History,* and *Managing the Jewish Classroom*.

AUTHORS

RICHARD ABRAMS graduated in 1994 from the Rhea Hirsch School of Education at HUC-JIR in Los Angeles with a master of arts in Jewish Education. Currently residing in southern California with his wife, Lori Price Abrams, Richard is the Assistant Director of Administration and Adult Programs at The Brandeis-Bardin Institute.

RICHARD A. BLOCK was ordained at Hebrew Union College-Jewish Institute of Religion, Cincinnati, in 1982. He has served as Senior Rabbi of Congregation Beth Am, Los Altos Hills, California, since 1987 and has authored several publications. He is currently a trustee of the Rabbinical Pension Board, a member of the UAHC-CCAR Commission on AIDS, and a member of the Boards of the Jewish Community Federation of San Francisco, The Peninsula, Marin and Sonoma Counties, UAHC Camp Swig, and the Mid-Peninsula Jewish Community Day School in Palo Alto.

KENNETH CARR is a fifth-year rabbinical student at HUC-JIR in Cincinnati. He graduated with a master of arts in Jewish Education from the Rhea Hirsch School of Education in 1994. He presently serves as the student rabbi for Congregation B'nai Israel in Grand Forks, North Dakota, and is an intern in the Youth Programs Department of HUC-JIR in Cincinnati.

SUSAN ELLEN COSDEN graduated from HUC-JIR in Los Angeles in 1994 with a master of arts degree in Jewish Education. She is currently the Educator at Congregation B'nai Israel in Sacramento, California.

LARRY CUBAN has taught at Stanford since 1981 and has served as Associate Dean of Stanford's School of Education. His research focuses on the history of school reform, teaching, curriculum, and administration. His publications include *The Managerial Imperative: The Practice of Leadership in Schools* (1988), *Teachers and Machines: The Use of Classroom Technology since 1920* (1986), and (with David Tyack) *Tinkering Toward Utopia* (1995).

JONATHAN E. KRAUS is the Rabbi of Beth El Temple Center in Belmont, Massachusetts, where he also serves as Director of Education for the religious school. He was the Founding Director of the Bergen Academy of Reform Judaism, a regional post-Bar/Bat Mitzvah program in northern New Jersey. He holds a master of arts in Jewish Education from the Rhea Hirsch School of Education in Los Angeles.

RIV ELLEN-PRELL, an anthropologist, is Associate Professor of American Studies at the University of Minnesota and is associated with the programs in Women's Studies and Jewish Studies. She is the author of *Prayer and Community: The Havurah in American Judaism* and coeditor of *Interpreting Women's Lives: Feminist Theory and Personal Narratives*.

JOSEPH REIMER is an Associate Professor in and Director of the Benjamin S. Hornstein Program in Jewish Communal Service at Brandeis University, where he teaches courses in Jewish education and family life. He has authored a book and numerous articles on how adolescents in the United States and Israel think about moral issues. Since 1990 he has continued his ethnographic research on synagogues and is completing a book, *When Synagogues Educate*, which will be published by the Jewish Publication Society.

EDDIE REYNOLDS, an independent executive and organization development consultant, works with companies and firms ranging from start-ups to Fortune 500 organizations throughout Silicon Valley, California. Consultations have focused on a wide variety of organizational, team, and personal topics, including organizational values and visions, new team start-up, transition and change management, executive coaching, and organization design and governance. Eddie has also been very active in Congregation Beth Am in Los Altos Hills, serving as Chair of the educational long-term task force and as President of the congregation.

SUSAN SHEVITZ is an Associate Professor at Brandeis University's Benjamin S. Hornstein Program in Jewish Communal Service, where she heads its Jewish Education Concentration and teaches courses in organizational behavior, evaluation, and planning, as well as Jewish education. She holds a Ph.D. from Harvard University in Educational Planning, Social Policy, and Administration.

LINDA RABINOWITCH THAL is Director of Education of Leo Baeck Temple in Los Angeles, California. She is a member of the clinical faculty at Hebrew Union College-Jewish Institute of Religion Rhea Hirsch School of Education and a consultant to the Experiment in Congregational Education. She has taught and written in the areas of family and *tzedakah* education, the use of art in Jewish education, interfaith family issues, and Judaism and spiritual growth. Linda was a 1994 recipient of the Covenant Award.

JONATHAN WOOCHER is the Executive Vice President of the Jewish Education Service of North America. He has also served on the faculty of Brandeis University and Carleton College. He is the author of *Sacred Survival: The Civil Religion of American Jews* and numerous articles on American Jewish religion, education, and communal affairs.

elements of a complete holiday celebration in the *sukkah*, including the *lulav* and *etrog, ushpizin,* the meaning of a *sukkah*, the requirements for building a *sukkah*, and the rituals performed and prayers recited in one. As families learn about *hiddur mitzvot* — beautifying the mitzvot — they can decorate the *sukkah* and end the day there with a festive community meal.

Chanukah After each family crafts a chanukiah from tag board, clay or wire, lead them on a hike through the history of Chanukah. At each of eight stops along the way, participants can engage in an activity that highlights an historical period, from coloring a mural of the elephants used by the Syrian armies to playing *dreidel* as a way to study Torah. At each station families can pick up one paper candle flame for the *chanukiah* that they will have made.

Tu Bishvat Invite families to a Tu Bishvat seder. During this festive meal families can eat the fruits and nuts of the land of Israel and drink four cups of juice, each a different color, celebrating the progression of nature from the barrenness of winter to the full bloom of summer. As families engage in the Tu Bishvat seder, they can sing songs, tell stories, and share beautiful poetry and readings — all of which celebrate God's gift of creation and nature.

Purim Create a life-size *Megillah* for your Purim celebration. Assign each family a portion of the Book of Esther. Through guided discussion parents can help their children understand the text and families can then artistically re-create their section on a huge piece of butcher paper or on cloth,

1

This material is provided as a service of the UAHC Department of Education

SUGGESTIONS FOR FAMILY HOLIDAY PROGRAMS

by Rabbi Judith Schindler

The possibilities for creative family programming are endless. Some of the following programs are appropriate for families with younger children, while others are suited for those with older children. Adapt each program to meet the needs of your community.

Selichot Create a program in which families visit various stations in order to draw up a spiritual and physical checklist for the High Holidays. Stations may include food preparation, a list of the steps to *teshuvah*, music and stories of the High Holidays, and *shofar* blowing. The program can end with a brief Selichot service during which the stories, foods, and music are integrated.

Rosh Hashanah Have a family *Tashlich* program to teach families about the ritual of *Tashlich*. Have each participant list the behaviors, attitudes, and events they would like to leave behind as they begin the New Year. Families can then go to a body of water and participate in a *Tashlich* service,symbolically casting away the items their list. Families with younger children might have a birthday party for the world. Families can work together to decide what birthday gift the world most needs, and can commit themselves to helping the world get it.

Sukot Hold a *sukkah*-decorating fair. At different sites families will collect and learn about the to cover the meaning of Yom Kippur, Kol Nidre, fasting, and the concept of *teshuvah*. Emphasize that for transgressions against God, we ask for God's forgiveness, but for transgressions against another person, we must ask for that person's forgiveness.

SHARING:

Have the students work in pairs to create collages on poster board. Have each pair draw a line down the middle of the poster board to divide it in half. Have them label one side "good" and the other side "evil." They can create their collages by cutting pictures from old magazines and gluing them on the appropriate space on their poster board. Have each student sign the collage. (You will find what the students perceive as good and bad very interesting.) While the glue is drying, move on to the learning activity on Yom Kippur.

On index cards, write the situations listed below. Have each student select a card, read it aloud, and then act out what s/he would do in the same situation. The group should then discuss the student's presentation and, if necessary, suggest a more positive approach.

- Someone pushes you. What do you do?
- You are caught telling a lie. What do you do?
- No one will talk to you. What do you do?
- Your best friend ignores you. What do you do?
- You are not invited to a friend's party. What do you do?
- Everyone laughs at you. What do you do?

20

1. Jewish Identity (Including History)

2120

OBJECTIVE: Identify the Origin of Jewish Life Activities, Including Holidays, Ceremonies, Symbols, and Customs

OPENING: Read Leviticus 23:27: "The tenth day of this seventh month is the Day of Atonement. It shall be a sacred occasion for you; you shall practice self denial and you shall bring an offering by fire to the Lord" (*The Torah—A Modern Commentary* [New York: UAHC, 1981], p. 929). Ask the students which holiday this passage refers to (Yom Kippur).

FOCUSING: Have the students take turns reading aloud from the story of Jonah. Periodically ask for volunteers to state in their own words what has happened in the story thus far. Explain that this is the Haftarah that is read on Yom Kippur and how appropriate the story of a society that is spared from destruction because of true repentance is to the Day of Atonement. It is also significant that the people of Nineveh are not Jewish, from which we learn that God's mercy and compassion extend to all peoples.

LEARNING: Provide some background on Yom Kippur. An excellent reference for Yom Kippur and other Jewish holidays and rituals is Daniel B. Syme, *The Jewish Home: A Guide for Jewish Living* (New York: UAHC, 1988). D...